BILL NYE

HIS OWN LIFE STORY

"A thoughtful, scholarly and choice fragment of modern architecture with lines
of care about the firmly chiseled mouth."

BILL NYE

HIS OWN LIFE STORY

CONTINUITY BY

FRANK WILSON NYE

Illustrated

 BOOKS FOR LIBRARIES PRESS

FREEPORT, NEW YORK

First Published 1926
Reprinted 1970

104622

STANDARD BOOK NUMBER:
8369-5434-3

LIBRARY OF CONGRESS CATALOG CARD NUMBER:
78-124246

PRINTED IN THE UNITED STATES OF AMERICA

To My Mother
CLARA FRANCES SMITH
BILL NYE'S "IDEAL WIFE," WHOM
HE THUS CHARACTERIZED

My ideal wife is a comrade who wins me from down town, and who agrees with me generally. And if not, it is quite likely to be because I am wrong. She is one who has repeatedly proved that her impressions are better than the expensive opinions of my attorney.

She sees where danger lies, while I am groping about, by means of cumbersome logic, to arrive later at the same conclusion.

She does not claim to be literary, but discovers at once when an author becomes artificial and writes from the head rather than the heart.

She is level-headed, rather than strong-minded. She knows when to applaud her husband without making a goose of him, and how to criticize without offending him.

She delights in benefiting the needy, whom she knows, rather than make blanc mange for the people on the upper Congo. She does not say kind words by long distance telephone, but anticipates the wants of the deserving in her own neighborhood.

She can give pointers to a professional cook, and compels good service because she is familiar with all the details of good housekeeping.

She can transact business when an emergency arises, but is glad to turn it over to the husband when he is at hand.

v

The ideal wife is also an ideal mother. She has no abnormal affection for wheezy dogs.

She is a good fellow with her husband, and the confidante and comrade of her sons and daughters.

She reveres the honest elements of religion without being a beggar or hustler for the church. She does not neglect her home or her children in order to wipe out a church debt, which should not have been incurred.

She is the kind of woman to encourage wedlock by her glorious example. She is the kind to make confirmed bachelors and old maids pity themselves.

Finally, she compels her husband to congratulate himself, and to wonder what he would have been without her.

She is unselfish. She is healthy in mind and body, and she is the mother of good citizens. She makes the world better for having lived in it, "and of such is the kingdom of Heaven."

FOREWORD

Hamlet's estimate of Yorick seems to be applicable to Bill Nye. "I knew him," and he was "a fellow of infinite jest." But something more. He was scrupulously careful that nothing of his should corrupt either the morals or the pure English of his readers or his hearers. He had no recourse either to slang or dialect. He wrote in our best English and was most amusing. Of course, upon occasion he quoted the native vernacular, but he did not depend upon it for his fun, as Josh Billings and many others did.

In the early and mid eighties, the humorists of the country made rendezvous at Chicago, and seemed to choose the "Daily News" office as their headquarters. Eugene Field was in the heyday of his "Sharps and Flats"; Will Vischer and Opie Read were living in the city. Peter Dunne was a reporter on the "Daily News," but had not yet immortalized the political saloon-keeper, Jim McGarry, and his friend Mike Finucane, of Archer Avenue, as Dooley and Hinnesy; George Ade and John McCutcheon were at Purdue University. Jim Riley was at Indianapolis and Bill Nye at Hudson, Wisconsin, but both made frequent visits to Chicago and occasional contributions to the paper. We all had jolly days together.

Then Joseph Pulitzer and John Cockerill, his managing editor, were organizing a staff for the "New York World." They took something like a dozen men from the "Daily News." There were George Harvey, the recent United States ambassador to England; John Fay, now Chicago correspondent of the "World"; Kingsbury, for years a conspicuous editorial writer of the "World"; a young man named Gay; and another named May. And Bill Nye joined the hegira. How he grew in fame every one knows. I saw him frequently in his new home. He was ever a devoted friend.

This life has all the sparkle of Nye's work. Indeed, it is practically an autobiography. It is well worth reading by any one who enjoys drollery rather than trash.

Melville E. Stone

REMARKS BY JIM NYE

Bill Nye's eldest living son, Frank Wilson Nye, whom his family and intimates have always called Jim Nye, tells a bit about this book, what it comprises, how it was fabricated, why it is published at this time, and those who aided in its preparation.

Is a biography of Bill Nye of interest to the American public to-day?

Bill Nye died in 1896, and thirty years are thirty years. The majority of those who read my father's weekly letters have joined that greater majority. Much of his writing dealt with matters of the moment. He wrote rapidly and seldom reread his manuscript. He did not consider himself literary. That he is remembered has surprised many and would, no doubt, surprise him if he knew.

The fact remains that he has not been forgotten.

Young men as well as their fathers are heard to preface remarks with, "As Bill Nye said." Newspapers and magazines still mention and quote the Laramie humorist. What he called his dome of thought remains a national landmark. Wagner's music continues to be better than it sounds. The dog Entomologist lives on in spite of the overdose of plaster. Even in this prohibition era there are those who can say with the sage of Buncombe County, once a year at least, "Yesterday I made New Years calls, I am told." Reprints of his two comic histories and his Red Book go on selling. Many of his remarks, sharply original in their day, have been dulled by use, but others are as fresh to eye and ear as they were the day they were made. And Bill Nye's philosophy, which was always the backbone of his wit, marches on, discerning, undimmed, ageless.

Soon after my father's death a "Life and Letters of Bill Nye" was projected by my mother. But she never went beyond the collection of some letters and few notes. At the time of her death I was twenty, and I did not feel qualified to sponsor such a work, but I continued to add to the material as opportunity offered.

On one of his visits to the United States, Sir Horace Plunkett, an old Laramie friend of my father, urged me to write the story of Bill Nye's life. Encouraged by him, I made a beginning. I had, of course, read everything of my father's I could lay my hands on. Before I got far I realized that Bill Nye had written his own biography. He hadn't known it, but in his letters to his personal friends, and to his other friends, the newspapers, he had forged every important link in the chain of his own life-story. He had set forth, more entertainingly than another could relate them, the interesting happenings of his life.

The difficulty was to assemble these bits of self-history in their proper order and with utmost readability. What was needed was a sympathetic hand to put together the episodes in a life which was, of itself, eventful and had been embroidered by Nye with "fancy's finger tip that dints the dimple now and kinks the lip."

I was only eight years old when my father died. My impressions of him were immature, but my recollection is vivid. A better chronicler might have been found. But, in any event, Bill Nye has narrated the happenings, and for another to tell the story in his own words would have been presumption, if not sacrilege. Some running comment was needed. This I have tried to provide, with speed and brevity; a veritable sprint.

Like a toast-master who knows that his speakers are more eloquent than he, I have set down only what seemed to be

needed in the way of a thread of continuity. And that has
not been easy, for my father jumped from subject to subject in a way that is at times as baffling as it is stimulating.

For this reason, and because humor that flashes and scin-
tillates cannot be enjoyed in large doses, I use his language
to suggest: "Do not read it all at once to see whether he
married the girl or not. Take a little at a time. If you
read it all at once and it gives you the heaves, you deserve
it. I will not bind myself to write the obituary of such
people."

As nearly as I can reckon, Bill Nye, in the forty-five
years that he lived, wrote more than three million words
for publication. Besides he wrote some fifty personal letters a week, never dictating. Hundreds of his letters,
hitherto unpublished, have been collected for this book, and
the best of them are included. For twenty years, he wrote
one or more newspaper stories each week. He contributed
to several magazines including the "Century," "Cosmopolitan," "Ladies' Home Journal," "Collier's" (then "Once
a Week"), "Good Roads," "Ingleside," "Northwestern
Miller"; wrote the two Comic Histories, two plays, and some
verse.

In writing of Bill Nye, Sewell Ford said truly: "The
adventures and happenings which he wrote about and which
most people thought had their existence only in his imagination were based largely on facts. Of course he added a
quaint exaggeration in the telling, but the foundations of
his funny tales were actual occurrences. Perhaps the very
fact that he wrote with such frankness misled his readers."

He wrote chiefly of himself, his doings, his thoughts. The
pronoun I is to be found in a majority of his paragraphs.
In nearly all of Nye's writing he is present to bear the brunt
of ridicule. In making folly appear foolish, he himself is

the lay figure or the heavy villain. When illustrations were added to his writings they caricatured Bill Nye. To me this selflessness is the outstanding difference between the humor of Bill Nye and that of other humorists.

Nowhere in his writings do I find his formula more lucidly stated than in the explanation:

> I always like to tell anything that has the general effect of turning the laugh on me, because then I know that there will be no hard feelings. It is difficult to select any one who will stand publicity when that publicity is more amusing to the average reader than to the chief actor. Every little while I run out of men who enjoy being written about in my chaste and cheerful vein. Then I have to come forward and take this position myself.

Edgar Wilson Nye had a wholesome self-respect and a high but not exaggerated opinion of his qualities. To him, *Edgar* Nye was not a buffoon; an opinion shared by all who knew him. But *Bill* Nye was another self. The personality of Bill Nye supplied a convenient vehicle, not alone to avoid giving pain to others, but to carry the burden of exposing and correcting shortcomings by making them humorously untenable.

Some time after Nye's death there appeared an editorial headed, "Wanted a Humorist":

Since the death of Edgar W. Nye the position of *National Humorist*, a place in every way desirable and with a large salary attached, has remained vacant, and so far no candidate of any merit has appeared to claim it. And so it seems likely that we are to suffer from a famine of humor and an overwhelming amount of seriousness unless some one is speedily found to fill the office. The Boston Sunday Herald declares that in the last fifty years so long a vacancy has not occurred in the humoristship, as one humorist has been ready to take the place of another without delay, and in some cases has even crowded the incumbent out of the chair before death came to put an end to his jesting. The situation is not, like a laureateship, in the gift of the Government, nor do the aspirants reach it through a regular competitive examination; but they are elected by acclamation of the populace, and he who can make the people laugh the loudest and longest wins the prize.

Since this tribute was paid, many new stars have flashed in the sky of American humor, but those best qualified to judge agree that Bill Nye's shoes are still vacant. I doubt if they will ever be filled, because the times that produced such a character have passed.

As the renowned educator, John Dewey, has said: "Bill Nye was a great satirist. Few Americans have done more to expose pretense and superstition."

Bill Nye is part and parcel of the social and industrial revolution. He was one of the leavening influences, national in scope, which helped to make the first quarter of the twentieth century more tolerant than the last quarter of the nineteenth century, which aided in improving public taste, which punctured the balloon of snobbishness, which contributed to make the present generation more natural, more democratic, broader, and better.

It was Nye's inherent honesty that gave him his power and multiplied the circulation of his writings. His honesty was so transparent it surprised and intrigued his followers. His integrity was the cornerstone of his philosophy, and it was this philosophy that constituted the foundation upon which all of his success as a humorous writer and speaker was built. His exaggeration was always to emphasize a homely truth. His writings are peculiarly free from cynicism. There are no poses. There is no sophistry. And, hand in hand with this sincerity, ringing always true in the hearts of his readers, went a gentle kindliness that made him millions of friends.

These qualities characterized his writing, and, quite as much, his living. Indeed, he was a better citizen, neighbor, friend, husband, and father than his public writings might suggest. In telling the story of his life it has not been my wish to use a whitewash brush. I have rather sought to include evidence of the little foibles which make a personality more human. Realizing that many of us are loved for our weaknesses and that none of us is without them, I have readily set down what there is to tell of Bill Nye's shortcomings. It is little enough.

I take this opportunity to express my gratitude to the many who have helped with this work:

My dear mother, who turned over to me much of the material that has been used.

My two sisters, Bessie Loring and Winifred Louise, who, older than myself, have been of inestimable aid in supplementing my own store of facts and impressions.

My cousin, Clara Mitchell Millspaugh, to whom were written many of the best Bill Nye letters and who has aided me with extraordinary zeal and sympathy in revising and editing this manuscript.

My younger brother, Douglas Day, who, though born just one month after my father's death, has helped me greatly with his enthusiasm and friendly criticisms.

My grandmother, Bill Nye's mother, with whom I spent many months and who aided me to visualize "Edgar," the boy and the son.

My father's brother, Frank Mellen Nye, whom I have "interviewed" so many times on the subject of this book.

James Whitcomb Riley, my father's old friend and partner, my own unofficial godfather, and one who took an intense interest in this contemplated biography, supplying me with many of the choicest morsels.

The many other relatives and good friends who have inspired or otherwise helped me, and including Cousin Solon Perrin, Cousin Frank Perrin, Aunt Mary Woodworth, Cousin Maria Field, Uncle A. J. Mitchell, Sir Horace Plunkett, Carey Abbott of Cheyenne, the Rev. Dr. Clarence S. McClellan, Opha Moore of Columbus, Don Seitz, Walter McDougall, Eugene Zimmerman, Captain Wade Mountfortt, Arthur Chapman, State of Wyoming Historical Department. And last but not least Mr. Melville E. Stone.

Such a book as this must contain errors of omission and fact. I have used every reasonable precaution to minimize these, but to guard against their repetition, I urge any one observing a mistake of any kind to write me at Spuyten Duyvil, New York City, and I will thankfully see to it that in any future editions corrections are made.

FRANK WILSON NYE.

CONTENTS

Book One

Book Four

Book Five

ILLUSTRATIONS

BOOK ONE

CHAPTER I

LOOKING UP THE FAMILY TREE

A MAN ought not to criticize his birthplace, I presume, and yet, if I were to do it all over again, I do not know whether I would select that particular spot or not. Sometimes I think I would not. And yet, what memories cluster about that old house! There was the place where I first met my parents. It was at that time that an acquaintance sprang up which has ripened in later years, into mutual respect and esteem. It was there that a casual meeting took place, which has, under the alchemy of resistless years, turned to golden links, forming a pleasant but powerful bond of union between my parents and myself. For that reason, I hope that I may be spared to my parents for many years to come.

Thus did Bill Nye write of Shirley, Maine, where he made his first observations of the world he found so amusing.

Nye was born August 25, 1850, on the same day of the same month, and eleven years later than the man responsible for his being called Bill—Bret Harte.

Many years later, upon being introduced to the late Senator Shirley of Maine, Nye remarked that he was born in a town of that name. In a rather offish manner the senator remarked that he had never heard of the place.

"Neither had I until I was born there," admitted Nye.

3

Nowadays Shirley is best known by hunters who go to the Moosehead region of Maine. In 1850 it was a red sawmill and a cluster of houses. It is said that the first minister in Shirley prefaced his prayer, "O Lord, here we are in Shirley, where the Lord never was and man hadn't ought to be, but let us pray."

Speaking of his birthplace, Nye quotes an old neighbor from that neck of the woods as saying to him:

"I have been told that you was born here. I am sorry to say that Shirley has never overcome this entirely. It has hurt her with other towns in the State, but you can see yourself that there was no way we could provide against it."

In the late eighties the same old wag visited us at Staten Island and informed my father that Shirley had at last waked up to its chief distinction, and was now so proud of the quality of humorist produced there that a tablet had been erected upon the Nye homestead. Naturally my father inquired as to the text of the inscription.

"Well," replied our visitor, "it says on the tablet, 'Eight miles to Greenville.' "

Nye left Maine too young to remember Shirley, but a generation later he went back there and observed:

Last week I visited my birthplace. I waited thirty years for the public to visit it, and as there didn't seem to be much of a rush, this spring I thought I would go and visit it myself.

How humble the home, and yet what a lesson it should teach the boys of America! Here, amid the barren and inhospitable waste of rocks and cold, the last place in the world that a great man would naturally select to be born in, began the life of one who, by his own unaided effort, in after years rose to the proud height of postmaster at Laramie City, Wy. T.

Here on the banks of the raging Piscataquis, where winter lingers in the lap of spring till it occasions a good deal of talk, there began a career which has been the wonder and admiration of every vigilance committee west of the turbulent Missouri.

There on that spot, with no inheritance but a predisposition to baldness and a bitter hatred of rum, with no personal property but a misfit suspender and a stone-bruise, began a life history which has never ceased to be a warning to people who have sold goods on credit.

It should teach the youth of our great broad land what glorious possibilities may lie concealed in the rough and tough bosom of the reluctant present. It shows how steady perseverance and a good appetite will always win in the end. It teaches us that wealth is not indispensable, and that if we live as we should, draw out of politics at the proper time, and die a few days before the public absolutely demands it, the matter of our birthplace will not be considered.

It is the only birthplace I have, however, and I hope that my readers will feel perfectly free to go there any time and visit it and carry their dinner as I did. Extravagant cordiality and overflowing hospitality have always kept my birthplace back.

After viewing the birthplace of the Adamses at Quincy, I felt more reconciled to my own birthplace. Comparing the house in which I was born with the houses in which other eminent philanthropists and high-priced statesmen originated, I find that I have no reason to complain. Neither of the Adamses was born in a larger house than I was, and for general tone and éclat of front

yard and cook-room on behind, I am led to believe that
I have the advantage.

I sometimes think that those who spend all their time
looking up their forefathers should be rewarded by being
allowed to join them. This sentiment coincides with my
father's ideas of ancestral worship.

"We once had a family coat of arms," said he, "but one
day while airing on the line it was stolen and never returned."

Since his death, a distant cousin with greater curiosity
hired some one to climb the Nye tree. A family crest, in an
excellent state of preservation, was discovered. The family genealogy was traced back, too, via Cape Cod and England, to Denmark and the thirteenth century.

In Denmark the name meant New or New-comer. Nye is
one of those unfortunate *punable* names. And the best pun
on it was perpetrated when my sister Bessie sought to
equalize the distance by marrying a man named Pharr.

Benjamin was the earliest American Nye. In the year
1635 the first Nyes were imported into this country. At
the age of fifteen Ben embarked on the good ship *Abigail,*
with Edmund Freeman's company, landing at what is now
Lynn, Mass.

Benjamin, John, Peleg, Joseph, Bartlett, Bartlett,
Franklin, was the father-son route to Edgar Wilson
Nye—better, oh, much better, known as Bill—who had this
to say about his British antecedents:

My ancestors are haughty English people from Piscataquis County, Maine. For centuries, our rich, warm
blood has been mellowed by the elderberry wine and
huckleberry juice of Moosehead Lake; but now and then
it will assert itself and mantle in the broad and inde-

structible cheek of our race. Ever and anon in our family you will notice the slender triangular chest, the broad
and haughty sweep of abdomen, and the high, intellectual
expanse of pelvic bone, which denote the true English-
man; proud, high-spirited, soaked full of calm disdain,
wearing checked pantaloons, and a soft, flabby tourist's
hat that has a bow on both ends, so that a man cannot
get drunk enough to put it on his head wrong.

Bill Nye's mother, Elizabeth Mitchell Loring, lived to a
ripe old age. She was largely responsible for the ambition, not only of Edgar Wilson, her eldest son, but also of
his two surviving brothers, Frank Mellen and Carroll Anderson. This pioneer woman early filled the souls of
her sons with an undying urge. All three essayed the bar,
and the world nearly lost one of its humorists in the making
of another attorney. No sacrifice was too great for this
woman to make that her sons might have books, newspapers,
magazines, and schooling.

In the history of the family, Bill Nye's mother's mother
was a notable character. They called her Grandmom. She
could not but have impressed her mark upon posterity.
Almost a six-footer, stern and capable, was this good
Yankee and forceful abolitionist. Her husband died leaving a large estate consisting solely of young children. The
Widow Loring never remarried but turned in and supported
the entire brood with her needle. I remember her well. She
died at the age of eighty-odd, with a record of many years
of independence, in possession of her own home and a sub-
stantial bank-account, and with her boots on.

I never saw my father's father. Those who knew him
remember a tall, slender man with brown eyes like gold-
stone. He was quiet, home-loving, fastidious about his

dress, scrupulously honest, and in money matters what the Yankee calls "prudent."

I get this description from the woman who knew him best, his wife. I asked her which side of the family she thought had the greater influence in the forming of Edgar's personality. (The family always called my father by his Christian name.)

"He was a blending of them both," she replied. "He got his dignity from his father's family, and his *genial glow,* if I may use such a term, from the Lorings."

Franklin Nye, my grandfather, was a handsome, hearty young lumberman from the Maine woods. As a girl Eliza had seen him attentive in turn to each of the teachers at the little district school. When she achieved this office, and with it his attentions, she would have none of him. He went away for a year, asking her if she would correspond with him. But she refused, saying that the fact that she had reached a point where she could teach school a bit was no reason for him to imagine her interested in *him.* This time, however, he was in earnest, and one night after his return, during a dance at the Corners, they "fixed it up." The marriage soon followed.

The year preceding my father's birth was the happiest of his mother's life, she told me.

CHAPTER II

LEADING HIS PARENTS WEST AND MAKING A
HOME FOR THEM

THE life of a Maine lumberman was anything but easy. At the first sign of winter my grandfather said good-by to his family and went into the woods to remain until the thaw.

When word came from a friend, who had sought the more friendly soil of Wisconsin, that here was a land where a living was to be had without the old hardships and the long separations, the Nye family arranged to leave Shirley.

My father's version of the happening was that at two years of age he took his parents by the hand and, telling them that Piscataquis County was no place for them, he boldly struck out for St. Croix County, Wisconsin, where the hardy young pioneer soon made a home for them.

Not only Nye but likewise Artemus Ward, Josh Billings, Bob Burdette, and Petroleum V. Nasby, though Easterners by birth, seemed to need the alchemy of new country to precipitate their precious metal. Some of Artemus Ward's relatives were neighbors of the Nyes in Maine, and an uncle went west with the Nye party.

To-day Honolulu is not as far from Maine as Wisconsin was in the early fifties. A railway journey to Buffalo, thence by boat through the Great Lakes to Milwaukee, again by rail to Madison, and from there by wagon, was a big undertaking for any family, and especially for these young pioneers of inexperience and slender resource.

9

The Nyes were aiming along the Wisconsin River for the new town of Richland. It was June, and Indian pinks dotted the unbroken prairie. For three days they drove through Dodge County, through the Dells, and along the shore of Devils Lake. The name and the beautiful country through which they drove gave a misleading foretaste of Richland. A two weeks' stay there sufficed to send the family in search of richer land in another part of the State.

The best thing the head of the family could find to do at Hazel Green, the next experiment, was to team flour over the State line to Galena, Illinois, returning with dry goods to Hazel Green. After a year and a half of this, my grandfather took his family up the Mississippi Valley to the wooded part of St. Croix County. Here, in the Kinnic Kinnic Valley, they chose the place that was to be their home for many years to come.

Nye's own explanation for leaving Maine was:

When I had utilized Maine as a birthplace, our business relations ceased, for I wanted to be a farmer, and I didn't like Maine for farming purposes.

The State of Maine is diversified and quite rugged, especially where I was born. Verdure of all kinds is late, and the little pewee wears his ear muffs till the Fourth of July.

The reason I left Maine to try other localities for farming was that in the summer of '52 I had my feet severely frost-bitten while mowing in the north meadow.

Selling out my little farm, I packed up a scythe and together with two split bottom chairs, and my trusty dog Yellow Fever, and taking a large accordion and my cyclopedia in a shawl strap, I went as far as the Mississippi Valley.

According to my father, the first year after the Nyes had settled at Kinnic Kinnic he drove the Indians out of the St. Croix Valley and suggested to the Northwestern Railroad Company that it would be a good idea to build to St. Paul as soon as the company could get a grant that would pay them two or three times the cost of construction. In the following year he adopted trousers and made $175 on the sale of wolf scalps.

In 1854 he established and endowed a district school in Pleasant Valley. (Bill Nye is still talking.) It was at this time that he began to turn his attention to the abolition of slavery in the South, and he wrote articles for the press signed "Veritas," in which he advocated the War of 1860, as soon as the government could get around to it.

In 1855 (he was now five) he graduated from the farm and began the study of law. He did not advance very rapidly in this profession. He was, however, a close student of political economy, and he studied personal economy at the same time, until he found that he could live on ten cents a day and his relatives, easily.

Of the same period in his life Nye said:

If I had thought of it in time I would have studied a great deal more by the light of the pine-knot but it did not occur to me until too late to be of use to me in an autobiography.

When I was a child I was different from other boys in many respects. I was always looking about to see what good I could do. I am that way yet.

If my little brother Frank wanted to go in swimming contrary to orders, I was not strong enough to prevent him, but I would go in with him and save him from a watery grave. I went in the water thousands of times and as a result he is alive to-day.

But he is ungrateful. He hardly ever mentions it now, but he remembers the Gordian knots that I tied in his shirts. He speaks of them frequently. This shows the ingratitude and natural depravity of the human heart.

My parents were blest with five bright-eyed and beautiful little boys, three of whom grew up and by that means became adults. I am in that condition myself. I was the eldest of the family with the exception of my parents. I am still that way. My early life was rather tempestuous in places, occasionally flecked with sunshine, but more frequently with retribution. I was not a very good roadster when young, and so retribution was always in the act of overtaking me. While outraged justice was getting in its work on me, the other boys escaped through a small aperture in the fence.

When we ran away from school to catch chubs, built a fire to cook them and the fire got into the tall, dry grass and burned four miles of fence and sixteen tons of hay belonging to a gentleman for whom I had a high regard, and I went back to put out the fire, the *other boys* escaped and have so remained ever since.

When a party of us had been engaged in gathering Easter eggs in the barn of a gentleman who was away from home at the time, and he returned just as we had filled our pockets with the choicest vintage of his sunkissed hens, the other boys escaped while I was occupying the attention of the dog, and I had to slide out of the second story of the barn. I wore my father's vest at that time and it was larger than was necessary. My father was larger than I, for I was only nine years of age and had not arrived at my full stature. In sliding down the batten I discovered that the upper end of it was loose and that my flowing vest had slipped over it, so that when I got down about four feet I hung with the board buttoned inside my bosom and scrambled eggs oozing out of my knickerbockers.

The batten had sprung back against the barn in such a way as to prevent my unbuttoning my vest, and while I hung there on the side of the barn like a coon skin, the proprietor came around and accused me of prematurely gathering his eggs.

I had heard truth very highly spoken of by people who had dabbled in it, and I resolved to try it in this instance. I admitted that such was the case. It was the best thing I could have done, for the man said as I had been so frank with him he would take me down as soon as he got his other work done. He was as good as his word. After he had milked nine cows and fed nine calves he came around with a ladder and took me down. He also spanked me and set the dog on me, but I did not mind that, for I was accustomed to it. To hang on the side of a barn, however, like an autumn leaf, trying to kick large holes out of the atmosphere, is disagreeable.

One of Uncle Frank's favorite stories of the childhood of Edgar and himself is given below in his own words:

Edgar was about thirteen, and I a year and a half younger. Father had bought a steer some eight or ten miles from where we lived and the steer had run away. The region south of us, where the steer was bought, was a wilderness. Father thought boys should be something besides ornaments, and he told us one morning to go and find that steer. It was a busy time and he couldn't go. It was hot weather in August. We started after breakfast, and got home the next morning just before breakfast. We were lost several times and nearly starved to death but found no steer.

Edgar recounted the perils and privations of the trip on our return, and intimated that the job was far out of proportion to the salary connected with it. Father said he had intended to compensate us according to the success of the undertaking.

Thirty years later, on a voyage to Europe, and in midocean, Edgar wrote me one of his characteristic letters. Towards the closing, he became serious, and discussed his plans for the future. He said he had an offer from a newspaper syndicate to take a trip around the world and write it up from his own viewpoint. "What do you think of it?" he asked. "I am a good deal taken with the idea. It will pay well financially, the experience would be valuable, and besides *I may possibly find that d—d steer.*"

CHAPTER III

LEARNING THE RUDIMENTS OF GREATNESS AND HOW TO THROW A PAPER WAD WITH PRECISION

TIME and place considered, my father had a fair education and one that cost him and his parents no little effort. After he had learned all that the district school had to teach him and the others in his class, the board voted to engage an instructor who was on speaking terms with the higher branches. Algebra, geometry, trigonometry, physical geography, and bookkeeping were mastered with the able instruction of this pedagogue. A sixteen weeks' term at the "academy" under a college graduate and two long terms at a military school in River Falls, where held forth some able teachers from Exeter, completed his class-room instruction.

One of Edgar's young aunts, Mary Loring Woodworth, writes of her appreciation of the young humorist:

Our amusements were few. If we had any fun we had to manufacture it. I remember best the wonderful performances we had in the old granary. We called it Loring's Sky Parlor. Both boys were born mimics, and a protracted experience meeting would give them wonderful material. Frank, as class leader, would call on Brother Mapes to testify. Brother Mapes habitually ended his testimony with "O Lord, if you will spare me the remainder of my days I will serve you while I live." Edgar would rise and with a long sanctimonious face and voice that sounded as if it came from the bottom of an empty barrel, give the testimony, word for word, as we had heard it at the last meeting; also imitating a peculiarity of making his under eyelids come half way to meet his upper lids when he closed his eyes in prayer. The latter was, for a long time, an accomplishment difficult to imitate.

Or better yet, were rainy days in the Loring kitchen, with the choice spirits gathered there and Edgar wrapped in his grandmother's white tufted counterpane for a toga, giving us Mark Antony's address or Spartacus with variations.

I heard James Perrin say one morning, "I drove my team home from town behind Pat Hawkins's rig last night. Pat had Mike Caffery in with him. They were mighty funny and I thought pretty well sprung. But they turned into Nye's gate and blamed if it wasn't them darn fool Nye boys."

Further evidence that Edgar Nye was a humorist at an early age comes from an old schoolmate, Judge Lauder, of Wahpeton, North Dakota:

I knew Bill Nye well. His father's farm was three miles from the farm on which I was reared. We were often together in the social events of the country, and were fellow students at the academy at River Falls. (River Falls was the village nearest to the Nye Farm.) In his case—and the same may be said of his distinguished brother, the prosecuting attorney of Minneapolis—"the boy was father to the man." The humorous bent of his mind was clearly marked early in life. In rhetorical exercises at school he always wrote and never spoke. His composition was usually the event of the exercises, and was almost always couched in a humorous vein. The ludicrous side of a situation never escaped him, and he was not at all particular as to the subject of his sport. The professors were quite as liable to figure in his essays and compositions as any other person.

BILL NYE'S FATHER, FRANKLIN
NYE

"I should look for Father to
be there and meet me with
the few words, but the warm
greeting, which he always
looked more than his tongue
said."

BILL NYE'S MOTHER,
ELIZA MITCHELL LORING NYE

"As the Mexican Indians, who have
been burden-bearers over the
mountains for many years, cannot walk or rest without a weight
upon their shoulders, so your idle
hands will instinctively reach out
into the empty air for the task
that is gone."

BILL NYE'S GRANDMOTHER LORING

"Your life has been one long, eloquent
prayer, not for exhibition purposes,
but for the comfort and pleasure of
those nearest to you."

Let Nye tell his own story of his school days:

In the midst of the hurry and distraction of business do you ever look far out across the purple hills, with misty vision, and think of the days, now held in the sacred silence of your memory, when you trudged through the June sunlight to the little log school house, with bare feet and happy heart?

Do the pleasant memories come thronging back to you now of those hallowed years in your history when you bowed your head above your spelling lesson, and, while filling your mind with useful knowledge, you also filled your system full of doughnuts and thought?

How sweetly return to us to-day, like almost forgotten fragrance of honeysuckle and wood violets, the recollections of the school-room, the busy hum of a score of industrious scholars, and, above all, the half-repressed sob of the freckled youth who thoughtlessly hovered o'er the bent pin for a brief, transitory moment. Oh! who can give us back the hallowed joys of childhood, when we ostensibly sought out the whereabouts of Timbuctoo in our geography while we slid a vigorous wasp into the pants pocket of our seat mate?

Our common schools are the foundation of America's free institutions. They are the bulwarks of our liberty and the glory and pride of a great republic. It is there that the youth of our land learn the rudiments of greatness and how to throw a paper wad with unerring precision.

Do you remember when you had no dreams of statesmanship and when the holy ambition to be a paragrapher had never fired your young blood? Do you remember when you had no aim except to be the boy who could tell the most plausible lie? Do you still remember with what wonderful discretion you sought out and imposed upon the boy you thought you could lick? And do you still call to mind the thrill of glad surprise that came over you when you made a slight error and the meek-eyed victim arose in his wrath and left you a lonesome ruin?

Do you ever stop to think of those glorious holidays you took without the teacher's consent? How you rambled in the wildwood all day and gathered nuts, and crab apples, and wood ticks, and mosquito bites? Have you returned tired and hungry at night and felt that your parents wouldn't be so tickled to see you as they might be?

Do you know of the day when you rashly resolved to lick your father, and he persuaded you to change your mind and let him lick you?

Who would rob us of those green memories of other days? Who would snatch from us the joy we still experience in bringing up those pictures of careless childhood when we bathed in the clear, calm waters of the smooth flowing river, or pelted each other with mud or dead frogs while the town people drove by and wondered why the authorities didn't take some measures to prevent boys from bathing in public places?

After I grew larger, my parents sent me to a military school. That is where I got the fine military bearing and stately carriage that I still wear.

My room was on the second floor, and it was very difficult for me to leave it at night, because the turnkey locked us up at 9 o'clock every evening. Still, I used to get out once in awhile and wander around in the starlight. I do not yet know why I did it, but I presume it was a kind of somnambulism. I would go to bed thinking so intently of my lessons that I would get up and wander away, sometimes for miles, in the solemn night.

One night I awoke and found myself in a watermelon patch. I was never so ashamed in my life. It is a very serious thing to be awakened rudely out of a sound sleep, by a bulldog, to find yourself in the watermelon vineyard of a man with whom you are not acquainted. I was not on terms of social intimacy with this man or his dog. They did not belong to our set. We had never been thrown together before.

After that I was called a great somnambulist and men who had watermelon conservatories shunned me. But it cured me of my somnambulism.

Nye became interested in one of the local belles and paid court to her. She evidently felt that she was doing the young farmer a distinct favor in allowing him to take up her time. But she was not so particular how she occupied his spare moments. In due time the inevitable invitation to a buggy ride was issued by the budding humorist and accepted by his admired.

The best turnout that the local livery offered stood before the lady's home promptly at the appointed hour. The steed, it must be admitted, was not of the latest model. Nye waited patiently in the hot sun while the finishing touches were placed upon the toilet of his best girl. A considerable period was thus occupied.

Meanwhlie the horse settled down in the shafts and Nye on the small of his back. At last, an hour or more late, a vision of loveliness appeared at the front door. No word of regret had she for her tardiness, but with raised eyebrows she took in the livery plug, remarking in a critical tone that the age of said plug was evidently advanced.

"Yes," said Nye, "this is an old horse now, but *when I brought him here he was young and spry.*"

Thus did Nye always hold his own. His ingenuous ways invited those who did not know him well to patronize him. But woe to her or him who so indulged. It was impossible to take offense at his rejoinders, but the more one considered his counter-thrusts, the more clear it became that he could give as good as he got. Before you turn the last page of this story you will have many more evidences of his gentle art of self-defense.

Oh, what a strange, wild thrill love brings!

And yet it is a good thing.

When not taken to excess.

I can still recall the first time I felt a wild, passionate desire to be loved.

It was a spirited heart pang and then all was over. I was going on seventeen. She was a widow. She had some property in her own right and a team.

I did not care especially for the team.

But she was a woman with a heart like an ox.

I did not then know what love was. If I had enough to eat I was all right.

One day I went to her house to borrow her hay-rack so I could finish up my stacking while the weather was good. As I turned to leave her at the gate, it was just twilight. The tree toads were sinking to rest and the katydids sang in a sleepy way in the tall grass. There was a slight breath of hay from the distant meadows, and the odor of plum-butter scorching a little on the kitchen stove.

She did not seem to care.

Her hand rested on the sleeve of my wammers.

I let it rest there.

For quite a while.

Finally I saw in the dim light a tear on her long lashes. I can stand most anything but that. I cannot bear to see anybody weep.

Especially a middle-aged person.

I asked her why she wept and she said it was for her dead. Her husband had died in the war. He had been an army contractor and died from exposure.

I took my handkerchief and wiped away her fast falling tears. As I started to go away, she caught me up and kissed me violently three times, stating that there was a grave between us. I told her I thought it couldn't possibly be a full-grown grave.

Often after that I used to go up there and borrow her farming implements or inquire about the aspect of the grave which seemed to separate us. She always said that she would be true to the memory of the deceased, but would be glad to meet me at any time for the wholesome interchange of thought.

Whenever I would think a new thought, I would try to remember it and tell her about it, and she did the same.

Considering that there was a grave between us, we were less gloomy than one would suppose. You get used to the presence of a grave after awhile and seem hardened to it.

She used to say that she felt just as if she would be willing to climb over a whole cemetery if I could be her'n, yet she would be true to him whose wife she was in the sight of heaven.

She had queer notions that way, I thought.

Evening after evening I would sit by the open casement while the day died and the new-born night with its sweet, baby breath stole through the heavy cheese-cloth

hangings and the rich foliage of the oleander.   Hour
after hour I would hold her large, heavy hands.

Tears sometimes welled up in her eyes, and fell upon
her gingham apron, but I did not reproach her.   How
could I reproach a person who was so much older than I?

Looking back at it now, after the lapse of years, I can
see that it is better as it is.

One of the horses got cast in his stall and tore out
several of his most desirable bowels.

Glanders garnered in the other horse.

Now there are three graves between us, and that makes
it awkward where people are of a strong, yearnful temperament and their heart cravings are deep-rooted and
their natures clinging and yet fractious.

And so it ended.   Years afterward I met a bright-eyed
girl between whom and myself I could find no disagreeable grave.   We were wed.

CHAPTER IV

DOING THE HEAVY FALLING, MAKING MONEY, AND OTHER YOUTHFUL ACCIDENTS

My father realized that he was one of those individuals for whom a perverse fate had planned a career consisting of one mishap after another, and he wrote of this predisposition:

Do you remember the boy of your school who did the heavy falling through the ice and was always about to break his neck, but managed to live through it all? Do you recall to mind the youth who never allowed anybody else to fall out of a tree and break his collar bone when he could attend to it himself? Every school has to secure the services of such a boy before it can succeed, and so our school had one. When I entered the school I saw at a glance that the board had neglected to provide itself with a boy whose duty it was to nearly kill himself every few days in order to keep up the interest, so I applied for the position. I secured it without any trouble whatever. The board understood at once from my bearing that I would succeed. And I did not betray the trust they had reposed in me.

Before the first term was over I had tried to climb two trees at once and had been carried home on a stretcher; had been pulled out of the river with my lungs full of water, and artificial respiration had been resorted to; been jerked around over the north half of the county

by a fractious horse whose halter I had tied to my leg,
and which leg is now three inches longer than the other.
My parents at last got so that along about 2 o'clock P. M.
they would look anxiously out of the window and say,
"Isn't it about time for the boys to get here with the
remains? They generally get here before 2 o'clock."

Accidents that involved physical suffering were not the
only kind of misfortunes that lent spice to the life of the
young humorist. One of Nye's specialties was losing money.
He has related a couple of true stories of mislaid lucre:

A man gave me two $5 bills once to pay a balance on
some store teeth and asked me to bring the teeth back
with me. The dentist was fifteen miles away and when
I got there I discovered I had lost the money. That was
before I had amassed much of a fortune, so I went to the
tooth foundry and told the foreman that I had started
with $10 to get a set of teeth for an intimate friend, but
had lost the funds. He said my intimate friend would,
no doubt, have to gum it awhile. Owing to recent shrink-
age in values he was obliged to sell teeth for cash, as the
goods were comparatively useless after they had been used
one season. I went back over the same road the next day
and found the money, although a hundred teams had
passed by it.

I lost a roll of a hundred dollars one spring, and
hunted for it in vain. I went over the road twenty times,
but it was useless. I then advertised the loss of the money,
giving the different denominations of the bills and stating,
as was the case, that there was an elastic band around
the roll when lost. The paper had not been issued more
than an hour before I got my money, every dollar of it.
It was in the pocket of my other vest. This should teach

us, first, the value of advertising, and, secondly, the utter
folly of two vests at the same time.

Hand in hand with his tendency toward accidents was
an element of good fortune which usually brought him
safely through his tribulations; as witness the above happy
endings to what might have been tragedies. My father
was lucky in many things that made for his progress and
prosperity. It would be unfair to attribute to the goddess
of fortune, however, any considerable part of his success,
which was due in a so much larger measure to his mental
alertness. Even as a boy this alertness was highly developed, though hidden behind an unsophisticated exterior.

One time at a circus he was approached by a flashy
stranger who wanted the country lad to throw for him at
the side-show lottery. The man explained that his luck
was so good the lottery manager wouldn't let him continue.
Edgar readily accepted the dollar offered, and the first
crack out of the box drew a silver cup and $20. Immedi-
ately the dapper investor elbowed his way in Nye's direction to claim the loot. But before he could reach this simple
lad, Nye had invested another dollar and drawn a brass
locket worth two bits a bushel. Nye had correctly diagnosed that the plausible come-on was a capper for the
lottery. And so he cheerfully gave his sporty acquaintance
the brass locket, explaining that the first dollar invested
was one he had received from his father.

CHAPTER V

FARMER, MILLER, LAWYER, TEACHER

I now budded into manhood. I was a great hit. I had obtained an education—that is, mostly a practical education. I had attended school off and on, between massacres, by working out in the summer by the month and then attending school winters, by dint of building fires and sweeping out the school-house for my board. Of course the board was not extensive, but almost every day some well-to-do and forehanded scholar would voluntarily give me a nice, durable boiled egg for writing his composition for him. And so I got along real well and always with a blithe heart. That is one thing which aroused the admiration of one and all, an admiration in which I was at last compelled to join; viz., I had a blithe heart.

Nye was not one of those fortunate geniuses who early in life realize that they are cast for one and only one occupation. He trod a thorny path to discover that he was really, after all, a humorist. One of the first misfits he adopted in the way of a vocation was that of miller.

I was about 18 years of age when I decided that I would be a miller, with flour on my clothes and a salary of $200 per month. This was not the first thing I had decided to be, and afterward changed my mind about.

I engaged to learn my profession of a man named Sam Newton, I believe; at least I will call him that for the sake of argument. My business was to weigh wheat, deduct as much as possible on account of cockle, pigeon grass and wild buckwheat, and to chisel the honest farmer out of all he would stand. This was the program with Mr. Newton; but I am happy to say that it met with its reward, and the sheriff afterward operated the mill.

On stormy days I did the bookkeeping, with a scoop shovel behind my ear, in a pile of middlings on the fifth floor. Gradually I drifted into doing a good deal of this kind of brain work. I would chop the ice out of the turbine wheel at 5 o'clock A. M., and then frolic up six flights of stairs and shovel shorts until 9 o'clock P. M.

By shoveling bran and other vegetables 16 hours a day, a general knowledge of the milling business may be readily obtained. I used to scoop middlings till I could see stars, and then I would look out at the landscape and ponder.

I got so that I piled up more ponder, after a while, than I did middlings.

One day the proprietor came upstairs and discovered me in a brown study, whereupon he cursed me in a subdued Presbyterian way, abbreviated my salary from $26 per month to $18 and reduced me to the ranks.

Afterward I got together enough desultory information so that I could superintend the feed stone. The feed stone is used to grind hen feed and other luxuries. One day I noticed an odor that reminded me of a hot overshoe trying to smother a glue factory at the close of a tropical day. I spoke to the chief floor walker of the mill about it, and he said "dod gammit" or something that sounded like that, in a coarse and brutal manner. He then kicked my person in a rude and hurried tone of voice, and told me that the feed stone was burning up.

He was a very fierce man, with a violent and ungovernable temper, and, finding that I was only increasing his brutal fury, I afterward resigned my position. I talked it over with the proprietor, and both agreed that it would be best. He agreed to it before I did. I rather hated to go so soon, but he made it an object for me to go, and I went.

I had started in with the idea that I would begin at the bottom of the ladder, as it were, and gradually climb to the bran bin by my own exertions; hoping by honesty, industry, and carrying two bushels of wheat up nine flights of stairs, to become a wealthy man. But I did not seem to accomplish it.

Instead of having ink on my fingers and a chastened look of woe on my clear-cut Grecian features, I might have poured No. 1 hard wheat and buckwheat flour out of my longer taper ears every night, if I had stuck to the profession.

After milling and at the age of twenty-four, came law. It was all the fault of too much maternal faith in phrenology. My grandmother was always willing to listen to the mysterious, the occult, the supernatural. My father has told the story as only he could.

I took my mother to a phrenologist to have her head looked over, feeling that as a parent she was not proving the success that I had hoped for. After I had counted out six dozen eggs for him, which I had brought to pay him for the work, he offered to examine my head and give me a written schedule of it for two pounds of butter which I had left over.

He wanted to please my mother, and so he spoke highly

of my talents—higher than they deserved, I think. He
said I had a high "forward," which reminded him of that
of Daniel Webster, whom he once examined. I said that
we were often mistaken for one another.

This phrenologist had a very hairy and Castle Garden
air, and when his paper collar peeped out from his jungle
of common, plastering hair you could see that when he
liked a collar he stuck to it.

Phrenology where I lived, in those days, had hardly
risen to the position of a science. It was merely a "job."
This man, whom I will call Prof. Biltong, had to combine
other things with his phrenology, such as chiropody and
the sale of fruit trees. Men had not learned to add
physiognomy and a general knowledge of human nature
to the science of phrenology, and thus read a man as we
would read a hotel register.

It was for that reason, perhaps, that Prof. Biltong
erred in reading me with a far-away look, and marking
out for me a future occupation.

Possibly it may interest the reader, especially the boy
or young man who reads this, if I tell him briefly how
Prof. Biltong erred in my case and how he caused me
thereby much annoyance and would have cost me a great
deal of money if I had had it. If any one can be led
to profit by my errors and thus dodge them at my expense
I am only too glad to aid him.

Prof. Biltong said that I would make a powerful and
eloquent lawyer. He said that alimentiveness, ideality
and secretiveness were just the right size, and that with
the Websterian dashboard, coupled with great inhabitive-
ness, I could not fail to jar the entire structure of the
bar, together with the crackers and cheese standing at
the end thereof.

I at once proceeded to prepare myself for the law. First I had to brush up a little in long division and spelling. This I did by taking a preparatory course at the Tidd school. This was called the Tidd school because it was endowed by Mr. Tidd during the plum season (without his knowledge), and we carried water from his well to quench the never dying thirst of the school.

Closing my term there with high honors and a baritone voice, which I cannot account for to this day, I got a place to study law and tidy up the cuspidors for a country lawyer whose name and memory are green and beautiful yet in the warmest corner of my heart.

While I did not make a lawyer of myself, it was not his fault. It was my own. And Biltong should have told me so on the start. That's what I paid him for. But in those days every boy who wore a big hat and got tired easily with manual toil was set aside for the ministry or the law.

Listening to the siren song of Prof. Biltong I read Blackstone all one summer, and his thrilling remarks about the right of piscary and the fee simple and fee tail and seizin which marred the history of the common law of England. I tried, oh so hard, to cuddle up to Justinian and to get intimate with Coke, and to enjoy commons of Estovers and commons of Turbary.

Meantime I swept out the office, ran of errands, got my board bill and trousers receipted and looked forward to the time when I should shake the resolution of the most stubborn and strong hearted juror that ever drew his little old $2 a day.

Days grew into weeks, weeks expanded into years. I was still reading one day what I easily forgot the next, thus storing my youthful mind with large quantities of echoing space which have since been very useful to me for other purposes.

There came a time, after two years of this sort of work, when people thought I ought to be "admitted." They talked as if it would be purely a matter of form; that I ought not to wait, for every moment I stayed outside of the profession was a loss to the American people.

The committee did not seem to think so. I went away by stage to a desolate and threadbare county seat and laid out my little stock of unripe knowledge before the committee. They sampled it one after another, and gently took me to one side, and instead of telling me, as they might, most truthfully, to go home and never fool with the law any more, they hated to hurt my feelings, and so they told me to study some more on this point and brush up on that.

So I returned, sold a pet heifer, and buying a set of Kent's Commentaries and a nice warm pair of hip boots read another six months and did general janitor work around the office, also drawing deeds, mortgages and portraits of the senior member of the firm.

At the end of that time I began to think I ought to be examined again. Every spring and fall term I would go through this ordeal, and then get bound over for examination the following term. Finally it got to be a part of the calendar. When the court was waiting for a witness or a juror it would put in the time by examining me. This ran on till I got tired of it and fled.

[The first time Nye failed of admission to the bar he asked the examiner if he could go on his own recognizance or would he have to give bond for his reappearance.]

In a new field, where the officials were being appointed by the president, and some of them knew even less than

I did, I felt at home right away, and finally one glad day in summer, with a joyful heart, though with many scars on the places where previous committees had knocked the bark off my soul, I signed the book and became a lawyer.

One of the old committee has kindly told me since that it made his heart bleed to refuse me, and that if he'd known how little damage I would do as a lawyer and how quiet I'd have been about it, blamed if he wouldn't have suspended the rules in my case and moved my admission.

Now I do not blame phrenology for this, but Prof. Biltong should have seen that while I had some of the prerequisites of a lawyer I lacked one great essential, and that was the ability to repeat a law, a ruling or a definition in the exact language of anybody else.

That ignorance on his part cost me many a reluctant, evasive and tear-dimmed dollar, and came very near landing me in the lap of an overworked and overburdened public, one of the most pitiful objects known to the entomologist, viz., a pettifogger.

Will A. Dudley gives some other slants on Nye's attempt at the study of legal lore:

In 1874 ex-Lieut. Governor Bingham, of Wisconsin, and John J. Jenkins were law partners at Chippewa Falls. One morning early in the fall of the same year, a young man with a sparsely grown beard and a bashful look walked into their office and without much ceremony applied for the position of law clerk. Mr. Jenkins stated to the young man that the present incumbent of that position was doing very nicely, and the firm could hardly afford any extra clerk hire. But the young man seemed eager to secure a position in a law office, he would

THE BIRTHPLACE OF BILL NYE AT SHIRLEY, MAINE
"There was where I first met my parents."

THE NYE FARMHOUSE AT KINNIC-KINNIC, NEAR RIVER FALLS, WIS.

plug hard to make a success. A second thought by Mr. Jenkins, and Edgar Wilson Nye was taken in to assist in the office duties of a leading law firm of northwestern Wisconsin.

He tried hard to be faithful in his chosen profession. He was bright and studious, but did not grasp the opinions of the English jurists and the voluminous reports of cases in the American law books. In the fall of 1875 he became uneasy. His wardrobe had dwindled. He slept on an old-fashioned lounge in the office that was opened up at night. Several blankets were kept in the vault during the day; also upon the occasion of one memorable night, when he forgot the combination, and was obliged to walk the floor to keep warm, the thermometer being down in the neighborhood of forty degrees below zero.

He informed his employers that he was thinking about going to Polk County to teach school, and then asked them if his services could be spared. It was agreed that he should be permitted to go.

The first school position my father held was a teachership in the same little St. Croix County school that he had previously attended. He held a first degree certificate and received the maximum salary for his kind of work then paid in those parts. Needless to say, the income did not pamper him.

Later he taught in Polk County. The salary was thirty dollars a month. From all I can learn of his experiences as a teacher, he never regarded teaching as anything but a pot-boiling means of livelihood.

Let Nye take up again the thread of the story of his life and tell us why boys in general leave home and why he in particular left the parental roof:

The day came on which I was gently but firmly invited to angle, cut bait, or go ashore. It was when I had outgrown the home nest. I was timid and of a shrinking nature. So were my clothes. At this time I was invited to buy into the farm with the privilege of allowing my wages to go in toward the payment of principal and interest—interest first, then principal, like the motto of a political patriot from New York. I made a few rapid calculations covering one side and part of one end of the barn, showing that I would have to give up operas, balls, cigars, wine, underwear, summer vacations at Newport, and my club; that I would have to let my beard grow, cover myself with metallic paint, and work very hard all the pleasant weather in the field, and all the bad weather in the barn or cellar. Thus, as crops and prices were, I found that my wages and my own share of the crop would pay the interest and leave a small sum each year which would help to make up the deficiency between the actual cost of the crop and price received.

So I said: "No, I think that farm life, of course, for those who can afford it, is the most independent, the most chaste and lonesome one of which I know; but I am not worthy of it. I am too restless. I am too dependent on my fellow-man. I want to see him and look in his face and catch his reflected sunshine. I cannot milk a cow a month without drying her up. I cannot impress my own indomitable spirit of push and enterprise upon the hens as some can. I cannot pay for a team each year with gopher pelts as others do. I am also too selfish to farm it, and besides, I haven't the money. Give my place to some worthy man."

There was another thing about it which made it seem imperative that I should go away. Where I lived I was still regarded as a boy. I saw that where I had grown up and been whipped repeatedly I should never be able to secure absolute reverence.   There are grizzly people there now, three score years old, who have not yet found out that they are men, because the community calls them "the boys" yet, and addresses them by their first names. And so they have never shucked their boyhood.   Thus the smell and the sound of the battle of life have never been borne to them.   They are silver-haired children yet, with big, fair, dimpled minds on which the world has made no scar.

One day, with tears, I turned my back upon the old home, which, although it had made rather a disagreeable specialty of industry, it seemed to me, yet held every element of a good home.   Not as a fugitive with bruises and bitterness only, to show for the past—that would have been easier; but as a boy whose home had been made always as cheerful for him as circumstances would permit, I plumed my wings for the wild and woolen west.

BOOK TWO

CHAPTER VI

THE "LARAMIE SENTINEL" CHALLENGES, THE WOOLSACK IS OCCUPIED, AND A DESERV-ING YOUNG WOMAN IS ENDOWED WITH HIS POVERTY

WHEN Edgar Nye left Wisconsin, pointed west, he was aiming at a broad target. He did not know exactly where he was going nor what he wanted to do when he got there.

Between his experiments with agriculture, milling, and law, he had dabbled in journalism. Of the small-town papers published in his part of Wisconsin he had been, at times, the smaller town correspondent. To most lads the gathering of such local items as the country-side yielded would have been hack work. To young Nye, the job was oddly congenial. As the Star Prairie correspondent of the "Hudson Star" and the "Chippewa Falls Weekly Herald" he acquired some facility with his pen, and traces of his wit sparkled through the stodgy record of news in these country journals.

One sample, recalled by his cousin, Frank Perrin, was Nye's description of a new method of corning beef. Nye said that some of the local characters, behind the swinging doors of the town corn whisky emporium, were trying the novel corning treatment upon themselves.

Upon the occasion of a local political convention Nye's humorous account had found its way into the columns of the "Chicago Times," and due note of this achievement had been taken by one who was destined to exert a marked influence upon Nye's future.

And so, before proceeding further west, Nye tried to connect with one of the dailies in the Twin Cities, his particular objective being the "St. Paul Pioneer Press." Failing to find a berth in Minneapolis or St. Paul he continued as far as his savings would carry him. An old and influential friend dwelt at Cheyenne, Wyoming. And as Nye had only a few dimes and nickels left when he reached this station it did not take him long to decide that he would halt and try his luck.

President Grant had appointed John J. Jenkins, of the Chippawa Falls firm in whose office Nye had read law, United States attorney for the territory of Wyoming. Before Jenkins had left for the west he had received a letter from his ex-clerk:

My wherewithal has been on the rapid decline or I would have been to see you. Nevertheless I hope that you will be able to get me some kind of place out West.

Mr. Jenkins had hardly settled down to his duties in Cheyenne when, returning to his office one day, he was told that a thin young man had been waiting for hours to see him.

That young man was the would-be lawyer from Wisconsin, the schoolmaster from Polk County, Edgar Nye. My father explained that he loved justice too well to become a jurist and that he had decided to try his hand at something—anything else in the Rocky Mountains.

Mr. Jenkins said that he hoped within a few days to get something for Nye to do. The latter explained that only heroic measures would save him from starvation.

You see, when I got off the train I had 35 cents in my pocket, but you were out of the city the day I arrived. My trunk is now at the Inter Ocean Hotel. Meals are a dollar apiece and rooms a dollar a night. My bill is now four dollars.

Mr. Jenkins had an idea that Nye would make good as a newspaper man; it was he who had noted the account of the convention that young Nye had written for the "Chicago Times." Furthermore, Mr. Jenkins happened to know that J. H. Hayford, editor of the "Sentinel" at Laramie City nearby, was in need of some one to share the troubles of his sheet. Judge N. L. Andrews, a friend of Jenkins, interceded with Dr. Hayford, and soon Nye was running the "Sentinel." His witty paragraphs were welcomed by the readers of the paper, and they began to talk about the new life that had been injected into it. Nye wrote to Jenkins:

I can now stand alone on two feet. Thanks for getting my trunk and securing my board. Enclosed find $5.

Years later Nye sketched this period of his career:

Securing second-class passage and not knowing exactly whither, so that it was west, I slept the nights away sitting upright in a coach, and landed finally in a territorial town accompanied by thirty-five cents, with which I desired to aid the flourishing young city in her wonderful growth. I was also associated with a pale yellow trunk which cost three dollars and had been rained on, so that when I landed at Cheyenne the inflated thing peeled.

I cannot think of anything sadder than to be associated with a trunk making claims to respectability which it is unable to maintain. This trunk when new had aimed to impress people with the idea that it was a *leather* trunk, but when adversity came, it surrendered and peeled. When the wall-paper came off, it was quite a plain trunk, and those who came in contact with it did not treat it with respect. I went to the best hotel, registered, and by some strange accident got a pretty good room; but I had to hurry and do it before my trunk got there.

It would take some time to tell how I got the money to pay this bill, and how the lonely little lop-eared, écru-colored trunk stood there in the baggage-room waiting for the day of its redemption to draw nigh; but suffice it that a lucky accident put me in the way of earning ten dollars by copying the minutes of a military court-martial then in session, and a tall angel with wings concealed under the cape of a Chumley overcoat was the means. His name was Remington, and I earnestly hope that he will find, when his life is over, that suitable arrangements have been made for his comfort.

Later I struck hard pan again, but the idea of despair did not enter my head. There is a general air of picnic and irresponsibility about a new country which certainly goes far to take the sting out of poverty. Stranded in New York, I would be tempted to fall from some elevated structure, perhaps, or with a shriek of despair to throw myself from the prow of some swift ferry-boat into the moaning tide; but where all is new, and where prosperity is ever generous, knowing that changes may in a few years or even months darken its own horizon, hope is the most hardy shrub that hangs upon the trellis of the heart.

If a boy could be made to believe that this one hour or day of battle with adversity may be the hand-to-hand fight of his life, compared with which all others following it will be mere skirmishes; if he could only know that the sky will never again be so somber, or his horizon so opaque—in nine cases out of ten, he would win; but he fears too often that this is the beginning only of a long life of despair and disappointment. At that time I fully expected for a few days that I would have to assist in taking care of the Union Pacific Railroad, as a lawyer friend of mine had already done—going to California in considerable style and returning by easy stages as a section hand.

The opportunity to do reporting came to the surface, and I improved it. The salary was not large; it was not impressive. It was not calculated to canker the soul. By putting handles on it every Saturday evening, I was enabled to carry it home by myself, the distance being short. I used it wisely, not running through it as some would have done. In this way at the end of the year, I had two dollars in money and a nice new set of whiskers. I also had acquired a gum overcoat, whose views one could easily get by being thrown in its society for a few minutes on a warm day.

The Sentinel was a morning paper. We printed it before sundown and distributed it before breakfast. Thus it had the appearance of extreme freshness and dampness. Old Jim Hayford was the manager of the paper.

He gave me $12 a week to edit the paper—local, telegraph, selections, religious, sporting, fashion, political and obituary. He said $12 was too much, but, if I would jerk the press occasionally and take care of his children, he would try to stand it. Perhaps I might have been there yet if I hadn't had a red-hot political campaign, and measles among the children, at the same time. You can't

mix measles and politics. So I said one day I would have
to draw the line at measles.

I collected my princely salary and quit, having acquired a style of fearless and independent journalism
which I still retain. I can write up things that never occurred with a masterly and graphic hand. Then, if they
occur afterward, I am grateful; if not, I bow to the
inevitable and smother my chagrin.

In the late spring of 1876, the town was called Laramie
City for the reason that the looks of Laramie herself would
never have suggested the appellation. The population was
about 2500. Laramie, the seat of Albany County, had been
settled by employees of the Union Pacific Railway in 1867.
Here the Laramie River cuts that system's right of way.
Laramie is fifty-eight miles west of Cheyenne, the State
capital, and is one of the stops regularly made by transcontinental trains. It is the shipping and trading center
of a large stock-raising and mining section.

When Edgar Nye and his écru trunk appeared, Wyoming had not achieved statehood. In fact, the country was
pretty wild. "Frontier" is not too strong a word to use
when you consider that the Custer Massacre occurred after
Nye went west.

The town consisted of a few hundred frame houses and
several brick and stone buildings on the Laramie plains,
clustered about the railway station. The altitude was
high; the assessed valuation was low. Liquor was plentiful
and water scarce.

There were many souls in Laramie congenial to Nye. A
few of the residents were living under assumed names, but
most of them, like Nye, had come to Laramie because they
were young and adventurous. Any one who has lived in

such a town can readily understand why Nye liked it. His talent was a new thing to him, and he had found out little about it or about himself. Like a nestling that tries its wings for the first flight, Nye was experimenting with his concealed yet revealed gift in the columns of the "Sentinel." His touch was light. His sensitiveness was keen. Wisconsin had been pioneer, yet it was already grown too conservative to bring Nye out. Then there was parental repression. Few are the places, and fewer the times, which could have supplied the field for Nye's first trial spins.

His readers were a small and unspoiled audience, many of whom he saw often. He was a good mixer. He made a host of friends. This gave him the chance to take frequent soundings. He knew quickly just how his readers were reacting to his writing.

Edgar's first squib in the "Sentinel" attracting more than local nótice was a report of an accident over which he put the head, "Presence of Mind." A workman was repairing the roof of one of Laramie's sky-scrapers when he took one sip too many from the flat bottle on his hip, lost his balance, and rolled off the roof. He fell a good many feet but without injury. Best of all he kept his pipe lighted all the while. Nye made quite a story of the roofer's imperturbability. What pleased him was that his story was reprinted by the "Pioneer Press" of St. Paul.

There was in Laramie a local humorist named Bill Root, who was the inspiration for several of Nye's first stories. Some of Root's admirers went so far as to say that Root discovered or made Nye. There were at least a score of men who claimed to have discovered Bill Nye—some of them with reason. But their very number shows that it was easier to do the discovering than to be worth the effort, and later to make good, as the discovered.

Perhaps the characteristic of Bill Nye's writings most often spoken of is his kindliness. There is no animus. This sprang from his tenderness of heart, a claim he did not advance, however, saying rather: "It's lots funnier to call yourself names. And besides, it's a lot healthier in Wyoming." And the epigram may have been inspired by an encounter with this same Colonel Root.

In one of his sallies, under the title, "A Monumental Liar," Nye said some things that were much funnier to the other residents of Laramie than to Bill Root. At that time Colonel Root was the leading story-teller and town character. So far did he forget his usual sense of humor as to arm himself and to take the war-path in search of the offending Nye. Those were the days in Wyoming when men were shot for less than this. I have been told that my father retired to the Homer ranch for a few days while Root's ire cooled. When the Colonel was himself again his laugh was the loudest. The two became better friends than ever, Nye continuing to write of Bill Root, but from that time on taking pains to avoid any unkind roast, such as a humorist's gift affords so many opportunities to use unjustly. And for his part, Root handed over the motley as Laramie's chief jester to one whom he now recognized as his superior.

Have you been wondering by what chance Edgar Wilson Nye became Bill Nye? Here is the answer in the form of a letter to a contemporary humorist, Eli Perkins:

Dear Eli:

You ask me how I came to adopt the nom de plume of Bill Nye, and I can truthfully reply that I did not do so at all.

My first work was done on a Territorial paper in the
Rocky Mountains and was not signed. The style, or
rather the lack of it, provoked some comment and two or
three personal encounters. Other papers began to wonder
who was responsible, and various names were assigned by
them as the proper one, among them Henry Nye, James
Nye, Robert Nye, and a general discussion arose, in
which I did not take a hand. The result was a compro-
mise by which I was christened Bill Nye, and the name
has clung to me. [Bret Harte's "Plain Language from
Truthful James" with its reference to "Bill Nye" had
appeared in 1870.]

I am not especially proud of the name, for it conveys
the idea to strangers that I am a lawless, profane and
dangerous man. People who judge me by the brief and
bloody name alone, instinctively shudder and examine
their firearms. It suggests daring, debauchery and de-
fiance to the law. Little children are called in when I
am known to be at large, and a day of fasting is announced by the governor of the state. Strangers seek
to entertain me by showing me the choice iniquities of
their town. Eminent criminals ask me to attend their
execution and assist them in accepting their respective
dooms. Amateur criminals ask me to revise their work
and to suggest improvements.

All this is the cruel result of an accident, for I am not
that kind of a man. Had my work been the same, done
over the signature of "Taxpayer" or "Vox Populi," how
different might have been the result! Seeking as I am,
in my poor, weak way, to make folly appear foolish, and
to make men better by speaking disrespectfully of their
errors, I do not deserve to be regarded, even by strangers,

as a tough or a terror, but rather as a plain, law-abiding
citizen, who begs leave to subscribe himself, yours, for
the Public Weal,   EDGAR WILSON NYE.

In his work for the "Sentinel" Nye had fun with the
Indians, and if his accounts are to be believed, some of
them had fun with him. There was Colorow, for instance,
chief of the Southern Utes. Nye called him his comrade
in arms, saying:

Have we not roamed over the North Park and Muddy
Pass and along Owl Creek and over Independence Mountain together, or nearly so, I being only two or three
mountains in advance?

Colorow once jumped one of my mines, but I did not
criticize him, for the day he jumped the mine, I jumped
the country. I had just gone down the gulch a little way
and was returning. As I strolled up the trail I burst
forth into song. My soul was full and seemed to swell
up in one of the most joyous little pianos that ever jolted
the geological formations of Colorado.

It was at this time that Colorow and I were thrown together. But there could be nothing in common between
two men of such opposite tastes. He was a thickset hairy
man with an immediate gun; I a tall, lithe blonde person,
less hairy than he, and ill-fitted for assassination.

As a result of his studies Nye had acquired an excellent
grasp of the fundamentals of the legal profession, and he
had been neither lazy nor careless in his attempts to master
the letter. But his mind was too effervescent to make for
a retentive verbal memory. Ideas rose from his mind like
bubbles from champagne. He couldn't keep his thoughts
static long enough to permit prosaic definitions to sink in.

And so, though he knew that he had many of the qualities of a successful attorney he hadn't passed the Wisconsin examinations. In Laramie, finding that his journalistic duties did not require all of his time or energy, he tried once more for admission to the bar and, somewhat to his surprise, made the grade. His way of putting it was:

When I went to the Rocky Mountains, it was my intention to practice law, although I had been warned by the authorities not to do so. Still I did practice in a surreptitious kind of a way, and might have been practicing yet if my client hadn't died. When you have become attached to a client and respect and like him, and then when, without warning, like a bolt of electricity from a clear sky, he suddenly dies and takes the bread right out of your mouth, it is rough.

Then I tried the practice of criminal law, but my client got into the penitentiary, where he was of no use to me financially or politically. Finally, when the judge was in a hurry, he would appoint me to defend the pauper criminals. They all went to the penitentiary, until people got to criticizing the judge, and finally they told him that it was a shame to appoint me to defend an innocent man.

During the brief period that my sheet-iron sign was kissed by the Washoe zephyrs, I had several odd experiences. One day I was figuring up how much a man could save in ten years, paying forty dollars a month rent, and taking in two dollars and fifty cents per month, when a large man with a sad eye came in and asked me if my name was Nye. I told him it was and asked him to take a chair and spit on the stove a few times, and make himself entirely at home. He did so. After allowing in a loud, tremulous voice that we were having rather a backward spring, he produced a red cotton handkerchief and took out of it a deed which he submitted to my ripe and logical legal mind.

I asked him if that was his name that appeared in the body of the deed as a grantor. He said it was. I then asked him why his wife had not signed it, as it seemed to be the deed to the homestead. Her name appeared in the instrument with that of her husband, but her signature wasn't at the foot, though his name was duly signed, witnessed and acknowledged. "Well," said he, "there's where the gazelle comes in." He then took a bite off the corner of a plug of tobacco about as big as a railroad land grant, and laid two twenty dollar gold pieces on the desk near my arm. I took them and tapped them together like the cashier of the Bank of England, and, disguising my annoyance over the little episode, told him to go on.

"Well," said the large man, "my wife has conscientious scruples against signing that deed. We have been married a year now, but not actively for the past eleven months. I'm kind of ex-officio husband, as you might say. After we'd been married about a month a little incident occurred which made a riffle in our domestic tide. I was division master on the U. P., and one night I got an order to go down towards Sidney and look at a bridge. Of course I couldn't get back till the next evening. So I sighed and switched off to the superintendent's office, expecting to go over on No. 4 and look at the bridge. At the office they told me that I needn't go till Tuesday, so I strolled up town and got home about nine o'clock, went in with a latch key, just as a mutual friend went out through the bed-room window, taking a sash that I paid two dollars for. I didn't care for the sash, because he left a pair of pantaloons worth twelve dollars and some silver in the pockets. But I thought it was such odd taste for a man to wear a sash without his uniform.

"Well, as I had documentary evidence against my wife, I told her she could take a vacation. She cried, but it didn't count. I suffered a good deal, but tears did not avail. It takes lots of damp weather to float me out of my regular channel. She spent the night packing her trousseau, and in the morning she went away. Now, I could divorce her and save all this trouble of getting her signature, but I'd rather not tell this whole business in court, for the little woman seems to be trying to do better, and if it wasn't for her blamed old hyena of a mother, would get along tip-top. She's living with her mother now and if a lawyer would go to the girl and tell her how it is, and that I want to sell the property and want her signature, in place of getting a divorce, I believe she'd sign. Would you mind trying it?"

I said if I could get time I would go over and talk with her and see what she said. So I did. I got along pretty well, too. I found the young woman at home, and told her the legal aspects of the case. She wouldn't admit any of the charges, but after a long parley agreed to execute the deed and save trouble. She came to my office an hour later, and signed the instrument. I got two witnesses to the signature and had just put the notarial seal on it when the girl's mother came in. She asked her daughter if she had signed the deed and was told that she had. The old lady said nothing, but smiled in a way that made my blood run cold. If a woman were to smile on me that way every day, I should certainly commit some great crime.

I was just congratulating myself on the success of the business, and was looking at the two $20 gold pieces and trying to get acquainted with them after the two women had gone away, when they returned with the husband and son-in-law at the head of the procession. He looked pale and care-worn to me. He asked me in a low voice if I had a deed there, executed by his wife. I said yes. He then asked me if I would kindly destroy it. I said I would. I would make deeds and tear them up all day at $40 apiece. I said I like the conveyancing business very much, and if a client felt like having a grand, warranty deed debauch, I was there to furnish the raw material.

I then tore up the deed and the two women went quietly away. After they had gone, my client, in an absent-minded way, took out a large quid that had outlived its usefulness, laid it tenderly on the open page of Estey's Pleadings, and said:

"You doubtless think I am a singular organization, and that my ways are past finding out. I wish to ask you if I did right a moment ago?" Here he took out another $20 and put it under the paper weight. "When I went downstairs I met my mother-in-law. She always looked to me like a firm woman, but I did not think she was so unswerving as she really is. She asked me in a low, musical voice to please destroy the deed, and then she took one of them Smith & Wesson automatic advance agents of death out from under her apron and kind of wheedled me into saying I would. Now, did I do right? I want a candid, legal opinion, and I'm ready to pay for it."

I said he did perfectly right.

Fifty years ago, as to-day, the red tape of the pension office was a governmental vice. And it was at this clumsy procrastination that Nye, in the story that follows, aimed one of his darts:

> When business in my office was not very rushing, and no dream of my present dazzling literary success had entered my mind, I rashly offered to assist applicants for pensions in attracting the attention of the general government, at so much per head.
>
> One hot day in July while I sat in my office killing flies with an elastic band and wondering if my mines would ever be quoted in the market, a middle-aged man came in and began to tell me about his service as a soldier, and how he was wounded, and wished to secure a pension.
>
> He said that several attorneys had already tried to procure one for him, but had failed to do so, giving up in despair. I examined the wound, which consisted of a large hole in the skull, caused by gun-shot. He was almost entirely prevented by this wound from obtaining a livelihood, because he was liable at any moment to fall insensible to the ground, as the result of exercise or work. I told him that I would snatch a few moments from my arduous duties and proceed to do as he requested me.
>
> Then I began a very brisk correspondence with the Interior Department. I would write to the Commissioner of Pensions in my vivacious but firm manner and he would send me back a humorous little circular showing me that I had been too hasty and premature. I never got mad or forgot myself but began a little farther back in the history of the world, and gradually led up to the war of the rebellion. In reply, the Commissioner would write back to me that my chronological table was at fault and I would cheerfully correct the error and proceed.

At this time, however, my client became a little despondent, several years having elapsed since we began our task. So to my other labors I had to add that of cheering up the applicant.

Time dragged its slow length along. Months succeeded months and the years sped on.

The Interior Department never forgot me. Every little while I would get a printed circular boiling over with mirth and filled with the most delightful conundrums relative to the late unpleasantness. These conundrums I would have my client answer and swear to, although I could see that he was failing mentally and physically. He would come into my office almost every day, and silently raise his right hand and with uncovered head stand there in a reverent attitude for me to swear him to something. Sometimes I had nothing for him to swear to, and then I would make him take the oath of allegiance and send him away. I wanted to keep him loyal if I could, whether he got his pension or not.

The last work had been nearly completed, and the claim had been turned over to the Surgeon-General's office, when the applicant yielded to the crumbling effect of relentless time, and took to his bed.

It was a sad moment for me. I could not keep back the silent tears when I saw the old man lying there so still and so helpless, and remembered how rosy, and strong, and happy he looked years and years ago, when he first asked me to apply for his pension.

I wrote the Department that if the claims could be passed upon soon, I would keep my client up on stimulants a short time, but that he was failing fast. Then I went to the bedside of the old man, and watched him tenderly.

When he saw me come into his room, although he could not talk any more, he would feebly raise his right hand, and I would swear him to support the Constitution of the United States, and then he would be easier. It seemed to me like a ghastly joke for the old man to swear he would support the Constitution of the United States, when he couldn't begin to support his own constitution.

At last the blow fell. The Surgeon-General wrote me that owing to the lack of clerical aid in that office, and a failure of Congress to make any appropriation for that purpose, he was behindhand, and could not possibly reach the claim referred to before the close of the following year.

Then the old man passed into the great untried realm of the hereafter. But he was prepared. With the aid of the government, I had given him an idea of Eternity and its vastness, which could not fail to be of priceless benefit to him.

After the government had used this pension money as long as it needed it, and was, so to speak, once more on its feet, the money was sent, and the old man's great-grand-children got it, and purchased a lawn-mower, a Mexican hairless dog and some other necessaries of life.

Of course Bill Nye caricatures himself as a lawyer. But those who knew him when he had his shingle out say that Edgar Nye took his cases seriously and handled them successfully. When he was in his study reading the law or preparing a brief, there was none in the household who had the temerity to disturb him. And it was not as a joke that his townsmen, and women—for women voted in Wyoming—elected and reëlected him justice of the peace. Young as he was, he was respected for his keen insight and undeviating fairness. He was addressed as "Judge Nye" with a

deference that would have surprised those who knew him
only through the columns of the "Sentinel." Of course his
own stories of his "judicial" activities are in a lighter vein.

It was at this time that I was chosen by the will of the
people to go and sit on the woolsack as Justice of the
Peace. I know that I trembled for fear that I should not
successfully fill my predecessor's place, and so I used to
go over to the penitentiary, where he was stopping for a
few years, to get points from him as to my course of
action. At first I sought to evade the great responsibility, and told the people to search far and wide, that
possibly they would find a more worthy man. They went
away and were gone quite a long time. Then they came
back and said "No," they could not find any one who
seemed to be raised up as I was to lead our people through
the doubts and dangers of the coming years, up into the
glorious light of peace and prosperity.

"Oh, go away," I was heard to say to them; "I fear
that you are joshing me."

I was elected quite vociferously, for the people of the
West are a humor-loving people and entered into the
thing with great glee. Therefore, on the first of January
I procured a compressed room with a real window in it,
through which the glad sunlight and 'most any other
medium-sized object came softly stealing. Furnishing
this room by means of a little bright red stove and a copy
of the Revised Statutes, I was ready to mete out sub-
stantial justice to those who would call and examine stock
and prices.

It was really pathetic to see the poor little miserable
booth where I sat and waited with numb fingers for business. But I did not then see the pathos which clung to

every cobweb and darkened the rattling casement. Possibly I did not know enough.

The office was not a salaried one, but solely dependent upon fees, the county furnishing only the copy of the Revised Statutes and a woolsack, slightly and prematurely bald. So while I was called Judge Nye, and frequently mentioned in the papers with great consideration, I was out of coal about half the time, and once could not mail my letters for three weeks because I did not have the necessary postage.

The first business that I had was a marriage ceremony. I met the groom on the street. He asked if I could marry people. I said that I could to a limited extent. He said that he wanted to get married. I asked him to secure the victim, and I would get the other ingredients. He then wished to know where my office was. It occurred to me at that moment that there was no fire in the stove; also, no coal; also, that the west half of the stove had fallen in during the night. So I said that I would marry them at their home. He maintained that his home was over eighty miles away and that it would consume too much time to go there.

"Where are you stopping at?" I inquired, using the Pike County style of syntax in order to show that I was one of the people.

"Well, we met here, Squire. She come in on the Last Chance stage, and I'm camped up in Gov'ment Cañon, not fur from Soldier Crick. We can go out there, I reckon."

I did not mind the ride, so I locked my office, secured a book of forms, and meeting the young people at the livery stable, went out with them and married them in a rambling way. The bride was a peri from Owl Creek, wearing moccasins of the pliocene age. The rich Castilian blood of the cave-dwellers mantled in her cheek along with the navy-blue blood of Connecticut on her father's side. Her hair was like the wing of a raven, and she wore a tiara of clam-shells about her beetling brow. Her bracelet was a costly string of front teeth, selected from the early settlers at the foot of Independence Mountain. With the shrewdness of a Yankee and the hauteur of the savage, she combined the grotesque grammar of Pike County with the charming naïveté of the cow-puncher. She was called Beautiful Snow. But I think it was mostly in a spirit of banter. She was also no longer young. I asked her, with an air of badinage, if she remembered Pizarro, but she replied that she was away from home when he came through. The cave-dwellers were a serious people. Their plumbing was very poor indeed; so also were their jokes. Her features were rather classic, however, and, I was about to say, clean-cut, but on more mature thought I will not say that. Her nose was bright and piercing. It resembled the breast-bone of a sand-hill crane.

The groom was a man of great courage and held human life at a low figure. That is why he married Beautiful Snow without any flinching; also why I have refrained from mentioning his name; also why I kissed the bride. I did not yearn to kiss her. There were others who had claims on me, but I did not wish to give needless pain to the groom. He had no money, but said that he had a saddle which I was welcome to. I did not have anything to put the saddle on at home, but rather than return empty-handed I took it.

It was soon after this I decided to give my hand in marriage to my present wife. Concluding that I had more poverty than one person was entitled to, I made up my mind to endow some deserving young woman with a part of it. There was really something rather pathetic in the transaction, viewing it from this distance across the level plateau of gathering years. But it did not seem so then.

The sorry office with its hollow-chested wood-box and second-hand stove, red with the rust of time and rain of heaven, the empty docket, the shy assault and battery, the evasive common drunk, the evanescent homicide, the faraway malice prepense, the long-delayed uxoricide, the widely segregated misdemeanor, the skittish felony—all, all seemed to warn me and admonish me against matrimony.

CHAPTER VII

HUSBAND, JUSTICE, JOURNALIST, AND COMMISSIONER

NYE went to Laramie in the spring of '76. One day of the following January, when the Cheyenne train arrived, he saw a young lady of about his own age alight. She was a petite girl with twinkly-brown eyes, wavy, dark hair, and a frank, engaging smile. To Nye the sight of this five feet of femininity was like a warm breeze from paradise. He correctly diagnosed his sensation as love at first sight. And as for Clara Frances Smith, she had already spied the tall figure of Edgar Nye upon the platform and, reading his face with the intuition for which her sex is renowned, she had the sudden conviction that her destiny walked abroad.

It is only truthful to say that each of these young people had been told of the other and that both were on the alert for observations. Fanny Smith was from Illinois. Her father and mother were York State folk from Lansingburg, now a suburb of Troy. In 1834, they, like Edgar's parents, had gone west. The father, Charles Day Smith, believing in the future of steam transportation, had entered the railroad business, and, according to family tradition, he became the first station agent in the city of Chicago.

Clara Frances, or Fanny, as she was generally called, was the youngest of five children. Her brother, Day K. Smith, was district superintendent of the Union Pacific at Cheyenne, and there Fanny had been visiting. She liked the new country and was thinking of putting her chief accomplishment, music, to work in one of these Wyoming towns. The wife of the publisher of the "Sentinel" was a friend, and it was to pay Mrs. Hayford a visit, and at the same time to investigate the possibilities for musical instruction, that Miss Smith went to Laramie. Mrs. Hayford was the kindly spirit who, knowing both the young people and correctly sensing their tastes, had told Edgar of her charming guest, at the same time not failing to pique the interest of Miss Smith in her husband's associate.

In a few weeks the young people saw as much of each other as many couples do in the same number of months. Their engagement came quickly, and the marriage followed so soon upon its heels that seven weeks from the time of their first meeting the "Cheyenne Sun," on March 7, 1877, carried this announcement:

The marriage ceremony of Miss Clara F. Smith to Mr. Edgar W. Nye was performed here at 6 o'clock this afternoon by Bishop Spaulding, of Denver, in the presence of a few friends. Dr. J. H. Hayford gave away the bride. There were some very handsome presents bestowed upon the newly married pair. The affair was a very solemn one. Nye forgot all his jokes suitable to the occasion, and will hereafter be known as the obituary editor of the Sentinel.

The marriage was a two-ring ceremony, and until death parted the twain both wore the plain gold bands with all of the affection and loyalty that this old-fashioned custom symbolized.

My father used to say that one of my mother's chief attractions was the fact that she was an orphan and he knew the mother-in-law joke would never be brought home to him.

Also he felt that there were too many Smiths, and he owed a duty to society to reduce the number in so far as possible.

> Thus I married, and one evening while the town lay hushed in slumber, and only the mountain zephyr from the grim old Medicine Bow range rustled the new leaves of the quaking aspen and the cottonwood, I moved. Not having any piano or sideboard, I did the moving myself. It did not take long.

This was the way the bridegroom described the commencement of housekeeping.

There was neither leisure nor the surplus for a honeymoon journey. This was postponed for many years and then—but that is another story.

I have before me in my mother's handwriting her first recollections of the bridegroom. Says she: "I thought his face kind, gentle and clever. I couldn't but notice the cheerful influence he had upon all he met. This quaint quality he carried with him always. He made you feel merry while you were with him, and when he left, you bubbled over, patting yourself on the back for discovering that you were really quite funny yourself."

In following the story of Nye, it is not difficult to see how his marriage helped and reinforced him. Not only was he given an objective but he had added to his own wavering confidence in his ability as a professional funny man the understanding faith of a partner in whose judgment he had implicit trust.

I have never known a more happily mated pair than my father and mother. He teased her about being four weeks older than himself. He would sometimes put into his stories subtle references with a family application. But there was always the closest comradeship between the two, and I never heard so much as a raised voice, much less a cross word. They married on an income of sixty dollars a month, and they lived on that salary. But their marriage marked the beginning of a steady increase in my father's earnings, continuing throughout their twenty years together. As Nye put it:

The legislature, seeing the county would have to provide for me in some way, decided to abolish one of the other justices. Then trade picked up. I was also ex-officio coroner. I would marry a quick-tempered couple in the morning, sit on the husband in the afternoon, and try the wife in a preliminary way in the evening for the murder. Thus business became more and more brisk. Sometimes a murderer would escape the grand jury and get lynched, but he did not escape me. If I could not try him in life's bright summertime, I could sit on him and preside over his inquest after the lynching. We had considerable excitement, too, in those days, for the town was young and laws were crude. Lawyers were still cruder. I rose early in the morning while the coyotes sang in the suburbs of the city.

The most attractive day's work that I remember was the preliminary examination of a band of stage-robbers, captured by Sheriff Boswell and a posse in the early morning. I examined them in the forenoon and held a double inquest in the evening on two gentlemen from a tie camp in the mountains. That was my busy day. I think Bronco Sam called that day also to be married to Mademoiselle Walk-Around-the-Block. I was too busy to marry him that day, and so he went elsewhere, fearing that if he put it off he might change his mind. Later he shot his wife, and then blowing out his brains instead of turning them off, he closed his career with the regular red fire and fortissimo bassdrum of the new West.

The stage-robbers had among them the gentlemanly, genial and urbane Irvin and the brainy but somewhat erratic and felonious "Kid." They were captured by a band of gritty frontiersmen under Sheriff Boswell. Boswell was not a toy frontiersman with long, accordion-plaited hair, tied back with blue ribbon, in which at springtime the swallows came to build their nests and rear their young. He was a plain, quiet man, with the scars of Indian arrows all over him, the record of an early day when you could not fight Indians by means of a Pullman car. I always admired him because he cut his hair and manicured his nails even in the early days. Boswell was not reckless of human life, and in fact killed very few people, but if a bad man had to be captured and brought to camp in good order, he generally had the job.

These road agents were a picturesque little party. They had probably not slept in a house for two or three years, and they needed repairs. They removed their spurs and piled them up in the corner of the room like a large bed of cactus. Their side-arms and Winchesters made a little hardware store on top of my desk. They were disagreeable men in some respects, and yet they did much to elevate the stage, especially the Rock Creek and Black Hill stages. Irvin was tried finally for some minor felony and got nine years. On top of this, in some way, he was also indicted for murder in the first degree and got a life sentence. The jailer found him in tears afterwards, in his cell.

"Why do you weep?" asked the gentle jailer, looking sadly into the uncertain light.

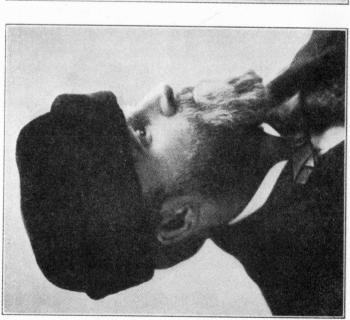

BILL NYE ABOUT THE TIME OF HIS MARRIAGE

"At the end of the year I had two dollars in money and a nice new set of whiskers."

MRS. EDGAR WILSON NYE

"Concluding that I had more poverty than one person was entitled to, I made up my mind to endow some deserving young woman with a part of it."

"Because," said the sobbing outlaw, "I shall be so busy serving out my life sentence that I do not see how in Sam Hill I am going to get time to serve out those nine years for plain robbery."

Of course, during the six years of my judicial life I met with many reverses, especially at the hands of the Supreme Court.

The income of a justice of the peace in a town like Laramie, even when supplemented by the salary of a newspaper man, would not sustain life in a growing family. And the Nye family had expanded by the addition of my two sisters, Bessie and Winifred. The household provider cast about for new sources of income, and discovering vacancies in government offices, proceeded, with the help of a growing circle of friends, to annex the office of U. S. commissioner and later that of postmaster.

His newspaper work now consisted of writing the "Laramie Sentinel" and acting as the Laramie correspondent of the "Cheyenne Sun." Encouraged by the fact that other Wyoming papers were copying his breezy locals, the idea entered Nye's mind of sending a sample of his work to the "Denver Tribune." Denver was the metropolis of the Rockies, and the "Tribune" of those days was in the hands of a notable coterie.

Eugene Field, who by the way was born the week after Bill Nye and died three months earlier than Nye, was doing paragraphs and poems. F. J. V. Skiff, later such a notable figure in exposition work; E. D. Cowan, Field's closest friend; F. O. Dickensheets, who later published the "Denver Republican," which absorbed the "Tribune"; O. H. Rothacker, a short-lived journalistic genius, whose work was attracting national attention at the time of his death—these were some of the notables who welcomed the Laramie funny man.

It was a crucial moment for Nye when his first letter came into the hands of Thomas F. Dawson, city editor. A rejection would have prolonged the period of early struggle. But Dawson had the insight, and Nye had the "goods." Dawson thought the letter well worth the fifteen dollars Nye asked for it. But Herman Beckerts, the owner, instructed Dawson to offer seven dollars. Nye was in no position to refuse and gladly supplied letters regularly at that figure. The first letter is still preserved in the files of the paper. It is a rambling, gossipy account of doings in Wyoming, full of laughs and snickers.

The "Denver Tribune's" exchanges were quick to discover the appeal that lurked in Nye's column, and soon Bill Nye was quoted and copied widely. The papers in Omaha and Salt Lake, the "Detroit Press," "Texas Siftings," "Peck's Sun," and many another took up the flare for the Laramie humorist, thus paving the way for the later success of the "Boomerang" and Nye's syndicate stories.

Nye's handwriting was full of individuality but not so full of legibility. He envied the penmanship of Eugene Field, of whom he said:

When you come to think of it, it is not surprising that so many newspaper men write so that no one but an expert can read it. The rapid and voluminous work, especially of daily journalism, knocks the beautiful business college penman, as a rule, higher than a kite.

I do not remember a newspaper acquaintance whose penmanship is so characteristic of the exacting neatness and sharp, clear cut style of the man, as is that of Eugene Field. As the "Nonpareil Writer" of the "Denver

Tribune," it was a mystery to me when he did the work which the paper showed each day as his own. You would sometimes find him at his desk, writing on large sheets of "print paper" with a pen and violet ink, in a hand that was as delicate as the steel plate of a bank note and the kind of work that printers would skirmish for. He would ask you to sit down in the chair opposite his desk, which had two or three old exchanges thrown on it. He would probably say, "Never mind those papers. I've read them. Just sit down on them if you want to." Encouraged by his hearty manner, you would sit down, and you would continue to sit down till you had protruded about three-fourths of your system through that hollow mockery of a chair. Then he would run to help you out and curse the chair, and feel pained because he had erroneously given you the ruin with no seat to it. He always suffered keenly and felt shocked over the accident until you had gone away, and then he would sigh heavily and "set" the chair again.

With the "Denver Tribune" letter added to his other chores Nye was now operating at high speed. And this is reflected in his own list of activities of that period.

My duties are manifold and exceedingly heterogeneous. By the time I saw wood enough to last during the day, curry and groom my favorite shanghai, write an ode in D sharp to his Excellency, the Governor [please note the new additions to the vocabulary of Fanny Smith's star music pupil], and compose a contralto fantasia in G, dedicated to the Secretary of Wyoming, and a little mezzo soprano symphony ranging from J on added line below up to about 135 ozs. to the ton, and arranged for Secretary Schurz, and then eat a lunch in F and write a little

Ute sonnet in A minor for the "Denver Tribune," and
a little Sic Semper Gloria Glafcke for the "Cheyenne
Sun," and cinch the common drunk $5 and trimmings,
run the regular routine of fragments through the police
court program in C, and write up a few fashion items
and give the Laramie cow a grand matinée in the "Times,"
and eat my supper, the day is so far spent and the night
is so extremely contiguous, that I don't have time to
write to my friends.

Reading over the old scrap-book which my father kept at
this time, I came across his description of the Laramie leap-
year ball of 1880. I cannot resist the pure joy of setting
down his description of the costumes worn by the leading
citizens. Their wives' gowns were ignored.

Henry Wagner wore an organdie paletot, with inlaid
burlaps, looped back with moire antique; hair done up
in Pompadour wad.

Otto Gramm was perfectly bewitching with both ears
tied in a hard knot behind his head, and top of head
polished and varnished; also decalcomania scrap book
decorations.

C. W. Spalding wore a gros grain Russia Iron ap-
pliqué, with corsage of tin roofing held in place with
buckskin strings.

E. A. Slack attracted a good deal of attention in a
tarletan costume with lambrequins of pale pink, and
housings of split leather, held in place with mucilage and
tarred rope.

Ed. Dickinson wore emerald socks, clocked with eight
day clocks, and medallion suspender buttons. He also
wore a majolica dolman with lap robe of imported gunny
sack, looped back with copper rivets.

G. B. Grow wore an elegant costume of clamshell gray and pollywog brown, with Italian dressing. The basque was trimmed with passementerie, stylishly scalloped and served with crabapple jelly.

E. W. Nye wore his seldom costume, looped back with Pompadour yoke of the same. He wore his hair as usual —very much banged and cut princesse.

Evidently Nye's first term as justice gave general satisfaction to his constituents, for in 1880, at the time of the presidential election, he was returned to the woolsack. Nye's newspaper announcement stated that he, Garfield, and Arthur had been successful at the polls.

Just one more of Nye's adventures as justice:

One night after I had retired and gone to sleep a milkman, called Bill Dunning, rang the bell and got me out of bed. Then he told me that a man who owed him a milk bill of $35 was all loaded up and prepared to slip across the line into Colorado, there to grow up with the country and acquire other indebtedness, no doubt. Bill desired an attachment for the entire wagon-load of goods and said he had an officer at hand to serve the writ.

"But," said I, as I wrapped a "Welcome" husk door mat around my glorious proportions, "how do you know while we converse together he is not winging his way down the valley of the Paudre?"

"Never mind that, jedge," says William. "You just fix the dockyments and I'll tend to the defendant."

In an hour Bill returned with $35 in cash for himself and the entire costs of the court, and as we settled up and fixed the docket I asked Bill Dunning how he detained the defendant.

"You reckollect, jedge," says William, "that the

waggin wheel is held onto the exle with a big nut. No waggin kin go any length of time without that there nut onto the exle. Well, when I diskivered that what's-his-name was packed up and the waggin loaded, I took the liberty to borrow one o' them there nuts fur a kind of momento, as it were, and I kept that in my pocket till we served the writ and he paid my bill and came to his milk, if you'll allow me that expression, and then I says to him, 'Pardner,' says I, 'you are going far, far away where I may never see you again. Take this here nut,' says I, 'and put it onto the exle of the oft hind wheel of your waggin, and whenever you look at it hereafter, think of poor old Bill Dunning, the milkman."

One of Bill Nye's little journeys into official life was as U. S. commissioner, to which office he was duly appointed as added evidence of the fact that, much though his friends laughed at his writings, as a citizen he was taken seriously. Let him tell a few of his experiences in this capacity; the story of Soiled Smith, for instance:

Years ago Soiled Smith ceased to exist in the capacity of a man, and began to mingle with the dust from which he came. I presume that since the early dawn of creation no man ever died who became at once so thoroughly identified with the geological structure of the earth as did Soiled Smith. He had prepared himself for it by careful training, and "dust thou art unto dust shalt thou return" had no terrors for him.

My first acquaintance with Soiled Smith was while I was sustaining one corner of the national fabric as United States Commissioner of the Second Judicial District of Wyoming and ex-officio notary public for Albany County. The office of United States Commissioner was fraught with the most innocuous desuetude that I ever laid a lip over. The first day after I was appointed I had all I could do to keep down a feeling of most violent intolerance and arrogance. That night I did not sleep much, because I expected at any moment to be called upon by the Government to try a case.

I had not held the office over a year when suddenly, like a clap of thunder from a clear sky, a case was brought up before for me for preliminary examination. Three greasers, named Don Colorado Jobacos, Jesus Fabricante and Tufa Fivecente Maduro, were charged with selling liquor to Indians on the reservation, and I tried them for four days with all the earnest and acquired momentum of a man who has been saving up his energies for nearly a year. I can truly say that I never tried more faithfully to sift the evidence and get at the truth in any case with which I have been connected. We did not spare mileage or per diem in our efforts to obtain all the knowledge we could. I issued subpœnas for people who were unable to come and people who wouldn't come. In answer to the demands of the plaintiff I sent every kind of a subpœna, writ, bench warrant or requisition that the statute allowed a fee for, and among the rest I subpœnaed Soiled Smith.

He did not come.

I issued a quo warranto, but he came not. I then made out a large blue requisition for him, with an acknowledgment and a green notarial seal on the back, but he sent in his regrets and went up into the Diamond Peak country for a change of scene and rest.

The case had to proceed without the evidenc of Soiled Smith, but, with the aid of the United States Attorney, I succeeded in convicting the greasers without leaving my seat. I was as successful in this trial as an old gentleman in Maine who said he "had served on the jury for forty years and never lost a case."

But the Government came very near disallowing my bill for fees because I omitted to put a double red line under my footings. This, however, was soon remedied. I revised the bill, adding $3 for an item that I had overlooked, put a double red line under the footings and got my money. The accuracy with which the Government works in the Department of Justice is truly remarkable.

I afterward learned that the reason Soiled Smith did not respect any of my writs was that he did not like to come within the jurisdiction of the court on account of an old indictment against him which was still in a good state of preservation.

A few months later I was sent out to take the deposition of Soiled Smith in another case. He had been subpœnaed, but just as court was about to convene he had broken his leg. I had never taken anybody's deposition before and so I felt a little nervous about it. Knowing that Soiled Smith was a quick, impulsive man, with a pie-knife down the back of his neck, I feared that if I took the deposition and it didn't look like him, he might get up and imbrue his hands in my gore.

But I was agreeably surprised in his appearance. He was not ferocious in his nature generally, but meek and gentle in his ways. Though he was alone when his leg was broken, he did not murmur or repine. He bore his great misfortune there in the lone foothills and made no moan. Whatever may be said against Soiled Smith socially, he never paraded his woes before men or begged assistance and sympathy of others. I recall now, as I write, also the triumphant air with which he showed us his poor broken leg, together with the new one he had made from a pick handle, just as much like the old one as it was possible for two wooden legs to be. While I took his deposition he gently took the spike out of his broken leg and put it in the new one. I learned afterwards that when he wanted his deposition taken he generally broke his leg.

At the end of two years in this responsibility, announcement was made that the portfolio would be surrendered.

Fearing that in the hurry and rush of other business our contemporaries might overlook the matter, we have consented to mention, briefly, the fact that at the opening of the court, Judge Blair will be called upon to accept the resignation of one of our most tried and true officials.

It has been our solemn duty to examine the greaser who sold liquor to our red brother, and filled him up with the deadly juice of the sour-mash tree. It has devolved upon us to singe the soft-eyed lad who stole baled hay from the reservation, and it has also been our glorious privilege to examine, in a preliminary manner, the absent-minded party who gathered unto himself the U. S. mule.

We have attempted to resign before, but failed. One reason was, that it was a novel proceeding in Wyoming, and no one seemed to know how to go to work at it. No one had ever resigned before, and the matter had to be hunted up and the law thoroughly understood.

Sometime during the ensuing week we will turn over the lead pencil and the blotting paper of the office to our successor. We leave the Indian temperance movement in his hands. The United States mule kleptomaniac also, we leave with him. With a clear conscience and an unliquidated claim against the government for $9.55, the earnings of the past two years, we turn over the office, knowing that although we have sacrificed our health, we have never evaded our duty, no matter how dangerous or disagreeable.

Yet we do not ask for any gold-headed cane as a mark of esteem on the part of the government. We have a watch that does very well for us, so that a testimonial consisting of a gold watch, costing $250, would be unnecessary. Any little trinket of that kind would, of course, show how ready the department of justice is to appreciate the work of an efficient officer, but we do not look for it, nor ask it. A thoroughly fumigated and disinfected conscience is all we want. That is enough for us. Do not call out the band. Just let us retire from the office quietly and unostentatiously. In the bosom of our family we will forget the turbulent voyage of official life through which we have passed, and as we monkey with the children around our hearthstone, we will shut our eyes to the official suffering that is going on all around us.

True to his promise Commissioner Nye followed his warning with his official resignation:

To the Department of Justice, Washington, D. C.:
Several months ago I resigned as United States Commissioner for this judicial district. The government did not accept my resignation, thus tacitly asserting that there was no one who was considered competent to take my place.
I now once more resign. I do not do so because I am displeased with the government, or because I am displeased with public life. There is no reason why the

government and myself should not continue to be friends, but under the régime for United States Commissioner of District Courts, I am compelled to retire from the official capacity which I have so long filled with skill and credit both to myself and the United States. The Department of Justice now requires me to furnish a detailed statement each month of all the business done by the Commissioner, with his official certificate attached. I am also required to keep a large volume in my office as a record of the United States cases examined by me. I am to do this at my own expense in order that the honor and high moral tone of the nation may remain unsmirched.

All these requirements I could of course comply with, but I am cursed with the horrible apprehension that in the future I shall be required to do more of this until the expense will be more than I can meet. I could now, of course, get little chores to do around town, enough for necessary funds to buy the records, etc., but before another year the government may require me to buy a marble-topped center table and two or three paintings by the old masters, in order to give the proper amount of terror to the United States Criminals. This would compel me to go without a new overcoat and underclothes, of which I am sadly in need. I had hoped that with the financial prosperity of the past year there would be one case, at least, for examination from which I could realize $6 or $7, and which would ease this branch of the Department of Justice temporarily, but I have been disappointed all the way through. I could squeeze along without the overcoat in order to get the required record this winter, but the underclothes I feel as though I ought to have.

I might die suddenly while on the bench, and it would

sound harsh if the telegraphic dispatcher were to state that the United States Commissioner had died from exposure and temporary stagnation of underclothes.

I will now turn the office over to the department. It consists of a pine box with some specimens of second-hand chewing tobacco preserved in sawdust and a bald-headed feather duster. The department will please send a receipt to me for these archives, as I desire to have everything done correctly and with the usual amount of precision and delay.

I find that I can starve to death just as successfully in journalism as I can in my official capacity, and I hope that the government will not feel hurt over my course.

Handling the amount of money that I have handled, being a United States Commissioner, has been a terrible strain on me, and I resign before it is too late.

I resign while I have the manhood still left to overcome my fiendish desire to embezzle the coal-hod and the front door of the office.

BILL NYE.

CHAPTER VIII

BOOMING THE "BOOMERANG"

A COMPANY incorporated itself and started a paper of which I took charge. The paper was published in the loft of a livery stable. That is the reason they called it a stock company. You could come up the stairs into the office or you could twist the tail of the iron gray mule and take the elevator.

Thus was Bill Nye's newpaper, the "Boomerang," described by its founder. Sundry reasons are given for naming it the "Boomerang." One was that so many copies came back. The fact is it was named for Bill Nye's mule, Boomerang. I find this account of the coming of the stray mule set down by my mother:

This funny little creature appeared on the streets of Laramie from no one knew where. It ambled up to Edgar and rubbing its nose against his sleeve, brayed earnestly in his ear. From that time on, the arrival was known as Bill Nye's mule, Boomerang.

My father regarded Boomerang as a mascot. In gratitude for services rendered, Nye's first published book was dedicated to the luck-bearing animal:

To My Mule Boomerang

whose bright smile haunts me still, and whose low, mellow notes are ever sounding in my ears, to whom I owe all that

77

I am as a great man, and whose presence has inspired me throughout the years that are gone,

This volume,

this coronet of sparkling literary gems, this wreath of fragrant forget-me-nots, and meek-eyed johnny-jump-ups, with all its wealth of rare tropical blossoms and high-priced exotics, is cheerfully and even hilariously dedicated

By the Author.

At another time Nye remarked:

Whenever the cares of life weigh too heavily upon me, and the ennui which comes to those who have more wealth than they know what to do with settles down upon me, and I get weary of civilization, I like to load up my narrow-gauge mule and take a trip into the mountains. I call my mule Boomerang because I never know where he is going to strike.

After five years in Laramie, Edgar Nye, to his fellow-townsmen, was a good citizen who could write funny things for the paper, rather than a humorist who held office merely to gather local color. It was as Republican and journalist, more than as a humorist, that his friends backed him to publish the "Boomerang."

The Republican "Daily Sentinel" had not been a financial success. It had been kept alive for political reasons. After the campaign of '78 the owners decided, while continuing the weekly, to suspend the daily.

The Democrats perceived their opportunity and organized the "Daily Times," the first issue appearing January 2, 1879. One consequence of these changes was that Nye was no longer attached to a local daily. Another result, coming in 1880, was the loss of most of the county offices by Republicans. The latter mishap aroused several of the political leaders to promote a new daily newspaper with friendly leanings. Edgar Nye was considered the logical man to manage and edit such a paper.

Fifty-seven subscribers to stock met at the court-house and organized a corporation capitalized for three thousand dollars; 120 shares of stock at twenty-five dollars each. A. S. Peabody was president and M. C. Jahren secretary. When the articles of incorporation were filed with the secretary of state, January 18, 1881, it might have been noted that the jurat was written in Nye's handwriting and the notarial seal bore his name.

The money having been collected, Nye went to Chicago, where for eighteen hundred dollars he purchased a Washington hand-press, a Gordon jobber, and type for the newspaper and job printing department. Nye had little more than one thousand dollars left with which to put the paper on a paying basis.

The "Boomerang's" first home was on the second floor of the Kidd Building. The press was of the type that used to be called a "lemon-squeezer" and its greatest output was 250 papers an hour, two pages at a time. There was only one mail train a day, each way. The train going west arrived at 4:45 P.M., and friendly relations with the post-office made it possible to mail the papers directly on the train. Every afternoon witnessed a race between the "Boomerang" and the 4:45.

Through Nye's friendship with officials of the Associated Press he was able to make an unusually favorable contract for telegraphic despatches. This advantage soon gave the "Boomerang" an excellent sale in the towns west of Laramie.

Vol. I, No. 1, of the "Boomerang" bore the date of March

11, 1881. President Garfield had just been inaugurated
and was soon plunged into his historic fight with Conkling
and Platt over the federal appointments in New York State.
Then followed the shooting of Garfield on July 2, which
resulted in his death on September 19. Such events kept
the telegraph wires humming and were made the most of
in the columns of Laramie's new paper.

Bob Head handled the local items admirably, doubling
as advertising solicitor. Bill Nye wrote a column of humor
each day, from which a page was gathered for the "Weekly
Boomerang." Nye also had the managerial responsibility
and kept the books. One small chamber had to do for the
editorial room, local editor's quarters, and business office.

The weekly soon pulled itself out of the red ink, but the
daily ate up revenue faster than the weekly could produce
it. About May 1 a pay-day came and went without the
ghost walking. But within a day or two Nye corraled the
cash somehow, and the business continued more smoothly
until the following winter, when another stringency developed. By selling the job printing business to Garrett &
Chaplin, who were running it for the "Boomerang," the
second financial crisis was passed.

Soon after this the paper was moved into A. D. Haines's
livery stable at Third and Garfield Streets. This was the
barn so often referred to by Nye. One of his associates
thought it ill advised to park the "Boomerang" in a stable.
But Nye considered it fitting that a journal named for a
mule should be housed accordingly.

Addressing a convention of editors some years after leaving Laramie, Nye narrated some of his experiences as editor
of the "Boomerang."

It wasn't much of a paper, but it cost $16,000 a year
to run, and it came out six days in the week, no matter

HERE YOUNG NYE TAUGHT SCHOOL

THE LITTLE METHODIST CHURCH
WHERE THE NYE BOYS WERE JANI-
TORS AND WHERE THEY PRACTICED
ORATORY

THE OLD SWIMMING HOLE
"We bathed in the clear calm waters of the smooth flowing river."

what the weather. We took the Associated Press news
by telegraph part of the time, and part of the time we
relied on the Cheyenne morning papers, which we procured from the conductor on the early morning freight.
We received a great many special telegrams from Washington in that way. And when the freight train got in
late, I had to guess at what Congress was doing and
fix up a column of telegraph the best I could. There
was a rival evening paper there, and sometimes it would
send a smart boy down to the train and get hold of our
special telegrams. Sometimes the conductor would go
away on a picnic and take our Cheyenne paper with him.

All these things are annoying to a man who is trying
to supply a long felt want. There was one conductor, in
particular, who used to go into the foot-hills shooting
sage hens and take our cablegrams with him. This threw
too much strain on me. I could guess at what Congress
was doing and make up a pretty readable report, but
foreign powers and crowned heads and dynasties always
mixed me up.

Still, we used to have considerable local news to fill up
with. The north and middle parks helped us out when
the mining camps were new. Those were the days when it
was considered perfectly proper to kill off the board of
supervisors if their action was distasteful. A new camp
generally located a cemetery and wrote an obituary; then
the boys would start out to find a man whose name would
rhyme with the rest of the verse.

There were two daily and three weekly papers published in Laramie City at that time. There were between
two and three thousand people and our local circulation
ran from 150 to 250, counting dead-heads. In our pros-
pectus we stated that we would spare no expense whatever

in ransacking the universe for fresh news, but there were times when it was all we could do to get our paper out on time. Out of the express office, I mean.

One of the rival editors used to write his editorials for the paper in the evening, jerk the Washington hand-press to work them off, go home and wrestle with juvenile colic in his family until daylight and then deliver his papers on the street. It was not surprising that the great mental strain incident to this life made an old man of him, and gave a tinge of extreme sadness to the funny column of his paper.

In an unguarded moment, this man once wrote an editorial that got all his subscribers mad at him, and the same afternoon he came around and wanted to sell his paper to us for $10,000. I told him that the whole outfit wasn't worth ten thousand cents.

"I know that," said he, "but it is not the material that I am talking about. It is the *good will* of the paper."

While Nye was editing the "Boomerang," Eli Perkins visited Laramie. Here is Eli's account of the meeting written some years later:

I met Edgar Wilson Nye while passing through Laramie. Mr. Nye was then practicing law and making his first reputation as a humorist through ditorials and paragraphs in his Boomerang. These editorials were irresistibly quaint. Every one was reading his newspaper and every one loved the genial writer. He never had but one enemy, and that was the editor of the Democratic newspaper across the way. He wasted columns weekly calling Nye, to his great amusement, "an idiot and a crack-brained rattlesnake editor from Moosehead Lake." Bill Nye was then, as ever afterward, a delicate and retiring man. When I asked him why the rival editor called him such names, he said:

"Well, he is a Democratic editor and has to be precise in his statements. I was born on Moosehead Lake, in Maine, and grew up among the Indians and rattlesnakes of the West."

On the occasion of my visit to Laramie Mr. Nye introduced me to my Laramie audience. His introduction was like this:

"Ladies and gentlemen, I am glad that it has devolved upon me to-night to announce that we are to have an interesting lecture on lying by one of the most distinguished [there was a pause, for Mr. Nye's inflection indicated that he had finished, and the audience roared with delight, so that it was some time before the sentence was concluded] lecturers from the East."

Mr. Nye continued: "We have our ordinary country liars in Laramie, but Mr. Perkins comes from the metropolis. Our everyday liars have a fine record. We are proud of them, but the uncultured liars of the prairie cannot be expected to cope with the gifted and more polished prevaricators from the cultured East. Ladies and gentlemen, permit me to introduce to you Eliar Perkins."

"Ladies and gentlemen," I said in reply, "I feel justly flattered by your Laramie humorist's tribute to my veracity, but truly I am not as great a liar as Mr. Nye," and then I seemed to falter. The audience saw my dilemma and applauded, and I couldn't finish the sentence for some moments, but finally continuing I said, "I am not as big a liar as Mr. Nye—would have you think."

A day or two after this I picked up the Boomerang and read this paragraph:

"When Eli Perkins was passing through Laramie, he said he was traveling for his wife's pleasure.

" 'Then your wife is with you?' suggested our reporter.

" 'Oh, no,' said Eli; 'she is in New York.' "

Among the notables whose paths crossed Nye's trail was General Sherman. But let Nye tell the story:

I presume that I could write an entire library of personal reminiscences relative to the eminent people with whom I have been thrown during a busy life, but I hate to do it, because I always regard such things as sacred from the vulgar eye, and I feel bound to respect the confidence of a prominent man just as much as I would that of one who was less before the people. I remember well my first meeting with General W. T. Sherman.

It was on the line of the Union Pacific Railway, at one of its eating-houses. The colored waiter had cut off a strip of the omelette with a pair of shears, the scorched oatmeal had been passed around, the little rubber door mats, fried in butter and called pancakes, had been dealt around the table. The cashier at the end of the hall had just gone through the clothes of a party from Vermont, who claimed a rebate on the ground that the waiter had refused to bring him anything but his bill. There was no sound in the dining-room except the weak request of the coffee for stimulants, or perhaps the cry of pain when the butter, while practicing with the dumb-bells, would hit a child on the head.

General Sherman sat at one end of the table, throwing a life-preserver to a fly in the milk pitcher.

We had never met before, though for years we had been plodding along life's rugged way—he in the war department, I in the postoffice department.

I remember, as well as though it were but yesterday, how the conversation began. General Sherman looked sternly at me and said:

"I wish you would overpower that butter and send it up this way."

"All right," said I, "if you will please pass those molasses."

That was all that was said, but I shall never forget it, and probably he never will. The conversation was brief, but yet how full of food for thought! How true, how earnest, how natural! Nothing stilted or false about it. It was the natural expression of two minds that were too great to be verbose or to monkey with social, conversational flap-doodle.

Once I was asked by a friend to go with him in the evening to the house of an acquaintance, where they were going to have a musicale, at which there was to be a noted pianist. I did not get the name of the professional, but I went. When the first piece was announced I saw that the light was very uncertain, so I volunteered to get a lamp from another room. I held that big lamp, weighing about twenty-nine pounds, for half an hour, while the pianist would tinky tinky with the right hand, or bang, boomy to bang on the bass. He snorted and slugged that old concert grand piano and almost knocked its teeth down its throat, or gently dawdled with the keys like a pale moonbeam shimmering through the bleached rafters of a deceased horse, until at last there was a wild jangle, such as the accomplished musician gives to an instrument to show the audience that he has disabled the piano, and will take a slight intermission while it is sent to the junk shop.

With a sigh of relief I carefully put down the twenty-nine pound light, and my friend told me that I had been standing there like Liberty Enlightening the World, and holding that heavy lamp for *Blind Tom*. . . .

The Grant party passed through this town. I had an excellent opportunity for observation, and saw how the great warrior conducted himself during his stay here. While eating I noticed that he has the same swing of the biceps muscle and downward and lateral motion of the elbow simultaneous with the falling of the jaw that Wellington is said to have had. He does not wipe his hands on the tablecloth while eating, as his enemies have represented, nor swear and kick the table when he burns his mouth with coffee.

Nye wrote frequently and industriously but never promiscuously. His convictions are well enunciated below:

The Paper World says there's no use talking, the newspaper men are to-day becoming more and more "color blind." In other words, they have lost that subtle flavor of description for which the public yearns. They have missed that wonderful spice and aroma of narration which is the life of all newspaper work.

We do not take this to ourself at all, but we desire before we say one word, to make a few remarks. The "Boomerang" has been charged with erring on the other side and coloring things a little too high.

There is an excuse for lack of spice and all that sort of thing in the newspaper world. The men who write for our dailies, as a rule, have to write about two miles per day, and they ought not to be kicked if it is not as interesting as "Uncle Tom's Cabin," or "Leaves o' Grass."

We have done some 900 miles of writing ourself during our short, sharp and decisive career, and we know what we are talking about. Those things we wrote at a time when we were spreading our graceful characters over ten acres of paper per day were not thrilling. They did not catch the public eye, but were just naturally consigned to oblivion's bottomless maw.

Read that last sentence twice; it will do you no harm.

The public, it seems to us, has created a false standard of merit for the newspaper. People take a big daily and pay $10 per year for it because it is the biggest paper in the world, and then don't read a quarter of it. They are doing a smart thing, no doubt, but it is killing the feverish young men with throbbing brains, who are doing the work. Would you consider that a large pair of shoes or a large wife should be sought for just because you can get more material for the same price? Not much, Mary Ann!

Excellence is what we seek, not bulk. Write better things and less of them, and you will do better, and the public will be pleased to see the change.

Should any one who reads these words be suffering from an insatiable hunger for a paper that aims at elegance of diction, high-toned logic and pink cambric sentiment, at a moderate price, he will do well to call at this office and look over our goods. Samples sent free on application, to any part of the United States or Europe. We refer to Herbert Spencer, the Laramie National Bank, and the postmaster of this city, as to our reputation for truth and veracity.

Nye was the postmaster.

Gold and silver were to be found in the hills of Wyoming and northern Colorado near Laramie. While Nye lived there Laramie was an outfitting place for prospectors, and mining was a favorite topic of conversation about the town. It was inevitable that Nye should join in the discussion. In his accounts of his mining properties he of course "salts" the vein considerably, but like most of his neighbors he did take a few small fliers in the mining game. The names he

gave his claims were the best thing about them.   One was
suitably christened the New Jerusalem.   He had little confidence in engineers and said of them:

> I have no faith in mining experts, and with all due
> deference to their knowledge of dips and geological for-
> mations and surface indications, I still prefer to take
> the light of day and go down into a shaft and see how she
> seems, in preference to purchasing the wisdom of a man
> who labors under the impression that he stood in with the
> Creator on the architectural designs of the universe and
> helped to lay the corner-stone of creation with appro-
> priate ceremonies.

Nye came into possession of another mine.   This one was
named the Vanderbilt.   Like the New Jerusalem, it was
soon for sale, however.

> I have decided to sacrifice another valuable piece of
> mining property this spring.   It would not be sold if I
> had the necessary capital to develop it.   It is a good mine,
> for I located it myself.   I remember well the day I climbed
> up on the ridge-pole of the universe and nailed my loca-
> tion notice to the eaves of the sky.
>
> It was in August that I discovered the Vanderbilt claim
> in a snow-storm.   It cropped out apparently a little
> southeast of a point where the arc of the orbit of Venus
> bisects the milky way, and ran due east eighty chains,
> three links and a swivel, thence south fifteen paces, three
> links of sausage and a half to a fixed star, thence north
> across the lead to place of beginning.
>
> The Vanderbilt set out to be a carbonate deposit, but
> changed its mind.   I sent a piece of the cropping to a
> man over in Salt Lake, who is a good assayer and quite a

scientist, if he would brace up and avoid humor. His assay read as follows, to wit:

Salt Lake City, U. T., August 25, 1877.

Mr. Bill Nye:

Your specimen of ore No. 35832, current series, has been submitted to assay and shows the following result:

Metal	Ounces	Value per ton
Gold	...	...
Silver	...	...
Railroad iron	1	...
Pyrites of poverty	9	...
Parasites of disappoint- ment	90	...

McVicker, Assayer.

Note.—I also find that the formation is igneous, prehistoric and erroneous. If I were you I would sink a prospect shaft below the vertical slide where the old red brimstone and preadamite slag cross-cut the malachite and intersect the schist. I think that would be schist about as good as anything you could do. Then send me specimens with $2 for assay and we shall see what we shall see.

Well, I didn't know he was "an humorist," you see, so I went to work on the Vanderbilt to try and do what Mac. said. I sank a shaft and everything else I could get hold of on that claim. It was so high that we had to carry water up there to drink when we began and before fall we had struck a vein of the richest water you ever saw. We had more water in the mine than the regular army could use.

When we got down sixty feet I sent some pieces of the pay streak to the assayer again. This time he wrote me

quite a letter, and at the same time inclosed the certificate
of assay.

Salt Lake City, U. T., October 3, 1877.

Mr. Bill Nye:

Your specimen of ort No. 36132, current series, has been
submitted to assay and shows the following result:

Metal	Ounces	Value per ton
Gold	...	...
Silver	...	...
Stove Polish	trace	.01
Old gray whetstone....	trace	.01
Bromide of axle grease.	stain	...
Copperas	trace	5c. worth
Blue vitriol	trace	5c. worth

McVICKER, Assayer.

In the letter he said there was, no doubt, something
in the claim if I could get the true contact with calcimine
walls denoting a true fissure. He thought I ought to
run a drift. I told him I had already run adrift.

Then he said to stope out my stove polish ore and sell
it for enough to go on with the development. I tried that,
but capital seemed coy.

The Vanderbilt mine, with all its dips, spurs, angles,
variations, veins, sinuosities, rights, titles, franchises, pre-
rogatives and assessments, is now for sale. I sell it in order
to raise the necessary funds for the development of the
Governor of North Carolina. I had so much trouble with
water in the Vanderbilt, that I named the new claim the
Governor of North Carolina, because he was always dry.

There were two famous Nye dogs, Kosciusko and Entomologist. The latter provided the topic for a part of
one of Nye's most successful lectures, thus:

Some dogs are prized for their faithfulness, others for their sagacity, and still others for their beauty. My dog was not noticeable for his faithfulness, because he only clung to me when I did not want him, and when I felt lonely and needed sympathy, he was never at home.

He was not very sagacious, either. He was always doing things which, in the light of calmer afterthought, he bitterly regretted. Thus his life was a wide waste of shattered ambitions and the ghastly ruin of what he might have been. Neither did I prize him for his beauty; for he was brindle where there was any hair on him and red where there was none. He had, at one time, dropped his tail into a camp-kettle of boiling water. When he took it out and looked at it sadly, he was surprised to see that it resembled a new sausage.

When visitors came to my camp on the Boomerang Consolidated for lunch, my dog would sit near them, look yearningly at them, pound the floor with his tail, lick his chops, and follow each mouthful of the lunch with such a hungry, hopeless look, that the visitors wished they were dead.

When I first went to the mining camp I did not have a dog. I was not poor enough. After a while, however, by judicious inactivity and my æsthetic love for physical calm, I got poor enough. I knew I ought to procure a dog, and thus herald my poverty to the world. I also desired a constant companion who would share my humble lot and never forsake me.

I secured a dog, which I named Entomologist. Do you know what an entomologist is? He is one who makes large collections of peculiar insects and studies their characteristics. Entomologist seemed to be entirely wrapped up in his collection of insects, and they were very much attached to him. He had a good many more insects in stock than he really needed, especially fleas. Entomologist introduced into the gulch a large, early, purple-top, Swedish flea that had an immense run in camp. Most everybody got some of them.

Entomologist had a wild, ungovernable desire for food that made him a good deal of trouble. He would keep this unnatural appetite under control for days and weeks together, and then yield to it and become its willing slave. He would eat too much during the day, and at night he would creep into my tent and fill the air with his vain regrets.

I used to try to make him overcome his corroding grief. At last I got to throwing pick-handles and drills and pack-saddles and large chunks of specimen quartz and carboniferous profanity at him in the night to see if I couldn't convince him that it was better to suffer on in silence and smother his woe than to give way to such wild and robust grief.

One night he did not come home, and I feared that he had fallen down the shaft into the lower level of the Boomerang mine. I found him, however, down at Dobe Abraham's trying to eat a twenty-five foot rawhide lariat.

It seems that he had swallowed fifteen feet of it before he observed that the other end was tied in a hard knot to an iron picket-pin. When he discovered this, he had moved to reconsider, but the motion was defeated. I untied the lariat, however, and let Entomologist swallow it and go home. Then I went to the owner and purchased the lariat. I had one at home just like it, but I thought that it would be well for Entomologist to have one of his own.

I would do anything for my dog. I did not wish to

neglect him while he was alive, for I knew I would regret
it some day, if he were to be taken from me.

One day in the mellow autumn I went over to town to
purchase grub for winter, and took Entomologist with
me. He ran around a good deal, and tasted almost everything. But he knew his weakness, and did not yield to it
at first. Finally he found some soft plaster of Paris that
had just been mixed near a new house. He had eaten a
good many things, but he had never tasted plaster before,
so he ate what there was.

It was the effect of a blind impulse, and not the result
of Entomologist's mature judgment. Ah, how rashly
the best of us sometimes fly into the face of Providence,
in later years struggling, with tears and agony of spirit,
to overcome the foolish action of an unguarded moment!

That's the way it was with Entomologist. Five minutes after he ate that plaster he felt as though years of
integrity and self-denial could not overcome this rash act.

He lost his old vivacity, and came to me no more to lick
my face with his warm, damp tongue, or put his cold, wet
nose in my ear and sneeze, as he was wont to do when he
was well. He gradually lost all interest in his fleas, and
allowed them to shift for themselves.

Although he did not moan or complain, I could see
that little Entomologist was climbing the golden stair.

One day, just as the sun was lighting up the west and
glorifying the horizon with its royal coloring, Entomologist rolled himself up into a small globular wad and died.

He died without a struggle, but I always knew that he
would die easy. If it hadn't been easy he wouldn't have
done it.

As I reflect, memory takes me back to those days of
the long ago; and while the scalding tear wells up to my

eyelids and falls upon the page before me, a large paper-
weight, white and symmetrical, is lying by my side, and
on it is written:

Plaster cast of Entomologist, taken by himself (interior
view). He bit off more than he could chew.

When the "Boomerang" entered its second year Nye's
writings were being read nationally. Subscriptions were
coming in from every state and from several foreign countries. Many notables were on its subscription list. Charles
Dana of the "New York Sun" sent ten dollars for the
"Daily Boomerang."

And yet the paper was n't booming. The equipment, for
one thing, was wholly inadequate. There was only one man
in Laramie strong enough to operate the press. He was a
negro called Buffalo; lazy and unreliable. He was duly replaced by a Boston hydraulic motor. But sometimes the
water pressure was more temperamental than Buffalo had
been. The publication quarters were almost untenable for
humans on account of the four-footed tenants on the ground
floor. When Nye discovered that the paper was not making
enough to pay his salary he offered to go without for a
while and give the business a chance to catch up. In addition to this he made the company a loan.

On top of these troubles he learned that there was a plan
on foot to control the stock. The man responsible was one
whose dictation would have made Nye's continuance impossible. The owners of the job department, Garrett and
Chaplin, were equally opposed to the coup. The three gathered at Nye's home one night and agreed to raise one
thousand dollars, which was to be used to purchase outstanding shares in an attempt to thwart the manipulator.
Many of the stockholders showed their friendship and gen-

erosity by turning their shares over to Nye and refusing to accept any payment. Other certificates were coming in satisfactorily when a new foe, cerebrospinal meningitis, put an end to Nye's "Boomerang" activities.

A year after Nye had quit the paper, rumor, especially "Boomerang" rumor, said circulation had doubled. But Nye was unable to collect his bill. So he brought suit. Thereupon the management, still advertising "Bill Nye's Boomerang," abused in its columns the man who had built it. The paper had been named, not wisely, but too fittingly, for a missile that frequently returns and smites him who has launched it.

Nye ignored the shafts of his unsuccessful successors, but their ingratitude hurt. The "Boomerang" without Bill Nye soon found its level as a commonplace small-town daily. The paper struggled along for years, later becoming the "Laramie Republican." It is still published under that name. Nye's fame went steadily forward. The "Boomerang" had served a useful purpose. It was the vehicle which had brought his writings to the attention of more notable and more widely circulated papers.

The success of his suit against the company may be judged by this remark of Nye's:

Many lawyers of our day would do well to read and study the illustrious example of Daniel Webster. He did not sit in court all day with his feet on the table and howl, "We object," and then down his client for $50, just because he had made a noise. I employed a lawyer to bring suit to recover quite a sum of money due me. After years of assessments and toilsome litigation, we got a judgment. He said to me that he was anxious to succeed with the case mainly because he knew I wanted to

vindicate myself. I said yes, that was the idea exactly.
I wanted to be vindicated.

So he gave me the vindication and took the judgment
as a slight testimonial of his own sterling worth. When
I want to be vindicated again I will do it with one of
those self-cocking vindicators that you can carry in a
valise.

Before Nye left the "Boomerang" there was one group
of admirers in Laramie who recognized the honor of their
home-town prophet. My mother told of their admiration·

Three acquaintances, after spending the evening together,
stopped at our house on their way home at about 1 o'clock A.M.
to tell Edgar what a *genius* he was. The house was dark and
we were sound asleep, but that made no difference. They
knocked on the front door while they rambled around with
their voices, trying to find a key in which to sing "Auld Lang
Syne."

Being suddenly awakened, Edgar failed to recognize his
friends' voices and demanded, "Who's there?" They apolo-
gized and assured him they hated to disturb him but, inasmuch
as he might not live till morning, that they must let him know
without delay that he was a *genius*. And one of them added
as he turned to go, "I don't care how much of a genius a
man is, he looks like the *devil* in his nightshirt!"

CHAPTER IX

POSTMASTER AND PATIENT

HUMORISTS are thought of as a happy-go-lucky lot. Possibly many of them are. Few of them have held responsibilities outside of their writing commitments. Nye was not only a hard worker; he had a keen sense of stewardship. Some thought that his appointment as postmaster of Laramie City in 1882 was merely an official joke on the part of General Frank Hatton. Not so. Nye took his job seriously, although some of his official documents did not show it.

Nye's old chief, Dr. Hayford, had been the postmaster, and his term of office expired during the summer of '82. Nye had publicly opposed Hayford's reappointment. The first assistant postmaster-general at the time was General Hatton, a newspaper man. For years he had been with the "Burlington Hawkeye" and had acquired some reputation as a humorist on his own account. He had met Nye and liked him. One afternoon a telegram came from General Hatton saying that Hayford would not be reappointed and offering Nye the privilege of picking the new incumbent. Nye had in his business office C. W. Spalding, a post-office man of ripe experience. With such expert help Nye decided that he himself could fill the requirements of the office creditably.

And so he telegraphed his selection, choosing Spalding as chief clerk. The official letter of acceptance which follows pleased Hatton so much that he took it over to the

White House, where President Arthur read it and joined in a hearty laugh:

Office of Daily Boomerang, Laramie City, Wy.
August 9, 1882.

My dear General:

I have received by telegraph the news of my nomination by the President and my confirmation by the Senate, as postmaster at Laramie, and wish to extend my thanks for the same.

I have ordered an entirely new set of boxes and post-office outfit, including new corrugated cuspidors for the lady clerks.

I look upon the appointment as a great triumph of eternal truth over error and wrong. It is one of the epochs, I may say, in the Nation's onward march toward political purity and perfection. I do not know when I have noticed any stride in the affairs of state, which so thoroughly impressed me with its wisdom.

Now that we are co-workers in the same department, I trust that you will not feel shy or backward in consulting me at any time relative to matters concerning postoffice affairs. Be perfectly frank with me, and feel free to bring anything of that kind right to me. Do not feel reluctant because I may at times appear haughty and indifferent, cold or reserved. Perhaps you do not think I know the difference between a general delivery window and a three-em quad, but that is a mistake.

My general information is far beyond my years.

With profoundest regard, and a hearty endorsement of the policy of the President and the Senate, whatever it may be,

I remain, sincerely yours,
BILL NYE, P.M.

The "London Daily News" saw the letter and commented seriously on it. This gave Nye a fine opportunity for a report in the columns of the "Boomerang." Nye quotes the editorial from the "News" and then proceeds to discuss it in his own way:

If ever celebrity were attained unexpectedly, most assuredly it was that thrust upon Bill Nye by Truthful James. It is just possible, however, that the innumerable readers of Mr. Bret Harte's "Heathen Chinee" may have imagined Bill Nye and Ah Sin to be purely mythical personages. So far as the former is concerned, any such conclusion now appears to have been erroneous. Bill Nye is no more a phantom than any other journalist, although the name of the organ which he "runs" savors more of fiction than of fact. But there is no doubt about the matter, for the Washington correspondent of the New York *Tribune* telegraphed that Bill Nye had accepted a post under the government. He has lately been domiciled in Laramie City, Wyoming territory, and is editor of the *Daily Boomerang*. In reference to Acting-Postmaster-Gen. Hatton's appointment of him as postmaster at Laramie City, the opponent of Ah Sin writes an extremely humorous letter, "extending" his thanks, and advising his chief of his opinion that his "appointment is a triumph of eternal truth over error and wrong."

While thanking our London contemporary for its gentle and harmless remarks, we desire to correct an erroneous impression that the News seems to have as to our general style. The British press has in some way arrived at the conclusion that the editor of this fashion-guide and mental light-house on the rocky shores of time, is a party with wild tangled hair, and an eye like a tongue of flame.

That is not the case, and therefore our English co-worker in the great field of journalism is, no doubt, laboring under a popular misapprehension. Could the editor of the News look in upon us as we pull down tome after tome of forgotten lore in our study, or, with a glad smile, glance hurriedly over the postal card in transit through our postoffice, he would see, not as he supposes, a wild and cruel slayer of his fellow men, but a thoughtful, scholarly and choice fragment of modern architecture, with lines of care about the firmly chiseled mouth, and with the subdued and chastened air of a man who has run for the legislature and failed to get there, Eli.

The London News is an older paper than ours, and we therefore recognize the value of its kind notice. The Boomerang is a young paper, and has only begun to do damage as a national misfortune, but the time is not far distant, when, from Greenland's icy mountains to India's coral strand, we propose to search out suffering humanity and make death easier and more desirable, by introducing this choice malady.

Regarding the postoffice, we wish to state that we shall aim to make it a great financial success, and furnish mail at all times to all who desire it, whether they have any or not. We shall be pretty busy, of course, attending to the office during the day, and writing scathing editorials during the night, but we will try to snatch a moment now and then to write a few letters for those who have been inquiring sadly and hopelessly for letters during the past ten years. It is, indeed, a dark and dreary world to the man who has looked in at the same general delivery window nine times a day for ten years, and yet never received a letter, nor even a confidential postal card from a commercial man, stating that on the 5th of the following month he would strike the town with a new and attractive line of samples.

Farming over the Divide.

Bill Nye,

There are several reasons why farming on the Laramie Plains has thus far, been attended by indifferent success and farms there may still be had at a low price. Being over 7,000 feet above sea level, the air is too cool even in midsummer to ripen even the most rapidly maturing cereals, while the mountains on all sides, break up the rain clouds and precipitate them in such a manner that the thirsty, sandy, plains are not benefited. A friend of mine who used the English language freely in his conversation and who took in prohibition

A page of Bill Nye manuscript

We should learn to find such suffering as that, and if we are in the postoffice department, we may be the means of much good by putting new envelopes on our own dunning letters and mailing them to the suffering and distressed. Let us, in our abundance, remember those who have not been dunned for many a weary year. It will do them good, and we will not feel the loss.

Nye's experiences as postmaster and justice at Laramie were made the subject of his first play, "The Cadi." One of the characters, Taylor Wellington, is described thus: "Wild, young son of a good Irish family. He gets busted and deals faro, ashamed to go home or write. Falls heir to fortune and title."

This character was drawn from one of Nye's Wyoming friends named Plunkett, later Sir Horace Plunkett, minister of agriculture for Ireland. I don't know how closely the characterization of Taylor Wellington fitted Sir Horace in his Wyoming days. In any event his later distinguished service gives ample evidence of the value of the training.

Another character in "The Cadi," Dora Stanley, is thus described: "Young, English girl who has been sealed to a Mormon Elder by her mother, but en route escapes from the herd of proselytes and is secretly sent East to school."

Dora Stanley represented a splendid and attractive young girl who did have such an experience and for a while had been taken into the Nye home by my mother until she found employment. The local train despatcher became interested in her. She was sent East to a girls' school and later married the railroad man. Her husband became president of an important Western railroad, and the girl achieved distinction as one of the prominent women of a large Middle-Western city.

Nye's new job supplied a wealth of copy for the "Boom-erang," as when he described the post-office pests:

The official count shows that only two and one-half per cent of those who go to the postoffice transact their business and then go away. The other ninety-seven and one-half per cent do various things to cheer up the post-master and make him earn his money. When I go to the postoffice there is always one man who meets me at the door and pours out a large rippling laugh into my face, flavored with old beer and the fragrances of a royal Havana cabbage-leaf cigar that he is sucking.

He asks me if my circus [one of Nye's journalistic stunts] was a financial success, and how my custard pie plants are doing, and then fills the sultry air with an-other gurgling laugh preserved in alcohol.

I like to smell a hearty laugh laden with second-hand whisky. It revives me and intoxicates me. Still, I am trying not to become a helpless slave to the appetite for strong drink in this form. There are other forms of in-temperance that are more seductive than this one.

There is also a boy who never got any mail, and whose relatives never got any mail, and they couldn't read it if they had and if some one read it to them they couldn't an-swer it. He is always there, too.

When he sees me he hails me with a glad smile of recog-nition, and comes up to me and stands on my toes and is just as sociable and artless and trusting and alive with childish glee and incurable cussedness as he can be. He stirs me up with his elbows, and crawls through between my legs until the mail is open, and then he wedges him-self in front of my box so that I can't get the key into it.

Some day when the janitor sweeps out the postoffice he

will find a short suspender and a lock of brindle hair and a handful of large freckles, and he will wonder what it means.

It will be what I am going to leave of that boy for the coroner to operate on.

There is also an amusing party who cheerfully stands up against the boxes and reads his letters, and laughs when he finds something facetious, or swears when the letter doesn't suit him. He also announces to the by-standers whom each letter is from, and seems to think the world stands quivering with anxiety to know whether his sister in Arkansas has successfully acquired triplets this year or only twins.

One day this man got a letter in a mourning envelope, and I heaved a sigh of relief, for, thought I, he will now go away and be alone with his great grief. But he did not. He stood up manfully and controlled his emotions through it all; and when he had finished he broke into the old silvery laugh. It seems that his brother in Oregon had run out of yellow envelopes, and had filled the one with the black border unusually full of convulsive mirth.

What a world of bitter disappointment this is anyhow!

There is a woman who playfully stands at the general delivery window, and gleefully sticks her fangs out into the subsequent week, and skittishly chides the clerk be-cause he doesn't get her a letter. He good naturedly tells her, as he has done daily for seven years, that he will write her one to-morrow.

She reluctantly goes home to rest so she can come and stand there the next day.

Then comes the literary cuss, who takes a weekly paper from Vermont with a patent inside. He reads it with the purest unselfishness to me, and points out the new-laid jokes that one always finds in the enterprising paper with the patent digestion.

He also explains the jokes to me, so that I need not grope along through life in hopeless ignorance of what is going on all about me.

There is a woman, too, who comes to the window and lavishly buys a three-cent stamp, runs out her tongue, hangs it over the stamp clerk's shoulder, lays the stamp back against the glottis and moistens it. She pastes it on the upper left-hand corner of the envelope, and asks the clerk to be sure and see that it goes. She thoughtfully tells him who is to receive it and gives a short biography of the sendee.

After a year, with the duties of postmaster added to running the "Boomerang" and his other miscellaneous chores, came the illness that resulted in my father's death twelve years afterward. Because of the high altitude, he was advised to leave Laramie. Thus the postmastership was resigned, and, characteristically, President Arthur was addressed on October 1, 1883, as follows:

Postoffice Divan, Laramie City, W. T.,
Oct. 1, 1883.

To the President of the United States:

Sir: I beg leave at this time officially to tender my resignation as postmaster at this place, and in due form to deliver the great seal and the key to the front door of the office. The safe combination is set on the numbers 33, 66 and 99, though I do not remember at this moment which comes first, or how many times you revolve the knob, or in which direction you should turn it first to make it operate.

There is some mining stock in my private drawer in the safe, which I have not yet removed. It is a luxury, but you may have it. I have decided to keep a horse instead of this mining stock. The horse may not be so pretty, but it will cost less to keep him.

You will find the postal cards that have not been used under the distributing table, and the coal down in the cellar. If the stove draws too hard, close the damper in the pipe and shut the general delivery window.

Looking over my stormy and eventful administration as postmaster here, I find abundant cause for thanksgiving. At the time I entered upon the duties of my office the department was not yet on a paying basis. It was not even self-sustaining. Since that time, with the active co-operation of the chief executive and the heads of the department, I have been able to make our postal system a paying one, and on top of that I am now able to reduce the tariff on average-sized letters from three cents to two. I might add that this is rather too too, but I will not say anything that might seem undignified in an official resignation which is to become a matter of history.

Acting under the advice of Gen. Hatton, a year ago, I removed the feather bed with which my predecessor, Deacon Hayford, had bolstered up his administration by stuffing the window, and substituted glass. Finding nothing in the book of instructions to postmasters which made the feather bed a part of my official duties, I filed it away in an obscure place and burned it in effigy, also in the gloaming.

It was not long after I had taken my official oath before an era of unexampled prosperity opened for the

American people. The price of beef rose to a remarkable
altitude, and other vegetables commanded a good figure
and a ready market. We then began to make active
preparations for the introduction of the strawberry-roan
two-cent stamps and the black-and-tan postal note. One
reform has crowded upon the heels of another, until the
country is to-day upon the foam-crested wave of permanent prosperity.

Mr. President, I cannot close this letter without thanking yourself and the heads of departments at Washington
for your active, cheery and prompt coöperation in these
matters. You may do as you see fit, of course, about in-
corporating this idea into your Thanksgiving proclama-
tion, but rest assured it would not be ill-timed or in-
opportune. It is not alone a credit to myself. It reflects
credit upon the administration also.

I need not say that I herewith transmit my resignation
with great sorrow and genuine regret. We have toiled
on together month after month, asking for no reward
except the innate consciousness of rectitude and the
salary as fixed by law. Now we are to separate. Here
the roads seem to fork, as it were, and you and I, and
the cabinet, must leave each other at this point.

You will find the key under the door-mat, and you had
better turn the cat out at night when you close the office.
If she does not go readily, you can make it clearer to her
mind by throwing the cancelling stamp at her.

If Deacon Hayford does not pay up his box-rent, you
might as well put his mail in the general delivery, and
when Bob Head gets drunk and insists on a letter from
one of his wives every day in the week, you can salute
him through the box delivery with an old Queen Anne
tomahawk, which you will find near the Etruscan water-

pail. This will not in any manner surprise either of these parties.

Tears are unavailing! I once more become a private citizen, clothed only with the right to read such postal cards as may be addressed to me, and to curse the inefficiency of the postoffice department. I believe the voting class to be divided into two parties; viz., those who are in the postal service, and those who are mad because they cannot receive a registered letter every fifteen minutes of each day, including Sunday.

Mr. President, as an official of this Government I now retire. My term of office would not expire until 1886. I must, therefore, beg pardon for my eccentricity in resigning. It will be best, perhaps, to keep the heart-breaking news from the ears of European powers until the dangers of a financial panic are fully past. Then hurl it broadcast with a sickening thud.

No misfortune could dim the luster of Nye's wit, although his "veterinarian" drove him almost to bitterness. Of his illness he wrote:

Up to the moment I had a notion of getting some meningitis, I had never employed physicians. Since then I have been thrown in their society a great deal. Most of them were very pleasant and scholarly gentlemen, who will not soon be forgotten; but one of them doctored me first for pneumonia, then for inflammatory rheumatism, and finally, when death was contiguous, advised me that I must have change of scene and rest.

I told him that if he kept on prescribing for me, I thought I might depend on both. Change of physicians, however, saved my life.

My wife says that while he was attending me I was as

crazy as a loon, but that I was more lucid than the physician. Even with my little, shattered wreck of a mind, tottering between a superficial knowledge of how to pound sand and a wide, shoreless sea of mental vacuity, I still had the edge on my physician, from an intellectual point of view. He is still practicing medicine in a quiet way, weary of life, and yet fearing to die and go where his patients are.

He would come and sit by my bedside for hours, waiting for this mortality to put on immortality, so that he could collect his bill from the estate. But one day I arose during a temporary delirium, and extracting a slat from my couch I smote him across the pit of the stomach with it, while I hissed:

"Physician, heal thyself."

I then tottered a few minutes, and fell back into the arms of my attendants.

When my father was told he could not live in such a high altitude, the Nyes went first to Greeley, Colorado, where my mother's brother was stationed at the time. What follows is taken from one of Nye's letters written after his convalescence:

The old Greeley Colony in Colorado, a genuine oasis in the desert, with its huge irrigating canals of mountain water running through the mighty wheat fields, glistening each autumn at the base of the range, affords a good deal that is curious, not only to the mind of the gentlemen from the States, but even to the man who lives at Cheyenne, only a few hours' journey to the north.

Still I didn't start out to write up either Cheyenne or Greeley; I intended to mention casually Dr. Law, of the latter place, who acted as my physician for a few

months and coaxed me back from the great hereafter.   I
had been under the hands of a physician who was also a
coroner, and who, I found afterward, was trying to treat
me professionally as long as the lamp held out to burn, intending afterward to sit upon me officially.

Sometimes it isn't entirely the medicine you swallow
that paralyzes pain so much as it is the quiet magnetism
of a good story and the snap of a pleasant eye.

While Nye lived in the Rocky Mountains, he collected
and arranged the material for his first three books.   The
first two were published while he lived at Laramie and the
third soon after his return to Wisconsin.   All three were
a good deal alike as to size and style.   Each was a selection
of his newspaper writings.   All were published by Belford,
Clark & Co., of Chicago, largely for news company distribution.

"Bill Nye and Boomerang" was published in 1881.   His
letter transmitting the material to the publisher is dated
"In My Boudoir, Nov. 17, 1880."   There was something
about the word "boomerang" that piqued Nye's imagination.   His mule, his mine, his newspaper, his book, all bore
the trade-mark.

Quoting the Sweet Singer of Michigan on his title page,
Nye asks the reader:

And now, kind friends, what I have wrote I hope you
will pass o'er, and not criticize as some has done, hitherto,
herebefore.

The sale of "Bill Nye and Boomerang" was gratifying
and warranted another volume in 1882.   This was called
"Forty Liars and Other Lies" and was illustrated by Hopkins.   In his "Overture," February 15, 1882, Nye says that

the sale of the first volume was more contagious than he had
dared to hope and that the royalties have enabled him to
move into a larger residence and to reduce his collection
of dogs to one cream-colored pet.

"Baled Hay," the third book, was illustrated by the budding young Fred Opper. The "piazza" to this volume gives
evidence of a keen merchandising sense on the author's part.
It is a bid for the good will and coöperation of the "news
butcher." Says Nye under date of September 5, 1883:

> There is one friend I always meet on the trains, the
> news agent. He comes to me with my own books in his
> arms, and tells me over and over again of their merits.
> He means it, too. What object could he have in coming
> to me, not knowing who I am and telling me of their great
> worth? That is one reason I travel so much. When I
> get gloomy I like to get on a train and be assured once
> more, by a total stranger, that my books have never been
> successfully imitated.
>
> Some people like to have a tall man with a glazed grip-
> sack selling their works. I like the candor of the train-
> boy. He leans gently over you as you look out the win-
> dow, puts some pecan meats in your hand and thus wins
> your trusting heart.

When Nye left the Rockies his Denver friends gave him
a banquet which is still talked of in newspaper circles of
that city. W. L. Visscher, a brilliant entertainer and a
friend of my father, was the toast-master and prefaced
Nye's speech by whetting the appetites of the diners for
some of Nye's funniest. The address of the guest of the
evening had been preceded by Cowan of the "Denver Press"
and other talks that were more or less "shop."

Nye's subject was "Wyoming." He was known to love this broad territory, and each man present had a mental picture of the kind of humorous yet enthusiastic tribute Nye would probably bestow. But he refused to run in the accustomed groove. When he took the floor, it was seen that his serious face was more solemn than usual. And he was armed with a thick volume. In sepulchral tones he proceeded to read to his audience the driest possible facts and statistics from the government records—area, population, altitude, rainfall, mean temperature, and such sparkling bons mots. His listeners were a little slow to tumble, but when they did comprehend the joke that Nye was playing on them the applause was all the greater.

The banquet continued until a late hour. Finally Nye retired to his room at the old Windsor Hotel, but the merry-making, under the leadership of Field, went furiously on. A line was formed, and they paraded to Nye's hotel, where the party, one after another, sent their cards to his room. He tried to bribe the bell-boy to leave him alone, but no use. Good-naturedly he put his clothes on and returned to the fray, which continued unabated until noon. It was at this banquet that John E. Leet prophesied that Field, still practically unknown, would one day achieve a fame equal to that of Nye.

Bill Nye had gone to Laramie a few months before the election of Rutherford B. Hayes to the presidency, and he returned to Wisconsin seven and a half years later, toward the end of President Arthur's administration. When he wiped the dust of the Wyoming plains from his shoes there were several things of greater importance that were left behind. Among them three in particular. His rugged health. Professional and business responsibilities. Active participation in politics.

His health was the only one of the three, the loss of which he ever had cause to regret. The elimination of politics and business cares were partly the consequence of his decreased strength. But there were other reasons. His mother and many relatives and close friends of both my father and mother were anxious to have him continue in the practice of law and in his other activities outside of his writing, feeling that what success he had achieved as a humorist was evanescent and not a sufficient base upon which to build a career. Probably it was my mother's unwavering faith in his genius and her willingness to gamble their all upon his future as a humorous writer, more than his own confidence in his talent, that led to the burning of all other bridges. To understand the significance of this decision it is necessary to go back a little.

The three Nye boys, Edgar, Frank, and Carroll, were born and reared when the old traditions of American statesmanship were the gospel of ambitious mothers. Webster and Lincoln were household gods. The legal profession was the vehicle in which Franklin and Eliza Nye's trio were to ride to political preferment. Frank and Carroll never turned aside from the path of law and politics. Carroll, to be sure, went Democratic. Nevertheless he pursued the course of law and politics, serving for many terms as mayor of Moorhead, Minnesota, and as these lines are written he occupies the bench in northern Minnesota. Frank served long as county attorney of Hennepin County, went to Washington as congressman from Minnesota, won the appelation of Orator of the House, and to-day, like Carroll, is a Minnesota judge.

The same home influences and early training which have held the other two brothers to bar and bench, urged the eldest toward a similar goal. In Wyoming he had not only gained admission to the bar and become an important factor in local politics, but beyond this he had made good friends among the higher-ups of the Republican party. He had traveled some distance on the road to that kind of success for which he had set out.

More or less by chance, he had achieved a measure of journalistic celebrity. Which was the stout staff and which the slender reed upon which to lean in the future? Not alone for the satisfaction of his personal ambition but for three daily meals required by a growing family? The question was not an easy one to answer. However, the time never came again when the legal profession, politics, or business responsibilities were allowed to interfere with the flight of Bill Nye's pen. And never again did Nye force himself to turn out a column a day as he had done for the "Boomerang."

In this my mother was his strong ally. Instead of permitting his breadwinning to interfere, she kept all domestic responsibilities within bounds, as only a truly coöperative wife can do, thus giving the freest play to his writing talent.

BOOK THREE

CHAPTER X

HUDSON, WISCONSIN, NYE'S WINTER RESORT

The seven years in Laramie had done much for Nye. There he found himself. There the public discovered him, but it was pleasant to be back in Wisconsin.

It was gratifying for Nye, a budding celebrity at thirty-four, to be among his old friends again. It was comforting to know that he had established an earning-power for his pen that meant not less than a good living. The stay at Greeley had done much for his health, and, had he been willing to loaf along easily, who knows but that Bill Nye would be alive and writing to-day? For a time he did go slow, but as he grew stronger he shifted to his shoulders more and more responsibility.

Nye bought a little house in Hudson, not far from his parents' farm. In this simple home my father and mother spent three happy years. And here it was that my brother Max, seventeen months my senior, and I were born. This "villa" was given the Nyesque name of "Slipperyelmhurst." Nye's feeling of peace at being again in the region of his rearing was reflected in a letter he wrote to an inquirer for a place where a young man could get a good living.

That depends upon what you call a good living. If your stomach would not revolt at plain fare, such as poor people use, come up and stop at our house awhile. We don't live high but we aim to eke out an existence. Come and abide with us. It's a good place to come.

117

Quiet but restful; full of balm for the wounded spirit and close up to nature's great North American heart. That's the idea. You may be a man who does not pant for the sylvan shade. Very likely you are a seaside resortist and do not care for pants. But I simply say to you that if you are a worthy young man, weary with life's great battles—beaten back, perhaps, and wounded—with your neck knocked crooked like a tom-tit that has run against a telegraph wire in the night, come up here into northern Wisconsin.

In correcting a published misconception of the scale upon which he lived in Wisconsin, Nye gives his own description of Slipperyelmhurst:

I would like to make an explanation at this time which concerns me, of course, more than any one else, and yet it ought to be made in the interests of general justice. I refer to a recent article published in a Western paper and handsomely illustrated, in which I find a pretentious picture of my residence.

The description states: "The structure is elaborate, massive and beautiful. It consists of three stories, besides basement and attic, and covers a large area. It contains an elevator, electric bells, steam-heating arrangements, baths, hot and cold, in every room, electric lights, laundry, and fire-escapes. The grounds consist of at least five acres, overlooking the river for several miles up and down, with fine boating and a private fish-pond of two acres in extent, containing every known variety of game fish. The grounds are finely laid out in handsome drives and walks, and when finished the establishment will be one of the most complete and beautiful in the Northwest."

No one realizes more fully than I the great power of the press for good or evil. Rightly used the newspaper can make or unmake men, and wrongly used it can be even more sinister. Knowing this as I do, I want to be placed right before the people. The above is not a correct description of my house, for several reasons. In the first

"The front part of the house runs back to the time of Polypus the First, while the L runs back as far as the cistern"

place, it is larger and more robust in appearance, and in the second place it has not the same tout ensemble as my residence. My house is less obtrusive and less arrogant in its demeanor than the foregoing, and it has no elevator in it. My house is not the kind that craves an elevator. An elevator in my house would lose money. If I were to put one in I would have to abolish the dining-room.

I have learned recently that the correspondent who

came here to write up this matter visited the town while
I was away, and as he could not find me he was at the
mercy of strangers. A young man who lives here, and
who is just in the heyday of life, gleefully consented to
show the correspondent my new residence, not yet completed. So they went over and examined the new Oliver
Wendell Holmes Hospital, which will be completed in
June and which is, of course, a handsome structure, but
quite different from my house in many particulars.

For instance, my residence is of a different school of
architecture, being rather on the Scandinavian order,
while the foregoing has a tendency toward the Ironic.
The hospital belongs to a recent school, while my residence, in its architectural methods and conception, goes
back to the time of the mound builders, a time when a
Gothic hole in the ground was considered the magnum
bonum and the scrumptuous thing in art.

The front part of the house runs back to the time of
Polypus the First, while the L runs back as far as the
cistern.

I am not finding fault with any one because the above
error has crept into the public prints, for it is really a
pardonable error, after all. Neither do I wish to be considered as striving to eliminate my name from the columns
of the press, for no one could be more tickled than I am
over a friendly notice of my arrival in town or a timely
reference to my courteous bearing and youthful appearance. But I want to see the Oliver Wendell Holmes Hospital succeed, and so I come out in this way over my own
signature and admit that the building does not belong to
me and that, so far as I am concerned, the man who files
a lien on it will simply fritter away his time.

Slipperyelmhurst needed a bit of fixing up. Nye undertook to double as a decorator:

I economized in the matter of paper-hanging, deciding that I would save the paper-hanger's bill and put the money into preferred trotting stock.

So I read a recipe in a household hint, which stated how one should make and apply paste to wall paper, how to apply the paper, and all that. The paste was made by uniting flour, water and glue in such a way as to secure the paper to the wall and yet leave it smooth. First the walls had to be "sized," however. I took a tape-measure and sized the walls.

Next I began to prepare the paste and cook some in a large milk-pan. It looked very repulsive, but it looked so much better than it smelled that I did not mind. Then I put above five cents' worth of it on one roll of paper, and got up on a chair to begin. My idea was to apply it to the wall mostly, but the chair tipped, and so I papered the piano and my wife on the way down. My wife gasped for breath, but soon tore a hole through the paper so she could breathe, and then she laughed at me. That is the reason I took another end of the paper and repapered her face. I cannot bear to have any one laugh at me when I am unhappy.

It was good paste, if you merely desired to disfigure a piano or a wife, but otherwise it would not stick at all.

Then a man dropped in to see me about some money that I had hoped to pay him that morning, and he said the paste needed more glue and a quart of molasses. I put in more glue and the last drop of molasses we had in the house. It made a mass which looked like unbaked ginger snaps, and smelled like the deluge did at low tide.

I next proceeded to paper the room. Sometimes the paper would adhere, and then again it would refrain from adhering. When I got around the room I had gained ground so fast at the top and lost so much at the bottom of the walls, that I had to put in a wedge of paper two feet wide at the bottom, and tapering to a point at the top, in order to cover the space.

I went to bed very weary, and abraded in places. I had paste in my pockets, and bronze up my nose. In the night I could hear the paper crack. Just as I would get almost to sleep, it would pop. That was because the paper was contracting and trying to bring the dimensions of the room I own to fit it. In the morning the room had shrunk so that the carpet did not fit, and the paper hung in large molasses-covered welts on the walls. It looked real grotesque. I got a paper-hanger to come and look at it. He did so.

"And what would you advise me to do with it, sir?" I asked, with a degree of deference which I had never before shown to a paper-hanger.

"Well, I can hardly say at first. It is a very bad case. You see, the glue and stuff have made the paper and wrinkles so hard now, that it would cost a great deal to blast it off. Do you own the house?"

"Yes, sir. That is, I have paid one-half the purchase-price, and there is a mortgage for the balance."

"Oh. Well, then you are all right," said the paper-hanger, with a gleam of hope in his eye. "Let it go on the mortgage."

Not long after Nye returned to Wisconsin he wrote a letter to his old friend, Mr. Slack, editor of the "Cheyenne

Sun," in which he philosophized concerning the life of a humorist:

> With more leisure than usual on hand I believe I am getting more negligent in the matter of letter writing. I suppose that everybody dislikes the business by which he obtains a livelihood. I used to think that there could be none of the dull and tedious detail of life about being a clown in a three ring circus, and yet when I got acquainted with a flesh and blood clown and conversed with him as I would with an ordinary man, I found that though he laughed in the ring and jumped around with joy in his Mother Hubbard pants, his heart was sometimes filled with woe. Ah, thought I, if *he* finds life irksome, then is it so indeed to all. If he, amid a perfect gorge of peanuts and lemonade, with a grand carnival of elephants and gooseneck camels and beautiful women walking the slack wire without fear or raiment; if he, I say, could at times be sad, then what a hollow mockery must life be!
>
> I write an hour or two in the morning and go afishing the rest of the day on good pay and still I am mad all the time because I have to dig my angle worms. Life has its little equity proceedings all the time and a court is constantly in session that requires us to submit to the statutes.

On the same subject of being a humorist, Nye said to an ambitious young writer who asked for advice:

> Do not be a humorist! If you are a humorist everybody else will have more fun out of it than you will. You will make some money if you have the genuine afflatus, but you won't have any fun. Humorists do not have fun.

It is all a mistake. I am acquainted with one, and he says he has not smiled for years. Once I heard of a humorist who had laughed twice in one summer, and I hunted him out.

He was not a humorist, but had some other trouble the name of which has escaped my mind.

About this time Nye revealed the true inwardness of his literary style:

So that boys who yearn to follow in my footsteps and wear a laurel wreath the year round in place of a hat, may know what the literary habits of a literary party are:

I rise from bed the first thing in the morning, leaving my couch not because I am dissatisfied with it, but because I cannot carry it with me during the day.

I then seat myself on the edge of the bed and devote a few moments to thought. Literary men who have never set aside a few moments on rising for thought will do well to try it. I then insert myself into a pair of middle-aged pantaloons. It is needless to say that girls who may have a literary tendency will find little to interest them here. Other clothing is added to the above from time to time. I then bathe myself. Still this is not absolutely essential to a literary life. Others who do not do so have been equally successful.

Some literary people bathe before dressing.

I then go downstairs and out to the barn, where I feed the horse. Some literary men feel above taking care of a horse, because there is really nothing in common between the care of a horse and literature. But simplicity is my watchword. T. Jefferson would have to rise early in the day to eclipse me in simplicity. I wish I had as much money as I have simplicity.

I then go in to breakfast. This meal consists almost wholly of food. I am passionately fond of food, and I may truly say that I owe much of my success in life to this inward craving, this constant yearning for something better.

During this meal I frequently converse with my family. I do not feel above my family; at least, if I do, I try to conceal it as much as possible. Buckwheat pancakes in a heated state, with maple syrup on the upper side, are extremely conducive to literature. Nothing jerks the mental faculties around with greater rapidity than buckwheat cakes.

After breakfast the time is put in looking forward to the time when dinner will be ready. From 8 to 10 A.M., however, I frequently retire to my private library hot-bed in the hay mow and write 1,200 words in my forthcoming book, the price of which will be $2.50 in cloth and $4 with Russia back.

A few minutes before six P.M., September 9, 1884, a violent cyclone swept down upon northern Wisconsin. Several killed and many injured were the toll of the storm. Bill Nye was among the wounded.

Nye's account of the cyclone, when he was able to write it, as usual held the funny glass up to misfortune.

I desire to state that my position as United States Cyclonist for this Judicial District is now vacant. I resigned on the 9th day of September, A.D. 1884.

I have not the necessary personal magnetism to look a cyclone in the eye and make it quail. I am stern and even haughty in my intercourse with men, but when a Manitoba simoon takes me by the brow of my pantaloons and throws me across Township 28, Range 18, West of the 5th Principal Meridian, I lose my mental reserve and become anxious and even taciturn.

As the people came into the forest with lanterns and pulled me out of the crotch of a basswood tree with a "tackle and fall," I remember I told them I didn't yearn for any more atmospheric phenomena.

My brother and I were riding alone in the grand old forest, and I had just been singing a few bars from the opera of "Whoop 'em Up, Lizzie Jane," when I noticed that the wind was beginning to sough through the trees. Soon after that, I noticed that I was soughing through the trees also, and I am really no slouch of a sougher, either, when I get started.

The horse was hanging by the breeching from the bough of a large butternut tree, waiting for some one to come and pick him.

I did not see my brother at first, but after a while he disengaged himself from a rail fence and came where I was hanging, wrong end up, with my personal effects spilling out of my pockets. At midnight a party of friends carried me into town on a stretcher. It was quite an ovation. To think of a torchlight procession coming way out there into the woods at midnight, and carrying me into town on their shoulders in triumph!

The cyclone is a natural phenomenon, enjoying the most robust health. It may be a pleasure for a man with great will power and an iron constitution to study more carefully into the habits of the cyclone, but as far as I am concerned, I could worry along some way if we didn't have a phenomenon in the house from one year's end to another. As I sit here, with my leg in a silicate of soda corset, and watch the merry throng promenading down the street, I cannot repress a feeling toward a cyclone that almost amounts to disgust.

Nye had a great deal of trouble with his broken member. The first setting wasn't straight and the leg had to be rebroken. When the bones were beginning to knit, the bed collapsed and the bones parted for the third time. It was then that Nye wrote the following letter to a friend:

I don't know that I owe you a letter, but I wanted to write and ask you if you still have that circular and price list of artificial limbs which was sent you during the summer while you were trying to grow a new leg.

Fortunately I am not so fat as you are, and the physicians have had no superfluous flesh to get in the way while the bone was getting set in its ways.

I do not know that I shall want a false leg, but it's always well enough to be prepared, and my idea was to get estimates on legs, and be thinking the matter over. I should want a long, slim leg, with reddish hair on it, and would like to pay a part in advertising. Perhaps it would be safer to take it a short time on trial. Of course I wouldn't want to take it and pay for it if I couldn't play on it.

My father was very fond of my mother's brother-in-law, A. J. Mitchell, the husband of her sister Anna. He lived for many years in the suburbs of Chicago where he held important responsibilities for the Rock Island Railway. Uncle Mitchell had a twinkle in his eye which, to me, accounted for the enjoyment my father seemed to get from corresponding with "Jake."

My mother had three brothers, David, Day and James. James had a deeply religious turn of mind. He had given

up a promising career in business to fill a small and poorly
paid pulpit in a Wisconsin village. It was to this same
James that my father referred in the letter below. The
letter, by the way, was illustrated with a small caricature
by Nye showing himself on crutches and signed, "B. Nye,
cyclonist." Subtitle: "Young man, go west and blow up
with the country."

The letter follows:

Dear Jake:

We got a letter from James recently in which he re-
ferred casually to the advantages held out by the New
Jerusalem as a residence. Somehow I feel that I do not
deserve so good a brother-in-law as James. What have
I ever done to entitle me to such distinction? Nothing.
Absolutely nothing whatever!

Your program was away up! I was mad, and so was
my wife, that we could not be there to enjoy it. If my
leg gets so I can walk on it this winter I'd like first rate
to read a few little "eppygrams" at such a *recherché*
feast of reason and flow of soul. I go to River Falls in
a few weeks to read between a couple of numbers. It
is a public concert for the benefit of St. Paul's Church
here and is in charge of the ladies. Some staving voices
among them, too. I told them that if Zion languished
it must not be attributed to me. I hope to appear in
public several times this winter if the swelling goes down
so that I can get my pink tights on over it.

Yours truly,

B. N.,
ExJudge

It was while living at Hudson that Nye wrote his "Dear
Henry" letters. These were supposed to be written by an

Nye at 23, Law Clerk

Nye at 16, Farm Boy

old-fashioned farmer to his new-fangled son. This gave Nye a chance to indulge in some of his most picturesque philosophy and humor. In one of the letters this advertisement of the old farmer's cow was sent for insertion in Henry's newspaper:

FOR SALE

Owing to ill health I will sell at my residence in this township, one crushed raspberry colored cow aged 6 years. She is a good milkster, and is not afraid of the cars—or anything else. She is a cow of undaunted courage and gives milk frequently. To a man who does not fear death in any form she would be a great boon. She is very much attached to her home at present, by means of a trace-chain, but she will be sold to any one who will agree to treat her right. She is one-fourth short-horn and three-fourths hyena. Purchaser need not be identified. I will also throw in a double-barrel shot-gun, which goes with her. In May she generally goes away somewhere for a week or two and returns with a tall, red calf, with long, wabbly legs. Her name is Rose, and I would prefer to sell her to a non-resident.

Bill Nye's friends often wondered where he got his ideas. Apparently he plucked them out of the blue. When he sat down to write he went at the job with decision, and an hour or so later the manuscript was ready for the printer. He seldom reread his sketches. He found that fussing over them did not improve them, but their spontaneity would vanish. He could take apparently trivial incidents and without prevarication convert them, by giving play to his incongruous association of ideas, into rib-tickling fun.

One day his brother Frank and he were taking a railway journey together, and the question came up of where Bill, or, as Frank called him, "Edgar," got his inspirations.

To oblige, Nye took a weeping woman on the train as his subject and wrote this:

I took a ride on the cars and it shook me up a good deal. A woman got aboard at Minkin's Siding. I noticed, as we pulled out, that this woman raised the window so that she could bid adieu to a man in a dyed mustache. I do not know whether he was her *dolce far niente*, or her grandson. I know that if he had been a relative of mine, however, I would have cheerfully concealed the fact.

She waved a little 2 x 6 handkerchief out of the window, said "good-bye," allowed a fresh zephyr from Cape Sabine to come in and play a xylophone interlude on my spinal column, and then burst into a paroxysm of damp, hot tears.

I went into another car for a moment, and when I returned a pugilist from Chicago had my seat. When I travel I am uniformly courteous, especially to pugilists. So I allowed this self-made man with the broad, intellectual shoulder blades, to sit in my seat with his feet on my new and expensive traveling bag, while I sat with the tear-bedewed memento from Minikin's Siding.

I asked the woman if I might sit by her side for a few miles and share her great sorrow. She looked at me askance. I did not resent it. She allowed me to take the seat, and I read a paper for a few moments so that she could look me over through the corners of her eyes. I also scrutinized her lineaments some.

This leads me to say, in all seriousness, that there is nothing so sad as the sight of a man or woman who would scorn to tell a wrong story, but who will persist in wearing bogus clothes and bogus jewelry that wouldn't fool anybody.

My seat-mate wore a cloak that had started out to bamboozle the American people with the idea that it was worth $100, but it wouldn't mislead any one who might be nearer than half a mile. I also discovered that it had an air about it that would indicate that she wore it while she cooked the pancakes and fried the doughnuts.

She seemed to want to converse and she began on the subject of literature, picking up a volume that had been left in her seat by the train boy, entitled, "Shadowed to Skowhegan and Back; or, The Child Fiend; price $2." We drifted on pleasantly into the broad domain of letters. Incidentally I asked her what authors she read.

"Oh, I don't remember the authors so much as I do the books," said she; "I am a great reader. If I should tell you how much I have read, you wouldn't believe it."

I said I certainly would. I had frequently been called upon to believe things that would make the ordinary rooster quail.

If she discovered the true inwardness of this Anglo-American "Jewdesprit," she refrained from saying anything about it.

"I read a good deal," she continued, "and it keeps me all strung up. I weep, oh, so easily!" Just then she lightly laid her hand on my arm, and I could see that the tears were rising to her eyes. I felt like asking her if she had ever tried running herself through a clothes wringer every morning. I did feel that some one ought to chirk her up, so I asked her if she remembered the advice of the editor who received a letter from a young lady troubled the same way. This young lady stated that every little while, without any apparent cause, she would shed tears. The editor asked her why she didn't lock up the shed.

We conversed for a long time about literature, but every little while she would get me into deep water by quoting some author or work that I had never read. I never realized what a hopeless ignoramus I was till I heard about the scores of books that had made her shed scalding tears, and yet that I had never, never read.

When she looked at me with that far-away expression in her eyes, and with her hand resting lightly on my arm in such a way as to give the gorgeous two karat rhinestone from Pittsburgh full play, and told me how such works as "The New Made Grave" or "The Twin Murderers" had cost her many and many a copious tear, I told her I was glad of it. If it be a blessed boon for the student of such books to weep at home and work up her honest perspiration into scalding tears, far be it from me to grudge that poor boon.

I hope that all who may read these lines, and who may feel that the pores of their skin are getting torpid and sluggish, owing to an inherited antipathy toward physical exertion, and who feel that they would rather work up their perspiration into woe and shed it in the shape of common red-eyed weep, will help themselves to this poor boon. People have different ways of enjoying themselves, and I trust no one will hesitate about accepting this or any other poor boon that I do not happen to be using at the time.

Surely there wasn't much for the superficial writer to glean from the incident of the weeping woman. Psychology and philosophy are required to weigh real values in such a situation and to differentiate unerringly between genuine sentiment and cheap sentimentality of such a traveler through this vale of tears. Nye's piercing perception had long since detected that all is not gold that glitters, nor bona fide sorrow that glistens in the human eye. Sermons in stones and books in running ducts had meaning for this acute observer and interpreter. He knew that many a tear is a drop of still-born perspiration. As he admired *real* people and *real* feeling, so he spotted and exposed a sham, no matter what the disguise.

"Come back, Sarah, and jerk the waffle-iron for us once more"

Nye was only one of millions who have worried along with the servant problem, but I doubt if a sufferer ever tried more earnestly to do his or her part in making amends to a prodigal "hired girl" than Nye did when he wrote:

Personal.—Will the young woman who used to cook in our family, and who went away ten pounds of sugar and five and a half pounds of tea ahead of the game, please come back, and all will be forgiven.

If she cannot return, will she please write, stating her

present address, and also give her reasons for shutting up the cat in the refrigerator when she went away?

If she will only return, we will try to forget the past, and think only of the glorious present and the bright, bright future.

Come back, Sarah, and jerk the waffle-iron for us once more.

Your manners are peculiar, but we yearn for your doughnuts, and your style of streaked cake suits us exactly.

We realize that you do not like children very well, and our children especially gave you much pain, because they were not as refined as you.

We have often wished, for your sake, that we had never had any children; but so long as they are in our family, the neighbors will rather expect us to take care of them.

Still, if you insist upon it, we will send them away. We don't want to seem overbearing with our servants.

We would be willing, also, to give you more time for mental relaxation. The intellectual strain incident to the life of one who makes gravy must be very great, and tired nature must at last succumb. We do not want you to succumb. If any one has to succumb, let us do it.

You ought to let us have company at the house sometimes if we will let you have company when you want. Still, you know best. You are older than we are, and you have seen more of the world.

We miss your gentle admonitions and your stern reproofs. Come back and reprove us again. Come back and admonish us once more, at so much per admonish and groceries.

We will agree to let you select the tender part of the steak, and such fruit as seems to strike you favorably, just as we did before. We did not like it when you were here, but that is because we were young and did not know what the custom was.

If a life-time devoted to your welfare can obliterate the injustice we have done you, we will be glad to yield it to you.

Come back and oversee our fritter bureau once more.

Take the portfolio of our interior department.

Try to forget our former coldness.

Return, O wanderer, return!"

CHAPTER XI

NYE AND RILEY, RILEY AND NYE, GRIN AND CHUCKLE, SOB AND SIGH

In the spring of 1885 Nye got his first taste of the footlights. In a letter to A. J. Mitchell, dated March 31, he describes the experiment.

We have just returned from a grand farewell tour of Duluth, Superior and Cumberland which took place last week and devastated the country. It was a dull season and I accepted a call to go to the three cities at an agreed price, taking with me several accomplished singists, among them my wife, Mrs. Price, a graduate of the Bosting Conservatory of Music and a piano virtuoso. Also some other voices and a common readist who wanted to go along and protect his wife. It was a congenial party of friends, all young and full of frolic and I took them for a grand picnic and a great moral walk around. It was immense. I paid all expenses, had $94 left and $200,000 worth of fun.

We sang and cavorted around on the stage of the Grand Opera House at Duluth like a thing of life. Fanny [Mrs. Nye] warbled like a hired man and at Cumberland appeared in a new cream colored satin and brocade dress and *arctic overshoes*, both cut low in the neck. (*Fact!*) She only wore the overshoes during the first duet. After that she knew that they had done their duty so took them off. She sang just as well without them, so far as I could see, and if I had shut my eyes I could not have told whether she had them on or not, though I have a wonderful ear for music. Mrs. Price and myself took in the encores and bouquets. She sang "Swanee River" so that it raised Lake Superior 9 inches in 9 moments. I read "The Bronco Cow" till it raised the price of board to $4 per day.

We are all well and hungry all the time. I go to Bosting latter part of April or early in May to be gone several weeks. I would give some cultivated and gentlemanly cuss $100 to take the job off my hands. Still I have an uncle on Tremont Street who writes that he will keep me in his barn till I get tamed down a little. He is certainly a good kind man. Love to all. Good-bye.

WM. NYE,
Chin Virtuoso.

One of the first Eastern newspaper publishers to recognize that Bill Nye was more than a provincial attraction was the late General Charles H. Taylor of the "Boston Globe." It was he who was chiefly responsible for the journey east in May, 1885. On this trip arrangements were made for weekly letters in the "Globe," the first of which appeared Sunday, May 31. From Boston the following letter was written to Uncle Mitchell:

I am well with the exception of a slight uneasiness in the abdomen and hope these few lines will find you enjoying the same great blessing. A large feed this evening, another tomorrow evening and a Press Banquet next Friday evening will not assist the abdominal program. How sad it is that fun and bellyache should go hand in hand down through this vale of tears!

I have been doing Bosting several days now, having

astonished New York so that she will not recover for some time. I like the people of Boston bully but I hate their blamed old town and their cussed climate. It is cold, wet, full of pneumonia and the nut brown flavor of the codfish. I make my home with my uncle and aunt here who are able to show me the village with great fluency. I shall go and see Mr. Howells and Jno. Boyle O'Reilly as a mere matter of form, having letters to them from George Parsons Lathrop. George is a cuss. He is also a poet. The trip has been chock full of regular old fashioned, genuine hospitality and I am mad that I did not do it before. It has not been the drunk and disorderly kind of hospitality either as might be inferred from the opening lines of this letter. Yesterday I went down to the old South Church and hefted the Sword of Bunker Hill, roamed over the Common and walked my legs loose. This P.M. we go over to Bunker Hill to see if anybody has carried it off while we were away.

Yourn,

BEAN EYE.

While in New York, Nye dropped in at the offices of the "Century Magazine." Some months later he wrote his doctor:

I was in the Century office several hours and the editors treated me very handsomely, but, although I have bought the magazine ever since, and read it thoroughly, I have not seen where they said that they "had a pleasant call from the genial and urbane William Nye." I do not feel offended over this. I simply feel hurt.

Before that I had a good notion to write a brief epic on the Warty Toad, and send it to the Century for publication, but now it is quite doubtful.

The Century may be a good paper, but it does not take the press dispatches, and only last month I saw in it an account of a battle that to my certain knowledge occurred twenty years ago.

In the fall of 1885 Nye had another slight accident— nothing serious this time. He refers to the spill in another letter to Uncle Mitchell, November 27:

Yourn is at hand and found us fairly well. Mrs. Nye is O. K. and I am a little bruised but getting along first class. Our tip-over was very odd. It was not a runaway or the fault of the said hoss. I had been down to the depot to meet my bride who had just made another of her farewell visits to St. Paul. (She is making a farewell visit to Stillwater as I write.) It was dark and in coming home we turned a corner too soon and ran up on a little embankment. The slight elevation, the speed, and Mrs. Nye being on the lower side, all conspired to spill us out. Fanny slid out easily on her elbows and knees without a scratch but I described a much larger arc and bumped one hip pretty hard. I do not suffer much and the fact that Fanny got off so easily makes me perfectly comfortable. I shall get myself a bustle before another fall. Estimates are now being made.

You must miss Paul [Mitchell, his son] very much since he has gone and I presume that he will be a little homesick. It is a good thing, though, for him to meet the average man and study human nature as it shows itself. I presume I shall not be able to give my boy a college education, but I want him to be more or less familiar with the practical working of the "everidge" two-legged man and to see and fully realize man's wholly lost and undone condition. Still we should not count our chickens ere they are hatched, I trow.   [This was written a few weeks before the birth of my elder brother, Max.]

My father and mother inserted their limbs under our mahogany yesterday and I spattered Thanksgiving stuffing over their smiling lineaments.   They seemed to like it.

Nye's growing popularity as a humorist and his trial spin in the Northwest justified a more ambitious lecture

A drawing by Bill Nye.
"I presume I shall not be able to give my boy a college education, but I want him to be familiar with the practical working of the 'everidge' two-legged man."

experiment. He was invited to come to Indianapolis and there go through the paces with James Whitcomb Riley as the first step in what became the extraordinarily success-

ful Nye-Riley combination. Before joining Riley, however, Nye held a dress rehearsal in Tarkio, Missouri. Rich-
ard S. Groves tells the story of this lecture:

When he came upon the platform that night, it was some
time before he could speak, and it was plain that he was almost
overcome with stage-fright. He spoke in a voice that could be
heard all over the room, and said the funniest things I have
ever heard from a platform, but nobody laughed. Bill Nye
was then known all over the Middle West, and the newspapers
were filled with his humor. Every person in the room had read
them, but not one of them had ever heard a humorist say them.
It was all new to them, and they sat enjoying it, but afraid to
laugh, fearing they would miss something he was saying.

Doctor Postlewait sat quite a distance away from me, but
we both realized, at the same instant, that Nye was becoming
more disconcerted every moment. We signaled each other, and
although there had been no previous arrangement between us,
we both broke out in a laugh at the end of Nye's next sentence.

The entire audience laughed with us, and made up for its
silence up to that time. Nye concluded his lecture under great
difficulties, for the audience laughed so long that he hardly had
time to say anything. He spoke more freely after the ice had
been broken and, although his first crude lecture was not the
finished product that he afterwards delivered from the platform,
it was just as humorous as anything he ever wrote or said.

Although the assembler of this biography was christened
Frank Wilson Nye, I answer better to the name of Jim.
The Frank comes from my father's brother, the Hon. Frank
M. Nye, of Minneapolis. My father bequeathed me his
middle name. But James Whitcomb Riley is responsible
for the handier handle, preferred by family and close
friends when paging the writer.

It happened this way: My brother Max, who antedated

me by seventeen months, was just beginning to feel the need
of a something by which to call me when Riley visited us.
My dad was "Jimming" Riley all over the place, and, as
admiring young sons will, Max felt called upon to ape his
idol to the extent of doing likewise with me. From that
time I was not only Max's Jim, but Jim to all Nye family
intimates.

Thus did Riley achieve a namesake. Nevertheless the
Jim we had in common became a bond between us; at
least it augmented a natural predisposition I had in
favor of Mr. Riley, fanning the glow of admiration into
the crackling blaze of hero worship. We children were
raised on Riley's verse as an improvement upon Mother
Goose.

Hardly a day passed that there was not some reference
to "Uncle Sidney." Even when there were long pauses
between his visits he lived in our hearts as a sort of super
Santa Claus and all-round household god. Then he flattered us boys greatly by including us in the poem:

> Max an' Jim
>   They're each other's
> Fat an' slim
>   Little brothers.
>
> Max is thin,
>   An' Jim, the fac's is,
> Fat ag'in
>   As Little Max is.
>
> Their Pa 'lowed
>   He don't know whuther
> He's most proud
>   Of one er th' other.

Their Ma says
    They're both so sweet—'m'—
That she guess
    She'll hav to eat 'em!

Mr. Riley also delighted our sisters as much as he had
pleased us in this poem by writing of an occurrence concerning them, which he called "The Robin's Other Name."
It went like this:

In the Orchard-Days, when you
Children look like blossoms, too,
Bessie, with her jaunty ways
And trim poise of head and face,
Must have looked superior
Even to the blossoms,—for
Little Winnie once averred
Bessie looked just like the bird,
Tilted on the topmost spray
Of the apple-boughs in May,
With the red breast, and the strong,
Clear, sweet warble of his song.—
"I don't know their *name*," Win said,-
"I ist *maked* a name instead."—
So forever afterwards
We called robins "Bessie-birds."

Riley was three years younger than my father, but about
the time Nye's writings became popular in the exchange
columns, Riley's verse in the "Indianapolis Journal" was
being copied widely. Riley liked Nye's homespun humor
and Nye saw rare merit in Riley's verse. Both had ex-
perimented a little in the lecture field. Nye had discovered
that an evening of unadulterated mirth was a strain on
the laughing muscles; while Riley's lectures, leaning largely

to pathos, though keenly enjoyed by his closer admirers, had been only moderately attended.

A meeting was arranged at Indianapolis in 1886. Eugene Field was there at the time, and the trio appeared before an Indianapolis audience. This affair was the beginning of the long and intimate "pardnership" of Nye and Riley.

In his book, "The Maturity of James Whitcomb Riley," Marcus Dickey tells of the first Nye-Riley entertainment:

As was expected, the three-star bill drew a full house; "packed it," Robert Burdette said, "until people began to fall out of the windows." A more delighted audience never laughed its approval. Aside from the regular numbers—Nye in the "Cow Phenomenon," and "Robust Cyclones"; Field in the "Romance of a Waterbury Watch"; and Riley in "Deer Crick" and "Fessler's Bees"—there was considerable sparring among the participants, which keyed the audience to the G string of enjoyment. According to the program the order of appearance was Nye, Field and Riley, but when the curtain rang up Riley came forward first. "I desire to make a brief statement," he said, "concerning my friend from Wisconsin. He is the victim of an hereditary affliction, which makes him morbidly sensitive. When the audience laughs he is not always certain whether they are laughing at his humor or his physical defect, and thus he is humiliated and embarrassed, sometimes to the extent of forgetting his lines. Out of consideration for his feelings I therefore ask the audience to refrain from laughing while he recites his piece. I will add that his affliction is a slight tendency to premature baldness."

Riley retired and, according to Burdette, the audience put on a decorous, sympathetic look when Nye came on making his first bow to an Indiana congregation. "He was bald as a brickyard. The house gasped and then incontinently roared." When he could command silence, Nye said that Riley had sum-

EUGENE FIELD, JAMES WHITCOMB RILEY AND BILL NYE
At the time of their appearance together at Indianapolis in 1886.

moned him to Indianapolis by telegram, a compliment indeed, and he was glad to come. As the entertainment proceeded, he explained, the audience would observe that he and Field would be in view on the stage at the same time, but he and Riley would

LITTLE WILLIE.

"Little Willie", he was called,
From his childhood on until
He grew funny, old and bald,—
Then they called him "Bill."

Words and pictures
by James Whitcomb Riley

not appear at the same time. The separate appearance of himself and the Hoosier "star" was explained in the Riley telegram, which with the permission of the audience Nye would read: "Edgar W. Nye.—

"Come and appear at my reception. Be sure to bring a dress suit.

"P. S. Don't forget the trousers. I have a pair of suspenders."

"For a moment," said Burdette, "the jest hung fire. Then somebody tittered, the fuse sizzled through the boxes, down the aisle, and then up into the gallery."

The auspicious start in Indianapolis was followed by a short swing through neighboring territory. On March 6 Riley wrote his friend George Hitt:

Last night we bagged the town—a success not even second to our Indianapolis ovation. Nye is simply superb on the stage—and no newspaper report can half-way reproduce either the curious charm of his drollery—his improvisations—inspirations and so forth. At times his auditors are hysterical with delight. We repeat tonight by special request of everybody. Newspapers all sent reporters, quite an audience in themselves, as they sat in betabled phalanx in the orchestra-pen, and laughed and whooped and yelled and cried, wholly oblivious of their duty half the time.

The first Nye letter to Riley in my possession is dated April 8, 1886, and was written soon after my father's return from the first tour. Nye, much taken with Riley's idea of decorating his epistles with a sketch or two, and likewise possessed of some talent as a sketcher, has adorned his letter:

I hasten to write a brief 'pistle to you and to express my pleasure and delight over your pomes. I often think that if I "could have wrote" such things when I was young, regarding the eyes of the opposite sex, I "would of" been married at a tender age or locked up for tampering with the feelings of said sex.

I now decorate all my stationery with unique designs

from the old masters—and mistresses. I spent so much time in decorating the letter that the letter itself is rather feeble. Those who use their talents in one way cannot expect to use them much in other directions. This picture represents an ancient tear jug. One of these jugs was found in an old ruin at Herculaneum not long ago. It was in a good state of preservation but the tears were not worth a damn.

You must not expect a long letter from me for two reasons; viz., I am very much driven with work—such as it is, and also because I am not a ready writer as you are. I saw this in a paper and I know it is so. I've seen you dash off one of your dashed poems in less than a week while I was sweating over a feeble effort that was cheerful but assumed.

BILL.

P. S.—A large Norman, all around stud hoss in Illinois has been named Bill Nye I see by the press. Our lecture will be a success.

One of the things that added to the pleasure of Nye's partnership with Riley was the liking for Riley's manager, Amos Walker. Walker had an impediment in his speech, but not in his mental processes. One of my dad's favorite stories was told by Walker—the one about having the dining-room wall-paper match the gravy. I often heard my father refer to Walker and recall amusing incidents of their travels together.

In preparation for their next lecture tour together Nye and Riley were writing to each other frequently.

My father, once he started, literally dashed off his "pieces for the paper." With Riley each bit of writing was an artistic production which must please the eye as well as

the heart; an expression of his love of form, which made
Riley in his early days a successful sign-painter and in his
later days a Beau Brummel.   But Riley, in a spirit of mischief, had told a reporter most solemnly that he was the
speed king, and Nye the literary snail.   The interview had
just been published.   So it will be seen that Nye's remarks
relative to writing speed are shot with irony:

April 18, 1886.

> [Caricature of Riley standing on
> an elevation, with his hand on
> Nye's head, inspiring a thought.]

Dear Riley:

Your noble words of encouragement were rec'd on my
return last evening.   You can never know how it makes
my poor heart beat again with hope to receive such kind
words from one who is able to compose rapidly.   Oh, sir,
could you know how a newfound joy, one that has hereto-
fore been a stranger to this luxuriant home, has sprung
up on my soul like a tiny little sprig of Jimson weed near
the woodshed of an emperor, as a result of your hopeful
letter.   Ah—if I could only compose rapidly!   If I could
only shed my talents and pour ambrosia all over the age
in which I live!   If I could only demonstrate to a dying
world the wealth of my thinker and my salivary glands as
you can!   (Riley was an ardent chewer of Star Tobacco.)
But alas, I cannot do it.   I must struggle on and on,
writing a word, erasing it, writing it yet again, and at
last, with my life work only half performed, roll up my
pantaloons and wade across the mysterious river.   I tell
you it is tough, James, mighty tough.

Little can you realize what it is to struggle with a
thought, grapple with it, spit on it and grapple yet again.
But you give me hope.   You bid me despair not.   Oh, sir,

a thousand Oh sirs, for your kind, kind words and gentle, patronizing manner, which I have tried in my poor weak way to illustrate!

Adieu, Kind Sir, Adieu.

BILL NYE.

It was in 1886 that Nye wrote his play, "The Village Postmaster." As originally produced, it was not a success. Later, as "The Cadi," it had a fair run. More of that later. That Nye was willing to learn what he could about the drama is shown by his letter to Mr. Marble, a dramatist who proposed the writing of a play jointly:

Hudson, Wis., 1886.

Scott Marble, Esq.

Dear Sir: I have just received your favor, in which you ask me to unite with you in the construction of a new play.

Would you mind telling me how you write a play? Do you write it with a typewriter, or do you dictate your thoughts to someone who does not resent being dictated to?

Do you write a play and then dramatize it, or do you write the drama and then play on it? Would it not be a good idea to secure a plot that would cost very little, and then put the kibosh on it? Or would you put up the lines first, and then hang the plot or drama, or whatever it is, on the lines?

But seriously, a play, it seems to me, should embody an idea. Am I correct in that theory?

If we are to make a comedy, my idea would be to introduce something facetious in the middle of the comedy. No one will expect it, you see, and it will tickle the audience almost to death.

On April 14, 1886, Nye wrote this letter to Riley:

For some time I have been very busy, a thing I especially dislike. To be actually engaged in doing something all the time, annoys me very much indeed. I have been squirting a few desultory remarks into the play of which I told you, and attending rehearsals. I will witness its first production on the traditional dog stage at Rochelle, Ill. After that I will go home and leave the company on the road under the management of Tony Denier, who puts up the funds and pays me a royalty. If successful the play will add considerably to my great wealth. Still I shall not be above using your (*) tobacco just as I have been doing before this great flood of prosperity came rolling in upon me. When I like a man, I borrow tobacco of him right along, through prosperity or adversity.

I am glad that the prospects are so good for another Indianapolis appearance and I have been thinking that inasmuch as Indpls. is known among show people as an unusually "bad town," we might make a good point among opera house men and show people by wiring the "Dramatic News Mirror" that the "house was packed to suffocation." The bare fact that in a bad season and a bad city we got on our second date all that the house would hold and turned people away, ought to mitigate the horrors of our sad fate.

As I write, the soft wet rain is coming gently down. I can hear it patter ever and anon.

But again——

Why should not the rain descend in a downward direction? Perhaps it is better so. Albeit adieu for the nonce.

My mother used to tell of a game of "catch" between Nye and Riley when the Hoosier first visited us at Hudson. I can't think of any incident more characteristic of the boyish antics of the two. The day being dull and rainy, and confinement within doors beginning to pall upon them, each took an umbrella and went out to play ball. They performed with funereal faces for the benefit of the family and neighbors. Had either allowed the trace of a smile to show itself, the effect would have been lost. Imagine, if you can, two intellectual-looking, bespectacled gentlemen, both well past the ball-playing age, each trying to keep off the rain with a large black umbrella, and at the same time jumping to grasp a wild throw or stooping to stop a grounder.

No less amusing were Mr. Riley's imitations of a monkey, given for the benefit of the children. From chasing imaginary fleas to taking off his shoes and shinning up an appletree, the "impersonations" were perfect. Another favorite method of entertaining the children was to help them dig up stones—entrances to wonderland, or if not that possibly the abode of a "Wunk" or a "Squidgicum-Squee."

In their lectures, Nye would usually make the first appearance. Sometimes his initial laugh was gained by saying to the audience, "I will talk to you in my inimitable way until *I* get tired, whereupon Mr. Riley will entertain you until *you* get tired." That was what he told the audience, but to his friends he said: "The people come to see me out of curiosity—but Riley gives the show, and wherever we play return engagements they come the second time to hear him. I know I am not in his class as an entertainer."

Nye's newspaper contributions gave him excellent opportunities to boost his lecturing activities without detracting

from the enjoyment of his readers.   This open letter to
Edwin Booth was not only good publicity for Nye and
Riley's Little Mammoth Lecture Stand, as they called their
show, but was eagerly seized and reprinted by Booth's press
agent:

Friend Booth:

I learn with some surprise that through a misunder-
standing between your manager and my own you are
billed for Cleveland on the same evening with Mr. Riley
and myself.

In order to give the people of Cleveland an opportunity to witness two of America's greatest tragedians
without inconvenience, I have decided to change my own
date, so as to avoid any annoyance by dividing the audience.   Sentiment in Cleveland, I find, is about equally
divided on the question of dramatic and tragic interpretation between you and me.   Some like your style of melan-
choly best, while those who have used mine say they would
have no other.   So I think it would be better to give each
and all an opportunity to judge fairly and impartially
between us.

I believe that while your stage sadness is the perfection
of masterly interpretation, it is not entered into so thoroughly and participated in by the audience as mine is.
I am introducing this winter a style of sad that is becoming popular and brings tears to eyes unused to weep.

Everywhere I go I hear you highly spoken of, however.
I think you are giving general satisfaction.   I will try to
hear you at Cleveland.   I have read the play before so it
will not be new to me, but I would enjoy going very much
and my presence might induce others to go.   It does not
matter much where I sit.   You can put me wherever you
think I would attract the most attention.   After the per-

formance is over I will come back on the stage and congratulate you.

Hoping that you are well, and that the awkward conflict of our dates may be satisfactorily adjusted so that your pecuniary loss will be merely nominal, I remain yours with kind regards.

After witnessing the performance, he reviewed it:

Last evening I went to hear Mr. Edwin Booth in "Hamlet." I had read the play before, but it was better as he gave it, I think. The play of "Hamlet" is not catchy, and there is a noticeable lack of local gags in it. There is considerable discussion among critics as to whether Hamlet was really insane or not, but I think that he assumed it in order to throw the prosecution off the track, for he was a very smart man.

Mr. Booth wore a dark waterproof cloak all the evening, and a sword with which he frequently killed people. He was dressed in black throughout, with hair of the same shade. He is using the same hair in "Hamlet" that he wore twenty years ago, though he uses less of it. He wears black knickerbockers and long, black, crockless stockings.

Mr. Booth is doing well in the acting business, frequently getting as high as $2 apiece for tickets to his performances. He was encored by the audience several times last night, but refrained from repeating the play, fearing that it would make it late for those who had to go back to Belladonna, O.

CHAPTER XII

NYE'S FIRST TRIP TO DIXIE

NOTWITHSTANDING the more leisurely life Nye led at Hudson, the fall of 1886 found him again in poor health. His lecture tour with Riley ended at Chicago on November 1. Here the family joined him, and they went to Asheville, North Carolina, for the winter. Nye did not fail to record a narrative of the trip. One who knew him well can easily detect in his comments upon the journey a tendency to find serious fault. Such an indulgence was with him so rare as to suggest how utterly fagged he must have been by the time Asheville was reached:

All night long, except when we were changing cars, we rattled along over wobbling trestles and third mortgages. The cars were graded from third-class down. The road itself was not graded at all.

They have the same old air in the coaches that they started out with. Different people, with various styles of breath, have used this air and then returned it. They are using the same air that they did before the war.

At one place where I had an engagement to change cars, we had a wait of four hours, and I reclined on a hair-cloth lounge at the hotel, with the intention of sleeping a part of the time.

Dear, patient reader, did you ever try to ride a refractory hair-cloth lounge all night, bare back? Did you ever get aboard a short, old-fashioned, black, hair-cloth lounge, with a disposition to buck?

I was told that this was a kind, family lounge that would not shy or make trouble anywhere, but I had only just closed my dark-red and mournful eyes in sleep when this lounge gently humped itself, and shed me as it would its smooth, dark hair in the spring, tra la.

The floor caught me in its strong arms and I vaulted back upon the polished bosom of the hair-cloth lounge. It was made for a man about fifty-three inches in length, and so I had to sleep with my feet in my pistol pockets and my nose in my bosom up to the second joint.

Soon after his arrival at Asheville, Nye gave a characteristic description of the locality in one of his newspaper letters:

As soon as I saw in the papers that my health was failing, I decided to wing my way South for the winter. So I closed up my establishment at Slipperyelmhurst, told the game-keeper not to monkey with the preserves and came here, where I am now writing. At first it seemed odd to me that I should be writing from where I now am, but the more I think it over the better I am reconciled to it, for what better place can a man select from which to write a letter than the point where he is located at the time?

Asheville is an enterprising cosmopolitan city of six or seven thousand people and a visiting population during the season of sixty thousand more. It is situated in the picturesque valley of the French Broad and between the Blue Ridge and the Alleghanies.

This region is from 2,000 to 7,000 feet above sea level

and is, in fact, a mountain country with a southern exposure.

Asheville is called the Switzerland of America. It has been my blessed privilege during the past twenty years to view nearly all the Switzerlands of America there are, but this is fully the equal if not the superior of any of them.

You can climb to the top of Beaucatcher Mountain and see a beautiful sight in any direction. Everywhere the eye rests on a broad sweep of dark-blue climate. Up in the gorges, under the whispering pines, along the rhododendron bordered margins of the Swannonoa, or the French Broad, out through the Gap, and down the thousand mountain brooks, you will find enough climate in twenty minutes to last a week.

The chief products of Western North Carolina are smoking tobacco and climate. If you do not like the climate you can help yourself to the smoking tobacco.

One of Bill Nye's most congenial relatives was his first cousin, Solon Perrin. They had been boys together in Wisconsin, and during Nye's years at Hudson the youthful friendship had ripened into mature fellowship. Cousin Solon was one of the first of my father's friends to preserve his letters, and he is one of those to whose foresight I am chiefly indebted for the letters quoted in this narrative. Nye wrote him:

Oh Sir!   On Thanksgiving Day, Morning Session.
    Your gentle and yet withal powerful epistle of 15th inst. was duly received and did me much good. It found us all quite well and happy, for those who do right will always be happy, both here and hereafter.

I was pained to hear that the great baritone of Kinnic Kinnic had decided to sit on the corner of a damp cloud and murmur Coronation, wearing a low cut collar and a swollen appearance. I agree with you that his upper register was a little dim and his lower notes were frequently protested. He was the pride of a pop-eyed family but with his voice unassisted by his dazzling beauty and strong personal magnetism, he would have died a poor and abstruse man. It was really his stage appearance and gentle demeanor that packed the houses when he sang.

We are having very nice autumn weather, and we frequently walk abroad into the persimmon vineyards and ivy-clad gorges of the Blue Ridge; the children and I. Sometimes the children ride me and sometimes they take a smaller, mouse-colored jackass, a mammal which is quite plentiful here.

But enough of this. I am still getting papers with pathetic references to my ebbing health. As a matter of fact, I am not in a critical condition and may be spared to my parents yet for years to come.

I cannot vouch for the veracity of all of the story which follows. Part of it is true. My father unquestionably took the walk into the woods in search of a holly-tree. Beyond that you will have to use your own judgment. I should feel that I were a poor chronicler, however, if I failed to record the episode.

Asheville, N. C., Dec. 13, 1886.

Last week I went out into the mountains for the purpose of securing a holly tree with red berries on it for Yuletide. I had noticed in all my pictures of Christmas festivities in England that the holly, with cranberries on it, constituted the background of Yuletide. A Yule-tide in England without a holly bough and a little mistle-toe in it wouldn't be worth half price. Here these vege-tables grow in great profusion, owing to the equable climate, and so the holly tree is within the reach of all.

I resolved to secure one personally, so I sped away into the mountains where, in less than the time it takes to tell it, I had succeeded in finding a holly tree and losing my-self. It is a very solemn sensation to feel that you are lost, and that before you can be found something is liable to happen to the universe.

I wandered aimlessly about for half an hour, hoping that I would be missed in society and some one sent in search of me. I was just about to give up in despair and sink down on a bed of moss with the idea of shuffling off six or seven feet of mortal coil when, a few rods away, I saw blue smoke issuing from the side of the mountain and rising toward the sky. I went rapidly towards it and found it to be a plain dugout with a dirt floor.

I entered and cast myself upon a rude nail keg, allow-ing my feet to remain suspended at the lower end of my legs, an attitude which I frequently affect when fatigued.

The place was not occupied at the time I entered, though there was a fire and things looked as though the owner had not been long absent. It seemed to be a kind of laboratory, for I could see here and there the earmarks of the chemist. I feared at first that it was a bomb fac-tory, but as I could not see any of these implements in a perfect state I decided that it was safe and waited for the owner to arrive.

After a time I heard a low guttural footstep approach-ing up the hill. I went to the door and exclaimed to the proprietor as he came, "Merry Christmas, Colonel."

"He showed me a new beverage that he had been engaged in perfecting"

"Merry Christmas be damned!" said he in the same bantering tone. "What in three dashes, two hyphens and an astonisher do you want here, you doubled-dashed and double-blanketed blank to dash and return!!"

The wording here is my own, but it gives an idea of the

way the conversation was drifting. You can see by his manner that literary people are not alone in being surly, irritable and unreasonable.

So I humored him and spoke kindly to him and smoothed down his ruffled plumage with my gay badinage, for he wore a shawl and you can never tell whether or not a man wearing a shawl is armed.

He was a man about medium height with clear-cut features and retreating brisket. His hair was dark and hung in great waves which seemed to have caught the sunlight and retained it together with a great many other atmospheric phenomena. He wore a straw hat, such as I once saw Horace Greeley catch grasshoppers in, on the banks of the Kinnic Kinnic, just before he caught a small trout.

I spent some time with him watching him as he made his various experiments. Finally, he showed me a new beverage that he had been engaged in perfecting. It was inclosed in a dark brown stone receptacle and was held in place by a common corncob stopper. I took some of it in order to show that I confided in him. I do not remember anything else distinctly. The fumes of this drink went at once to my brain, where it had what might be termed a complete walkover.

I now have no hesitation in saying that the fluid must have been alcoholic in its nature, for when I regained consciousness I was extremely elsewhere. I found myself on a road which seemed to lead in two opposite directions, and my mind was very much confused.

I hardly know how I got home, but I finally did get there, accompanied by a strong leaning towards Prohibition.

Early in December there was a heavy fall of snow at Asheville, a record-breaking storm, in fact. This was a

great opportunity for Nye. He made the most of the incongruous weather in a letter to the "New York World."
This letter, "In My Sunny Southern Home," became the
turning-point in Bill Nye's career. Nye was without training as a draftsman, but he was not without talent as a
caricaturist. He accompanied this letter with his own
crude drawing. Colonel John A. Cockerill, then managing
editor of the "World," and Mr. Joseph Pulitzer decided
that a man who could produce such humor as this while
convalescing should be in the exclusive employ of the newspaper with the biggest circulation of the day. So a telegram was despatched, and Nye was invited to come to New
York at the expense of the paper to discuss a contract.
In due time Nye went. He was offered $150 a week and
permitted to contribute to a few magazines under the name
of Edgar Wilson Nye. He offered to work for $1,000 a
year less if the "World" would let him live in North Carolina, but it was thought best that he report to New York.
Here is the story as it appeared in the "World":

In My Sunny Southern Home,
Asheville, N. C., Dec. 6, 1886.

To the Editor of the "World":
I write these lines from the South. I came here in
order to evade the severe winters of the North. I have
tried to show in the inclosed sketch how I appear while
in the act of evading the severe winters of the extreme
North. It is, of course, only a rough draught, but that
was the kind of draught we were having when I made the
sketch.
The tracks in the foreground are only ideal tracks.
They did not exist in reality at the time I made the sketch.
In the left middle foreground stands the author of these

lines, wrapped in earnest thought and a pair of adult ear-muffs. He is about to become the author of the tracks shown in the foreground. These tracks lead to the kitchen, where there is a warm fire.

A large magnolia grove may be seen by going over the range of hills shown in the extreme background and bear-

As Bill Nye saw himself.
"It is a rough draft but that is the kind of a draft we were having"

ing off to the left about three hundred miles. In the house there is a case of Budweiser beer and a case of croup.

The earnest gentleman in the foreground has just been out playing in the snow with a fire-shovel and is about to return it to the owner. He is less fluent with this instrument than with the poker game, of which he is passionately fond.

In the background, to the left of the toboggan slide,

may be seen a family of Christmas trees in repose. This region is noted for its Christmas trees, rhododendrons and rheumatism.

Many people come here to spend the winter and what spare change they may have on hand at the time.

Beyond the farthest line of hills at the back of this picture, and extending as far as the eye can reach, may be seen a broad expanse of climate. Climate here is as free as air. Such as it is, every one may help himself to it.

I thought before I came that I would find the oriole flitting through the soughing boughs of the magnolia and the mocking-bird cooing to its mate, but as I write the snow is nearly two feet deep on a level, trains are not expected for six days and the snow is still falling.

Imagine a slight, almost girlish, figure like my own, clad in a crinkled seersucker, a Mackinaw hat and a fire-shovel battling with the elements and digging holes through the virgin snow in order to get to the grocery store.

I had thought that the odor of the orange blossom and the mint julep would float along upon the gentle brow of the soft and voluptuous air. I had pictured to myself a land of gentle suns and soughing breezes, instead of which I seem to be the principal sougherer myself.

I was fool enough to imagine this a broad and beautiful green State, with here and there a dark red isothermal line across it, but the whole surface of the earth is covered knee-deep with the same kind of snow that people select up in Manitoba when they decide to perish and want something in which to do up their remains.

For thirty-five years and in various parts of the United States I have been the victim of unusual winters. I came here to evade this very thing. I said to my family last

fall: "It looks now as though we are going to have another of those unusual winters here. We will go South
just as soon as we can and see how it will be there."

The result is that old-timers say they never had such
an unusual winter since they have been here, although
the winters have been growing more and more unusual
for ten years.

I thought that here I would sit on the vine-embowered
porch all the livelong day and smoke a cob pipe, while
drowsy influences and enervating sloth would soothe my
troubled breast. So far it has been different. The houses
are made to resist the mild cold of what may be termed a
usual winter, but, greatly to the surprise of every one,
there hasn't been a winter of that kind since before the
war.

Therefore the raw and chilling blast comes stealing up
through the shrunken floors and seeks out the Northern
gentleman who has left his winter underwear at home in
his trunk.

What I reproach the Southern builder for is his absolute
failure to build houses that will protect people from the
cold. Last winter people ate their breakfasts clothed in
fur overcoats and mittens in Florida. Here comes a little
flurry of snow, lasting three days already, and still falling, while three tobacco warehouses have fallen in with
the weight of snow on their roofs. The houses that will
be erected here next summer will be thrown together in
the same wild and reckless manner by carpenters who yet
fondly hope to witness a winter that will fit their perforated style of architecture.

If you will excuse me I will cease writing in order to
nail a bed quilt up to the window where too much climate
is now gently stealing in and freezing some of my children.

Perhaps it was the telegram from New York that
prompted Nye's assertion, made in this letter of December
14, that wealth and invalidism go hand in hand:

No sooner does a man become wealthy than he at once
develops some kind of high-priced disease. This is not
alone my own experience, but it is also the experience of
many other wealthy men. Wealth always costs all the
assessor counts it at, and often even more.

So when I cast my eye about me as I write, and as it
rests on all the environments of luxury, I say to myself, "Of how little value is it all to one who may not
survive more than forty-five or fifty years more at the
furthest?"

Of what avail is the gayly colored "hit-or-miss" carpet
whereon my foot falls with a wild and startling echo like
the wail of the damned? What matters it that a costly
prayer rug embraces my footstep as I bound from my bed
in the early morning? Of what use is it to me that at night
I repose in a costly couch which at the first approach of
dawn, by pressing a secret spring, becomes an upright
piano?

Will all or any of these minister to a pain-racked and
pampered person devoid of hair? Will costly cuspidors
and large red-yarn mottoes worked in a framed sheet of
perforated cardboard minister to a moody and morose
mind? Can the mellow tones of a voluptuous organette
or the plaudits of the autograph purveyor woo back to
peace and contentment the surfeited and sin-sick soul?

The United States to-day has a large army of wealthy
invalids, an army that seems to be on the increase, too,
and one that goes moaning up and down over the land
seeking health and finding none. Wherever location and

climate have anything to offer, or healing waters contain aught of good to assist nature in her struggle to lengthen out the days of those who have more ducats than digestion, there you will see the anxious eye and the halting gait of those who have fought the fight for gain, and now, crowned with victory and misery, find themselves in the great national hospital. The patients of this itinerant sanitarium move about from Moosehead Lake to Tacoma, to Los Angeles, to Jacksonville, to Duluth, to Denver, to Asheville, to Minnetonka, to Santa Fé, to the Hot Springs and the Cold Springs, to the Iron Springs and the Soda Springs, to the dry air of the mountains and the wet air of the sea, with no home that they can call permanent and no sure thing for the future but a will contest and the long, starless night of death.

There is a beautiful opportunity presented here for the moralist, but the reader would hardly forgive me if I referred to anything of a serious nature. If I were a moralizer instead of a light and frothy writer and advance agent of the overworked fool-killer, I would say that the average American almost works himself to death for forty years in order that he may stagnate and suffer for the other ten or fifteen years.

Healthy farmer-boys, who work in the open air in the morning of their lives and eat what they can get, go into trade, professional life, or politics, and wonder at last why they cannot eat pie three times a day with impunity and do nothing. American pie with impunity won't do. Moreover, it will not answer for any man to crowd all his physical exercise into twenty years in order to bestow himself upon a sanitarium for the remainder of his life.

Next, an optimistic letter to Solon, dated December 15, 1886:

Your letter of the 8th inst. was received with much pleasure. It found us in the midst of a genial snow storm which the old time people here stated to me was unprecedented.

An unprecedented snow storm is a very disagreeable thing. To me it looked like one of our old fashioned Kinnic Kinnic snow storms such as we used to have when we had been a little dilatory about getting in our corn. It was a cold kind of snow and became moist when placed in contact with the human body. But when such a snow storm gets over Messrs. Mason and Dixon's line, it is called an unprecedented storm and attracts a great deal of attention.

The weather has been below zero only twice, however, for a few hours, since we came here, and the snow rapidly went off, leaving the grass green and the birds singing in the boughs. I really like this climate very much and have had no neuralgia whatever since I came here. In consequence of which I weigh ten pounds more than before. The town is not pretty in and of itself, but is flourishing, and times are good.

Agriculture here, aside from the propagation of tobacco and niggers, is still in its infancy, and it would tickle you to see the average North Carolina granger coming into town wearing a chip hat with a Nubia tied on his ears, driving a two-year-old heifer harnessed to a buck-board; or parading the streets with a live hen in each hand, offering them for sale to the affluent humorist of the frost-bitten North.

We are all well and eat like a thrashing crew all the time so that my trenchant pen is kept busy in order that we may win bread for eating purposes. Lately we have reveled in quail, sweet potatoes and the best smoking tobacco that grows.

Last week, the kindergarten where Bess and Win soak themselves full of knowledge caught fire and was completely gutted, as the papers say. It affords me much pleasure to state that none of the children was consumed. I am passionately fond of my children and would have been keenly mortified had they been incinerated. An incinerated child is a sad sight. If they must be consumed, let them be consumed by something more worth while; a thirst for knowledge or religion or something harmless like that.

From the middle of December until the end of January, 1887, Nye did practically no writing. He wasn't well enough. And that meant he was truly miserable. Then his father died in Wisconsin. Nye was too ill to make the journey. The best he could do was to write. But his letter to his mother on this sad occasion, though written while Nye suffered greatly, was long cherished by my grandmother. The fourth paragraph she learned by heart and often repeated to me. Never did a letter of condolence mean more to a bereaved one than these words of cheer meant to Eliza Nye.

Jan. 25, 1887.
My Dear Mother:
Frank's second letter confirming all our worst apprehensions came yesterday and found me ill as I have been for six weeks. It was not possible for me to write at once and I can hardly do so now.

It would be unnecessary to write how the news fell upon us even though we had been warned. We still hoped that Father's strength, which had borne him through so much, would bring him out at this time. The children are passing through their first bitter experience with death to one they loved. Our own tears mingled with the first great sorrow of these childish hearts. Winnie was broken hearted when Fanny told her and Bessie was equally shocked but controlled herself better.

I hardly know what I can write to you that will make your heart lighter. But with the fresh experience and distinct memory of pain that does not yield as in my own case, I cannot wish poor Father back again. I am sure that in later years he suffered far more than his nearest neighbors or best friends knew. Modestly and gently but bravely, he fought this long fight, and death, though it overcame him, did not terrify him.

Doubly somber and deserted will the days seem to you after the long years of devotion to him because he needed so much care. As the Mexican Indians, who have been burden-bearers over the mountains for many years, cannot walk or rest without a weight upon their shoulders, so your idle hands will instinctively reach out into the empty air for the task that is gone.

I hope that you will go to Frank's for the present at least and stay away from your own home as long as possible. I wish we were home to be with you to try as best we could to get you used to this new experience. For myself, I cannot sense it all yet and if I were to go to the old home, I should look for Father to be there and meet me with the few words but the warm greeting which he always looked more than his tongue said.

We all send our dearest love to you, Mother, and want

to see you very much. Can I do anything for you in the way of money? If so, do not hesitate to let me know and I will divide with you. When you see Frank and Carroll, give them our love and tell them I will write as soon as I can possibly do so. This is the first letter to anyone I have written for a long time and my work is away behind.

Good-bye, with love from Fanny and the children, as well as from your affectionate son,

EDGAR.

One week later, Nye wrote James Whitcomb Riley:

The rumour to which you referred was too sadly and sorrowfully true. I need not tell you how your letter was the first streak of day after a long black night for I have been physically miserable for some time and could not with safety have made the journey north even had I known in time how near my father was to his end.

It has seemed all at once to make an old man of me, for in his presence I was always a boy. When I went home the hour was never too late for a welcome from him, not a wordy welcome for he said little, but I would walk and have walked ten miles mainly to *see* the welcome that comes alone from the heart; a welcome that I will sadly miss till we meet again.

Frank was with him through the brief illness and wrote me as best he could in the gray morning that stole in on the heels of death.

For forty years my father and mother had buffeted the billows of poverty or reveled in the brief sunshine of prosperity and now one is taken and the other left. You can faintly picture to yourself in your sympathetic poetic heart how the tall tree lies prone in the solemn hush of the forest while the wind-tossed tendrils of the ivy reach out blindly for the rugged boughs that for nearly half a century supported it. I car, even in my misery, see that it is not like hers. Another home has grown about me and little voices and little hands break that awful hush that hangs about the old home today. I can now look forward to the trying time in my own life when one by one the children have gone and then in the unnatural stillness my wife or I will fall and the other, whichever it may be, will stand mute and terrified, alone on the lonely site of what was once our home.

I cannot thank you enough for your letter. I have had a good deal to make me anything but gay this winter. I've been in fact sick for about two months, and now, though better, I am not well by a long way. I am getting the "Indianapolis Journal," and though it is not addressed by you, I feel as I might if you had told Harry New or George Hitt that I would like to see it and they had sent it. I see your work, though less of it than I would anywhere else in the world. Booth's manager is using my letter as an advertisement and so it did not injure him materially. My new book is out but the first edition has some errors and the next edition will follow forthwith and be better. Then I will send you one to criticize.

Good-bye, my dear partner. May your life be as full of joy as it deserves and you will have all you can attend to in that line.

We all send our love and hope to hear from you soon.

The new book mentioned in the last letter was "Remarks by Bill Nye." This fourth compilation of writings was prefaced by the author with "Directions":

Some of my best thoughts are contained in this book. Whenever I would think a thought that I thought had better remain unthought, I would omit it from this book. For that reason the book is not so large as I had intended. When a man coldly and dispassionately goes at it to eradicate from his work all that may not come up to his standard of merit, he can make a large volume shrink till it is no thicker than the bank book of an outspoken clergyman.

This is the fourth book that I have published in response to the clamorous appeals of the public. Whenever the public got to clamoring too loudly for a new book from me, I would issue another volume. The first was a red book, succeeded by a dark blue volume, after which I published a green book; all of which were kindly received by the American people.

But I had long hoped to publish a larger, better and, if possible, a redder book than the first, one that would contain my better thoughts, thoughts that I had thought when I was feeling well; thoughts that I had emitted while my thinker was rearing up on its hind feet; thoughts that sprang forth with a wild whoop and demanded recognition.

This book is the result of that hope and that wish. It is my greatest and best book. It is one that will live for weeks after other books have passed away. Even to those who cannot read, it will come like a benison when there is no benison in the house. To the ignorant, the pictures will be pleasing. The wise will revel in its wisdom, and the housekeeper will find that with it she may easily emphasize a statement or kill a cockroach.

The range of subjects treated in this book is wonderful, even to me. It is a library of universal knowledge, and the facts contained in it are different from any other facts now in use. I have carefully guarded, all the way through, against using hackneyed and moth-eaten facts. As a result, I am able to come before the people with a set of new and attractive statements, so fresh and so crisp that an unkind word would wither them in a moment.

I believe there is nothing more to add, except that I most heartily endorse the book. It has been carefully read over by the proof-reader and myself. We do not ask the public to do anything that we were not willing to do ourselves.

When Nye had regained his health and weighed 175 pounds "as the crow flies" he wrote Riley:

Glad you are talking to them all the time, though it is not so blasted pleasant to roam over the land all by yourself, studying time tables when you want to read other things, and creeping in through the back way to the stage accompanied by an apprehensive man who is going to introduce you, and whose mouth is very, very dry, and you glide softly with him among mouldy scenes and decayed properties that smell like a haunted house. Oh, Sir, is it not joyous? Is it not fraught with merriment and chock-full of mirth?

In a letter to his mother, dated February 16, Nye says:

I wish you had some of our beautiful weather. So long as you are by yourself, nice bright weather would be good to have. We dread going home, the change will be so great even in April. If all my matters were in shape to remain here, I am quite sure I would do so, but this summer at least we cannot be moving and torn up.

I am quite well now. I take a horseback ride every

afternoon and it does me a deal of good.   I am getting to
be quite a horseman.

Occasionally we all go out together for an hour or
two's drive and Max enjoys it hugely.   He is just on the
point of walking and is very entertaining.   He stands
alone but doesn't take any steps yet.   He eats like a hired
man and grows like a weed.   If you ask him now to tell
what the donkey says, he can bray first rate and keep it
up.   He is a great boy for animals and cares more for
horses and dogs than any little child I ever saw.

I think honestly that we would all be better here all
the time, and they say the summers are beautiful, but we
cannot well move now, and the house we have is not convenient or well furnished.

In a letter, also to his mother, on February 26, he speaks
of the "World" offer:

I have a fine offer to become a member of the staff of
the "N. Y. World," the largest paper in America, with a
circulation of 252,000.   I may accept it.   If so, I will
have to live in New York City.   I would not move the
family if I went, until September, however.   Of course
this is all unsettled but I must go where I can do the best.

Nye was charmed with the Tar Heel State.   He hated
to leave it.   He returned to make his home there as soon
as that was possible.   Notwithstanding the early snow-storm,
the balmy breezes and stimulating sunshine of the French
Broad Valley were in pleasing contrast to the hard winters
of Wisconsin and the hard knocks of Wyoming.

BOOK FOUR

CHAPTER XIII

A MAN OF THE WORLD

At the time the "World" engaged Bill Nye to write a weekly story, this New York daily had begun to blossom under the skilful hand of Joseph Pulitzer. It was the talk of newspaperdom. And yet Nye had many misgivings.

Colonel John A. Cockerill, Pulitzer's managing editor, was a man whom my father greatly liked and admired, but Nye did not accept the "World's" offer until careful thought had been given to the problem of pleasing metropolitan readers and there had been consultation with his journalistic friends in the West. Mr. Melville E. Stone told me recently that he was approached by my father for an opinion on the wisdom of the change. Mr. Stone was then editing the "Chicago Daily News" and had been a staunch Nye supporter. Without hesitation he advised Nye to accept what he regarded as an offer no Western newspaper could afford to duplicate. Colonel Cockerill afterward said:

I had to use a great deal of persuasion to get him to take up his abode in New York and become a regular member of the "World" staff. He was afraid of the big city. He thought that his homely humor would not be appreciated here, and that he would lose touch with things rural. I convinced him that the Metropolis was made up of country born men, and that our active, potential citizens loved the smell of dog-fennel, the hum of the bee and the sweet incense of the haymow on wet days. It was only when satisfied that there was a great deal of human

177

nature in the Metropolis that he consented to come at all,
and even then he pitched his tent down on Staten Island,
where he could romp with his children and keep a cow.

In the spring of 1887, leaving the family at Hudson,
where my arrival was momentarily expected, the humorist
of Wyoming and Wisconsin reported for duty on Park Row.

A McDougall caricature.

"Everywhere I go I find people who seem pleased with the manner in
which I have succeeded in resembling the graphic pictures
made to represent me"

Among the first of Nye's New York acquaintances was
Walt McDougall, who had been assigned to the job of illustrating the Bill Nye stories.   Until the "World" contract,
few of Nye's articles had been printed with illustrations.
The idea of the caricature illustrations had been suggested

by the Asheville blizzard story in which Nye had incorporated his own rough pen drawing. Rather, the sketch had been made by my father purely for the amusement of the children, who, as we often did, had asked him to "draw something." Then the story had been written to "illustrate" the picture. Thus it happened that the inspiration for the picture part of my father's newspaper tales grew directly out of a bit of recreational nonsense.

McDougall added so much to the comedy by his quaint caricatures that he remained my father's partner in producing the weekly letter from that time on. The business partnership ripened into a close friendship, of which Mc-Dougall gave evidence in an account written nine years later, but which is given here because of the faithful likeness to the humorist as seen by a keen observer who had the opportunity to study him at close range:

On the day of his arrival I met him, and upon his removing his hat I recalled a funny little story anent a bald-headed Irishman which was then current, and that story made us friends instantly. The short cut to Nye's heart was a funny, a really funny story, and no man, unless it be Depew, ever had more offered to him.

No one could be more appreciative of a really new yarn nor give it a more hearty welcome and in the retelling of it add more flavor to its spiciness. He had the knack of illustrating his remarks in private conversation by stories that were so appropriate and so varied as to be amazing, and so funny that some of his hearers lost in their appreciation of his humor the application of it to the argument.

Of the many men with whom I have been intimate there is not one who has worn so well, for whom an honest admiration has increased rather than lessened with intimacy.

The day he came I went with him to the Court of General

Sessions to witness some notable criminal's trial. I made a sketch of Nye there to which I adhered in all the pictures I have of him, several thousand in number, devoid of hair, spare and angular in appearance; although in late years he grew quite portly.

Yet so like his general appearance was this caricature, to which only Mrs. Nye in her love and admiration objected, that often I have been tickled to see people point Bill out on the elevated and eagerly nudge their neighbors, as they whispered, "That's Bill Nye."

Of all the men widely known to the general public, and he was among the very first, I doubt if there is one who allowed himself fewer real intimates. Everybody took him as he was, free, unreserved and unaffected. Many called him Bill almost on sight, yet there was a certain dignity about him that kept the choice heart inside for a few. I think even the people who presumed upon his affable nature realized how little they knew of him.

He was bored by well-meant but annoying attentions, and compelled to dine with flattering strangers and meet uninteresting but obtrusive people, until he grew to have a sort of outer shell to all but his close friends.

Yet at home, at the head of his own table, alone with his family, what a fountain of good-humor and wit and gentle badinage he was!

To see him unbend and dance the Virgina reel with a dozen youngsters, with a wealth of gesture, comic genuflexion and capering, would have amazed those who have seen him only upon the lecture platform. The children would simply forget to dance and stand there roaring at him as he solemnly went through his capers with a face as grave and set as a judge on the bench.

We once spent a week with the Shinnecock Indians, whose sense of humor, he said, had been removed by a surgical operation. At the end of the visit we stayed the night at a Southampton farm-house, into which mirth had not entered for twenty years. An aged couple abode there and gave us lodging.

After supper we sat in the quaint, stiff parlor and as the silence and solemn gloom began to enshroud and chill us Nye talked and led the two old people into conversation. It was like trying to melt an iceberg with a candle. Never a smile thawed those ancient features. We batted jests from one to the other and grew in deadly earnest in our effort to make those people smile.

The door opened and an old sea-dog entered, whose round, red face shone like a polished apple. Nye's countenance brightened as the old captain seated himself, and he took a fresh grip.

The faces of the old people wore a grave look of wonder as they listened, but in a few minutes Bill captured the captain, who laid back and roared aloud. Then the faces of the others cracked and wrinkled into smiles as the mariner testified to the character of Nye's fun, and soon the old, musty homestead reëchoed with peals of laughter. It was a veritable triumph, and we sat there, all of us, until two in the morning listening to Nye's stories and enjoying the excitement of those two fossils.

In the morning the old woman told Bill that he had made her happier than she had been for years and that the house seemed brighter, as if, in her own words, "somebody had been and brushed a lot o' cobwebs out of it."

He was one of those men whom prosperity does not make ashamed of former poverty nor warp into affected mannerisms. He would have chatted with an Emperor with the same freedom and dignity that characterized his conversation with a farm-hand, yet he had earned with his own brain a fortune that would have made most men haughty and pompous. He had nothing of that theatrical self-assertiveness that marks so many famous men. He never posed nor tried to attract attention at any time, although he enjoyed, as all men must do, the large meed of fame and applause that came to him.

I have made fun of him in the most ridiculous ways I could devise in my pictures, yet with a loving and admiring hand that lingered always over his gentle, strong face, whose every line I know by heart.

He once told an audience to which I introduced him in Newark that I deprived his portrait of hair in order to avoid work, and on another occasion he powdered his hair and the top of his head, thus creating a most vivid resemblance to the caricature, and when he appeared before the audience there was a thrill of recognition that was delightful to my own vanity. I drew this comic portrait on an envelope, wrote "New York" under it, nothing more, and so well was his face known that he received the letter the next morning, much to his own astonishment.

In England he was a source of much wonder and speculation. His jokes were taken with the usual British amazement and speculation, then carefully pondered over, digested and finally comprehended, but he never wearied of narrating how some of his remarks were taken seriously. At the Wild West banquet somebody referred to "flowing hair," which is one of the Wild West "props." Nye remarked that he once had flowing hair, but his "had long since flown." This little jest was pondered over for many moons by the Englishmen present, who endeavored to find a concealed meaning in it.

Here is what Nye thought of McDougall's handwork:

Everywhere I go I find people who seem pleased with the manner in which I have succeeded in resembling the graphic pictures made to represent me in the "World." I can truly say that I am not a vain man, but it is certainly pleasing and gratifying to be greeted by a glance of recognition and a yell of genuine delight from total strangers. Many have seemed to suppose that the massive and undraped head shown in these pictures was the result of artistic license or indolence and a general desire to evade the task of making hair. For such people the thrill of joy they feel when they discover that they have not been deceived is marked and genuine.

These pictures also stimulate the press of the country to try it themselves and to add other horrors which do not in any way interfere with the likeness, but at the same time encourage me to travel mostly by night.

And perhaps you will be interested in some of Nye's remarks for the "World" on the occasion of his visit to the Shinnecock reservation with McDougall.

There can be nothing more pathetic than to watch the decay of a race, even though it be a scrub race. To watch the decay of the Indian race has been with me, for many years, a passion; and the more the Indian has decayed the more reckless I have been in studying his ways.

The Indian race for over two hundred years has been a race against Time, and I need hardly add that Time is away ahead as I pen these lines.

I dislike to speak of myself so much, but I have been identified with the Indians more or less for fifteen years. In 1876 I was detailed by a San Francisco paper to attend the Custer massacre and write it up, but not knowing where the massacre was to be held I missed my way and wandered for days in an opposite direction. When I afterwards heard how successful the massacre was, and fully realized what I had missed, my mortification knew no bounds, but it might have been even more so if I had been successful. We never know what is best for us.

But the Indian is on the wane, whatever that is. He is

disappearing from the face of the earth, and we find no
better illustration of this sad fact than the gradual fading
away of the Shinnecock Indians near the extremity of
Long Island.

In company with the "World" artist, who is paid a
large salary to hold me up to ridicule in these columns, I
went out the other day to Southampton and visited the
surviving members of this great tribe.

Neither of us knows the meaning of fear. If we had
been ordered by the United States Government to wipe
out the whole Shinnecock tribe we would have taken a
damp towel and done it.

The Shinnecock tribe now consists of James Bunn and
another man. But they are neither of them pure-blooded
Shinnecock Indians. One-Legged Dave, an old whaler,
who, as the gifted reader has no doubt already guessed,
has but one leg, having lost the other in going over a
reef many years ago, is a pure-blooded Indian, but not
a pure-blooded Shinnecock. The Shinnecocks have not
been rash enough to break out since they had the measles
some years ago.

Nye's ability to live down to the comic trade-mark of Bill
Nye, which his caricaturists devised, was useful on one occasion at least. He was calling at a certain bank:

I asked for a certificate of deposit for $2000, but I had
to be identified. "Why," I said to the receiving teller,
"surely you don't require a man to be identified when he
deposits money, do you?"

"Yes," that's the idea. Hurry up, please don't keep men
waiting who have money and know how to do business."

"Well, suppose I get myself identified by a man I know
and a man you know and a man who can leave his business

and come here for the delirious joy of identifying me.
How would it be about your ability to identify yourself
as the man you claim to be?"

"Oh, we don't care especially whether you trade here
or not. Our rules are that a man who makes a deposit
here must be identified."

"All right. Do you know Queen Victoria?"

"No, sir; I do not."

"Well, then, there is no use in disturbing her. Do you
know any other of the crowned heads?"

"No, sir."

"Well, then, do you know President Cleveland, or any
of the Cabinet, or the Senate or members of the House?"

"No."

"That's it, you see. I move in one set and you in
another."

I then drew from my pocket a copy of the Sunday
"World" which contained a voluptuous portrait of myself. Removing my hat and making a court salaam by
letting out four additional joints in my lithe and versatile
limbs, I asked if any further identification would be
necessary.

Hastily closing the door to the vault and turning the
combination, he said that would be satisfactory. I was
then permitted to deposit in the bank.

I do not know why I should always be regarded with
suspicion wherever I go. I do not present the appearance
of a man who is steeped in crime, and yet when I put my
trivial, little, two-gallon valise on the seat of a depot
waiting-room a big man with a red mustache comes to
me and hisses through his clenched teeth: "Take yer
baggage off the seat!" It is so everywhere. I apologize
for disturbing a ticket agent long enough to sell me a

ticket, and he tries to jump through a little brass wicket
and throttle me.   Other men come in and say, "Give me
a ticket for Bandoline, Ohio, and be damn sudden about
it, too," and they get their ticket and go aboard the car
and get the best seat, while I am begging for the oppor-

"I then drew from my pocket a copy of the Sunday 'World' which
contained a voluptuous portrait of myself"

tunity to buy a seat at full rates and then ride in the
wood box.   I believe that common courtesy and decency
in America need protection.   Go into an hotel or a hotel,
whichever suits, and the commercial man who travels for
a big sausage-casing house in New York has the bridal
chamber, while the meek and lowly minister of the Gospel

gets a wall-pocket room with a cot, a slippery-elm towel, a cake of cast-iron soap, a disconnected bell, a view of the laundry and a tin roof at $4 a day.

One of Nye's early assignments was to visit Washington, D. C., and report what was going on at the opening of the spring session of Congress. Before hearing much about government, the "World," through its cashier, received this letter, marked "Personal."

> Along toward morning, 1887.
> Washington, D. C.

Cashier, World Office, New York.

My dear sir: You will doubtless be surprised to hear from me so soon, as I did not promise when I left New York that I would write you. But now I take pen in hand to say that the Senate and House of Representatives are having a good deal of fun with me. You will wonder at first why I send in my expense account before I send in anything for the paper, but I will explain that to you when I get back. At first I thought I would not bother with the expense account till I got to your office, but I can now see that it is going to worry me to get there unless I hear from you favorably by return mail.

I have not written anything for publication yet, but I am getting material together that will make people throughout our broad land open their eyes in astonishment. I shall deal fairly and openly with these great national questions, and frankly hew to the line. Candor is my leading characteristic. If you will pardon me for saying so in the first letter you ever received from me, I believe there is nothing about my whole character which seems to challenge my admiration for myself any more than that.

I have been mingling with society ever since I came here, and that is one reason I have written very little for publication, and did not send what I did write.

Yesterday afternoon my money gave out at 3:20, and since that my mind has been clearer and society has made fewer demands on me. At first I thought I would obtain employment at the Treasury Department as exchange editor in the greenback room. Then I remembered that I would get very faint before I could go through a competitive examination, and, in the meantime, I might lose social caste by *wearing my person on the outside of my clothes*. So I have resolved to write you a chatty letter about Washington, assuring you that I am well, and asking you kindly to consider the enclosed tabulated bill of expenses, as I need the money to buy Christmas presents and get home with.

So far I have not been over to the Capitol, preferring to have Congress kind of percolate into my room, two or three at a time; but unless you can honor the inclosed way-bill I shall be forced to go over to the House to-morrow and write something for the paper. Since I have been writing this I have been led to inquire whether it would be advisable for me to remain here through the entire session or not. It will be unusually long, lasting perhaps clear into July, and I find that the stenographers as a general thing get a pretty accurate and spicy account of the proceedings, much more so than I can, and as you will see by inclosed statement it is going to cost more to keep me here than I figured on.

My idea was that board and lodgings would be the main items of expense, but I struck a low-priced place, where, by clubbing together with some plain gentlemen

from a distance who have been waiting here three years
for political recognition, and who do not feel like sur-
rounding themselves with a hotel, we get a plain room
with six beds in it. The room overlooks the District of
Columbia, and the first man in has the choice of beds,
with the privilege of inviting friends to a limited number.
We lunch plainly in the lower part of the building in a
standing position without restraint or finger-bowls. So
board is not the principal item of expense, though of
course I do not wish to put up at a place where I will be
a disgrace to the paper.

I saw Mr. Cleveland briefly last evening at his home,
but he was surrounded by a crowd of fawning sycophants,
so I did not get a chance to speak to him as I would like
to, and don't know as he would have advanced the amount
to me anyway. He is very firm and stubborn, I judged,
and would yield very little indeed, especially to

Yours truly,
BILL NYE.

P.S. The following bill looks large in the aggregate,
but when you come to examine each item there is really
nothing startling about it, and when you remember that
I have been here now four days and that this is the first
bill I have sent in to the office during that time, I know
you will not consider it out of the way, especially as you
are interested in seeing me make a good paper of the
"World," no matter what the expense is.

I fear you will regard the item for embalming as ex-
orbitant, and it is so, but I was compelled to pay that
price, as the man had to be shipped a long distance, and
I did not want to shock his friends too much when he
met them at the depot.

Expense Account

To rent of dress suit for the purpose of seeing life in Washington in the interest of the paper.......	$4.50
To charges for dispersing turtle soup from lap of same	1.00
To getting fur collar put on overcoat, in interest of paper	9.00
To amount loaned a gentleman who had lived in Washington a long time and could make me a social pet (I will return same to you in case he pays it before I come back).................	5.00
To lodgings two nights at 25 cents..............	.50
Six meals at 15 cents...........................	.90
Pen and ink....................................	.20
Postage on this letter..........................	.08
Bronchial troches, in interest of paper...........	.20
Car fare......................................	.60
Laundry work done in interest of paper	.30
Carriage hire in getting from humble home of a senator to my own voluptuous lodgings..........	2.00
To expenses of embalming a man who came to me and wanted me to use my influence in changing policy of the paper......................	180.00
To fine paid for assault and battery in and upon a gentleman who said he wanted my influence, but really was already under other influence, and who stepped on my stomach twice without offering to apologize	19.00
Paid janitor of jail next morning................	1.00
Paid for breaking the window of my cell..........	.50
Paid damage for writing humorous poetry on wall of cell so that it could not be erased.........	2.00
Total.............................	$226.78

Instead of New York cramping Nye's style he soon discovered that here was a wealth of new material. The incongruities of Gotham were doubly apparent to him who had never lived in a sizable city. Central Park, the Brooklyn Navy Yard, the Academy of Design, and all of the obvious sights of New York furnished him with scenery and properties for comedy. His picture of New York's slavish adherence to fashion in the matter of heraldic decoration of equipages is Nye in his best satirical mood:

I violate no confidence in saying that spring is the most joyful season of the year. But June is also a good month. Well has the poet ejaculated, "And what is so rare as a day in June?" though I have seen days in March that were so rare that they were almost raw. Central Park is looking its very best, and opens up with the prospect of doing a good business this season. A ride through the Park is a delight to one who loves to commune with nature, especially human nature.

The nobility of New York now turns out to get the glorious air and ventilate its crest. I saw several hundred crests and coats-of-arms the other day in an hour's time, and it was rather a poor day, too, for a great many of our best people are just changing from their spring to their light summer coats-of-arms.

One of the best crests I saw was a nice, large red crest, about the size of an adult rhubarb pie, with a two-year-old Durham unicorn above it, bearing in his talons the unique maxim, "Sans culottes, sans knockemonthegob, sans ery sipelas est."

And how true this is, too, in a great many cases.

Another very handsome crest on the carriage of the Van Studentickels consisted of a towel-rack penchant, with cockroach regardant, holding in his beak a large red tape-worm on which was inscribed: "Spirituous fru-menti, cum homo tomorrow."

Many of the crests contained terse Latin mottoes, taken from the inscriptions on peppermint conversation candies, and were quite cute. A coat-of-arms, consisting of a small Limburger cheese couchant, above which stood a large can of chloride of potash, on which was inscribed the words, "Miss, may I see you home?" I thought very taking and just mysterious enough to make it exciting.

Polka-dot or half-mourning dogs are much affected by people who are beginning to get the upper hand of their grief. Much taste is shown in the selection of dogs for the coming season, and many owners chain their coach-man to the dog, so that if any one were to come and try to abduct the dog the coachman could bite him and drive him away. A good coachman to take care of a watch-dog is almost invaluable.

Many New York gentlemen who are fond of driving take their grooms out to Central Park every afternoon for an airing. This is a wise provision. Those who have associated with grooms will agree with me that a little airing now and then is just what they need.

The first personal letter written by my father after he went to New York is addressed to his cousin Solon Perrin under date of June 23, 1887:

I frequently sigh for the cool evenings of my little cabin home, where children cluster 'round my door at a great rate. A man has to be quite facetious, I sometimes think, to keep a large family full of buckwheat cakes the year around. I like my position quite well and begin to feel more at home than I did.

NYE OF LARAMIE

NYE OF NEW YORK

NYE OF LONDON

NYE OF BUCK SHOALS

The demand for buckwheat cakes in the Nye family had been increased on June 6 by my arrival, and by the end of August a place for us had been found on Staten Island and arrangements were being made to transport the other Nyes from Hudson. Here is another letter written to Cousin Solon on August 27, 1887:

Dear One!

If you think you are the only party who has had watermeloncholic, you are off. I've had the cholic of clams, the cholic of green corn, and the plain, low-browed bellyache of the common people. If you have it again, take about three fingers (your own fingers) of best brandy. Drink it in silence, looking neither to the right nor to the left, and you will experience a healthy glow in the pit of the stomach in a short time that will make your cholic hunt its hole. Seriously it is the best and swiftest remedy according to the doctor here, and I've nearly died of cholic twice this summer before I could get relief.

That is all I can think of at this time, except that you can do me a great favor if you will; and if you refuse I shall still respect and esteem you. Could you, without groveling or debasing yourself, get passes for the family over your line and the Northwestern to Chicago? I shrink from asking this, God knows, for I am proud and haughty, but Mrs. Nye will have her hands full, and I want to make it as easy as possible for her.

Any favor you show Mrs. Nye will be almost like showing the same to me, though she is really no blood kin of mine.

Judging by the next letter to Solon the railway passed up passing out the passes.

False Thing!

Your groveling and lickspittle letter of late date was duly received. I note your abject demeanor and fawning, sycophanting sentences behind which I discover your true nature, your low, coarse instinks. Curses deep, long and lasting, light upon your false and degenerate rail road, a road lined with ruin, bull thistles and corruption; a road leading from Elroy to the struggling flour mills of Minneapolis; a road fraught with danger, flood and fire; a road soaked with slimy, pent up malaria and the unavailing tears of its misguided patrons; a road that extends its lecherous grasp beneath the outskirts of the pure and virgin town of Hudson; a road that turns its back upon Stillwater yet courts the wanton smiles of Mrs. S.; a road that hasn't a center-board; a road that will not go out of its way to oblige; a road that runs over cows and spreads desolation and crude tripe over the fair face of nature.

Pish! Avaunt! Git out! You are the fitting representative of such a road, the proper pal of such a soulless corporation. When you come here I will not put your name in the paper. You can come and go and I will conceal the fact from the world. I will feed you while here, but I will not introduce you to our set. You low thing! You may "be prospered" in life but if you continue to conduct yourself as you have, you must not depend on the assistance or endorsement of God or myself.

My deluded family still believe that you are what you purport to be and I cannot undeceive them though I may betray your treachery some night in my sleep. But I want to give you another chance. Will you improve it or will you still defy the best man in the United States, who begs leave to sign himself,

BILL NYE.

P.S.   All the foregoing is Youmor.

As he went about the city Nye saw much to intrigue his interest:

> Yesterday, a poor man at the Battery came up to me and asked for two cents with which to mail a letter to his wife. He talked in a broken voice, and his nose also had been broken. He held the letter in his hand. It was soiled and looked as though he had been trying a long time to get postage for it.   I took it in my hand, stuck a two-cent stamp on it, and mailed it in a big red box that stood near for that purpose.   I thought he would wring my hand and ask God to bless me, but he was as mad as a wet hen because, as I afterwards learned, I had robbed him of his only means of support.

A letter written to Riley after Nye moved to New York is dated July 2, 1887, and is headed with a caricature of himself clothed in a pair of tight swimming-trunks and a palmleaf fan:

My Dear Riley:

   I'm only going to draw off a few lines to say I am tolerable well and hope that these tottering lines will find you enjoying the same great duty.   (As I hear said here in the effete East.)   God grant that in pitching my tent in this growing town I may not become effeter than I now am and that my clothes will always continue to be large enough for me.

It is most thundering hot here but I really have an easy nice time and so it does not worry me much. I can almost do as I'm a mindter. In fact, do less work and for more pay than ever before and have all the latitude and longitude I need or want. Do not have any office in the building and do not want any. I read some of your crisp and blithesome sayings down there. "The mouth like a stab in the dark," for instance, and "The child violinist who plays Home Sweet Home like a picked mine." Give my love to Amos, the man with the moss on the north side going in, and tell him that when the weather gets cooler I will answer his letter without fail. Remember also that if you or Amos ever grew cold toward me it will be through no fault of mine and I hope I may be spared to you both for many happy years. I would like, oh, so much to drop quietly into the back seat some evening and hear you oncet more. I've got to do the single act at Long Branch, Red Bank and another fashionable undressing and wetting place the name of which I have forgotten.

Goodbye Jamesie

Yourn,
BILL.

CHAPTER XIV

JAMESIE AND BILL

BILL NYE's removal from the Middle West to the metropolis was not allowed to interfere with the development of the fellowship between him and James Whitcomb Riley. Their letters to each other became more interesting as they were more frequent.

Under the spell of Riley's personality the "Dear Riley" salutation changed to "My Dear Jamesie," and in the next letter, dated September 21, 1887, you will detect evidences of that hearty palship which made notable the intimacy between these two men, who had so accurately caught and were so faithfully reflecting the spirit of their times.

My Dear Jamesie:

And so you have been sick all this time while I was mildly cussing you under my breath for not writing to me!

I wish you knew how many friends you have in this young and growing town. It would make you well. I went into a Broadway office the other day and heard a publisher recite "The Harelip." I had never heard it and I was pained to hear anybody recite one of your poems in the "O-mother-may-I-go-to-school-with-brother-Charles - today - the-air-is-very-soft-and-cool-do-mother-say-I-may" style, but his admiration was mighty sincere and you could see that you had reached his large, dark red heart.

I wish that you and I might give a little show here together this winter under favorable auspices, for if I do say it as ought not, I believe that I've got a good many N. Y. people . . .

[Then follows a passage not intended for publication.]

When I started this letter, Jamesie, I thought I would write one that you could put in your autograph album and point to with pride, but I see now that it is not that kind of a letter. It is low and coarse in its tone, and when I have been garnered in at last and sit on the right hand of the Throne, scared half to death for fear that the Almighty will introduce me to the audience and ask me to make a few remarks, I hope, Jamesie, that you will not produce this letter and humiliate me.

I feel the deepest sympathy for you in your sickness, for the Lord knows I've been through it and looked the ceiling out of countenance for months at a time, till I got so thin that my Etruscan legs looked like the legs of a camera, but I was sick at *home*, and to be sick at *home* is not really a calamity compared with being sick "at Lodgings" as we say in Piccadilly. I do not advise you to marry, because I don't know that it would be congenial to your tastes, but if you're going to be sick much I would do so without delay. A kind wife with a cool, soft hand and a tender, velvet voice and the odor of violets about her, and a weak attempt at authority, and a gentle apology for her severity and above all a deep and undying loyalty that defies and disarms death itself, will do more to make "the King of Terrors" ashamed of himself than all else beside.

By the way, Catalpa [Mrs. Nye] is here, also Silberberg and the rest. They love and reverence your memory and your later poems are our delight. The Hearse poem is great. Gordon and I enjoyed it together when he was here. I am going to give Amos Jay Cummings material for a syndicate letter soon and devote most of it to you, and the Little Mammoth Lecture Stands. It will do you no harm. If you will notice my efforts, you will see the footprints of your brain across my later geological strata like the eccentric trail of a drunk and disorderly Icthyosaurus going to his preadamite roost. This is not intended to cast any reflections on you in the matter of the demon Rum, but more to show you how great has been your influence on the better class of literature.

I will now draw this letter to an untimely end, hoping it will find you well and basking in the smile of friends. Certainly there is no better or more satisfactory article of dress than the friendly basque. All my tribe send love to you and already yearn for another letter.

Goodbye, my dear Jamesie, with the best of wishes and the assumer that I will always use my influence for you at the Throne of Grace.

Many wondered why Riley never married. It certainly was not because he did not have affairs. There is in Indiana to-day many a white-haired lady who firmly believes that Riley regarded her as his first, last, and only "Old Sweetheart of Mine." When we knew him, Riley had not become indifferent to the sex.

Shortly after the appearance of Ella Wheeler Wilcox's "Poems of Passion," Nye became cognizant of the fact that letters were passing between their author and his fellow-pilgrim. The correspondence increased. At last the opportunity came for Riley to meet the lady face to face.

Which one was the more disillusioned, I do not know. Suffice it to say that the affair did not continue. Later

Riley's trunk containing the love-letters was destroyed in a station fire. My father never ceased tormenting Riley with his theory of the cause of the blaze: "spontaneous combustion of the letters from Miss Wheeler," was his diagnosis.

One day my mother took courage to ask Mr. Riley why he never married. "I feel too sorry for Mrs. Riley," was his reason.

James Whitcomb Riley seldom used his pen with greater eloquence than in writing tributes to his partner, none of which will be more slowly forgotten than the sonnet:

O, William, in thy blithe companionship
What liberty is mine—what sweet release
From clamorous strife, and yet what boisterous peace!
Ho! ho! it is thy fancy's finger tip
That dints the dimple now, and kinks the lip
That scarce may sing in all this glad increase
Of merriment! So, pray thee, do not cease
To cheer me thus, for underneath the quip
Of thy droll sorcery the wrangling fret
Of all distress is still. No syllable
Of sorrow vexeth me, no teardrops wet
My teeming lids, save those that leap to tell
Thee thou'st a guest that overweepeth, yet
Only because thou jokest overwell.

Nye reciprocated in kind:

With your countenance provoking
  An endless wealth of fun;
With your badinage evoking
  A laugh from everyone;
With your legs so bowed and slender,
  With your humor all so wily,

With your pathos quaint and tender,
    Catching hearts of every gender,
    Which you juggle with so slyly,—
        Can anybody wonder
    That we think of you so highly,
        Mr. Riley?
        No, by thunder!

That fall, 1887, Nye appeared alone on the New England circuit. Summing up his trip to Riley, he said:

I wore a plug hat, but conversed freely with the common people. Everywhere I went I was received with passionate reserve and shown the public schools and the mean temperature.

In a letter of October 21, 1887, Nye urges Riley to appear with him at an affair in Washington:

My Dear Jamesie:
I am counting real hard upon seeing you on the 28th, unless one of us should miss our train. Why can't you and I make the program for the 28th, also? You will have the hides of the dear ones on your hands when I get there. Would it not make a double song and dance if we were both to work the old business? O Jamesie, God nose I hate to do the act alone. Go with me to the end. Go with me down to the dark valley and with me climb the barbed wire fence that encloses the lecture field. The 28th is Friday and we can meet around one common altar on Saturday and converse in low passionate tones of the dear, dead and swelled-up past.
Before I forget it let me say that your last letter before this containing a little pome which you claim to have let in the presence of Catalpa [Mrs. Nye] or addressed

to her, I incautiously read to our genial and urbane managing Editor who greedily snapped it up for the Sunday
"World," but so far the Insane Asylum, and the Bacon-
Shakespeare Controversy have crowded out everything
else but the advertisements. I do not know that I did
right in allowing him to take it. Did I? Your name is
a household word at the "World" office, and if you were
to come in here on a busy day, you would have to fight
just as hard to get up the elevator as Col. Fred Grant
or Tom Ochiltree.

If you hear me this winter, you will be charmed with
the same program to which I have so religiously adhered
in the past. So if you are going to wait at Washington,
Pa., to hear my speech, you will be bitterly, oh *so* bitterly
disappointed.

I am glad you are once more well, my boy, and trust
that you will ever thus continue. Above all I hope you
will shun the demon rum. What sad ruin Rum has rot
in our midst! How it arouses all our dark red nature
and stirs passions which will assert themselves no matter
what the price! How it puts a feather edge on our
breath, so that when we hiss our hot words into the ears
of those we love, it scorches the cotton in their ears!
Moreover, I do not like the taste of rum.

Now if you can, come in with me on the double racket
at Wash., do it and we will have fun once more as we
erst did. Amos writes that Grand Rapids and Chicago
desire our dual dinklets, if I may be allowed to coin a
term. So in February we will again combine. I am
getting along well here and meeting with unqualified
success and many other people as I pass up the crowded
street. The "World" has already asked me to go to
Europe and ascertain what the feeling is there among

the crowned heads. I may go next summer awhile in order to become more polished in my manners. And now with my richest and most juicy benison on you, pardner, I will thank you again for your kind attendance and attention and bid you good night.

The Nye member of the Nye-Riley mutual admiration society gives further expression to his warm regard in a letter of November 11, 1887:

A few days ago I sent you a column and a half criticism of R. Watson Gilder by Nym Crinkle. It was quite sarcastic and yet in some places just, I thought, and I knew that you would appreciate it thoroughly as you are more familiar with poesy than I am. Really I am a coarse son of song and only hang on to literature by the eyebrows, as it were, through my valued personal friendships with such men as Harris, Hunt, Huddle and Hutchins. But to you, James, I look with an eye that glitters with pride for I can truly say before a notary public that in you I have an acquaintance of a literary character which does me good whenever I think of it. When I refer to you, I can truly say that I have slept with America's greatest living warbler, a man who did not get Bacon to do his amanuensis business. For I have seen you engaged in thought.

Oh, sir, should any future historian state that Mr. R. Lew Dawson wrote your poems and then worked in a cipher to prove it, God grant that I may live to state that it is false.

I still bear in mind what we talked about in the matter of illustrating the "Flying Islands of the Night" [the contemplated Railroad Guide] and will soon see an artist who has a little more imagination than the balance [Zim].

The most of them have no more idea of constructing a
thing *in toto* than an angleworm, but prefer to imitate.
Won't you suggest a New York artist whom you have
watched somewhat and whom you think the kind of man to
do the "Flying Islands," and I will see him for you?

As the weather gets cold I begin to feel badly again
and wish I might wing my way to a warmer clime. I have
more, many more lectures offered for the winter than I
can possibly do, including Boston, Philadelphia and other
large towns. I still hope to do about $5000 worth, how-
ever, and keep my other business going.

D——, who published my book, is here as the employe
of Mrs. Frank Leslie. Between ourselves, I do not know
how the two will come out together as each regards himself or herself as the one on whom the gaze of the great
American Public is riveted. Mr. D—— would make a
good man to try coats on at a ready made clothing bazaar,
and Mrs. Leslie would look well behind a plate glass window clothed in a pair of Ball's Corsets and a Rhinestone.

I am almost glad sometimes that God gave my beauty
to Mrs. James Brown Potter and my hair to the Suther-
land Sisters, for now I can put in my time thinking burn-
ning thoughts and following the steaming "spoor" of a
disabled idea while professional beauties stand pensively
before a large mirror practising on a wide wet smile that
will reveal their new and juicy bright red gums to a lost
and undone world.

I will write no more at present but close by hoping that
you are well and that you will not forget me in the first
glow of your wonderful "Afterwhiles."

Riley was upon the eve of the great triumph of his career.
He had been invited to appear at a benefit for the Interna-

tional Copyright League, to be held at Chickering Hall on
November 28 and 29. What more natural than that he
should make the Nye home his headquarters? So he wrote
his good friend on November 11:

Just now there is an invitation to me to come and "say a
piece" at the Authors' Readings. Consulting my own intentions about the matter, I find that I can go, and thus hasten
to warn you of the fact, so's you can have your chores at
home purty well off your hands and the house red up perpari-
tory-like, as the feller says, to receive me with corroberatin'
eclaw; and, last but not least, to ast you if I hadn't better
fetch along a extry shirt, and buy my tobacker here, as I have
heard my kind is not to be had there fer love er money. I wish,
too, that you and Catalpa and the fambly would meet me at
the depot—wherever I git off at, so's I won't git carried past
and run on into some other town where I hain't got kith ner
kin. I'm the blamedst fool travelin', I reckon, they is outside
o' the durn lunatic asylum—'bout not gittin' trains, er gittin'
the wrong one, and all sich aggervations that-away.

Mr. Johnson mysteriously postscripts invitation to keep
Reading in the dark for a few days—wonder why, and what
'ud become of a feller if he'd take it back, and I'd not get to go
there after all. Reckon though, it's all right, as I bet on his
friendship among the first. Write me soon and allus believe in
me.

And Nye replied on November 18:

Your note received hyst as I was embarking for a
little lecture "spirt" and now that I am back again I
will write to say that I will meet you at whatever train
and time you say and welcome you with a big and pronounced welcome then and there. I went over to Boston
and jerked a few remarks for them the other evening.
Kind friends came and laughed heartily.

There was a brief announcement the other day in the papers of the Copyright Benefit but only a partial list of the attractions. It is a big thing, one of the best in a literary way in the Union and will be presided over by our friend, James Russell Lowell, who, as you know, is the author of "The Old Swimmin-Hole and 'Leven More Poems."

Write me at once and tell me accurately, giving me your motif and time table and how and when and where to meet you at Jersey City or the other depots of our young and thriving town, so that I will be there an hour or two beforehand walking up and down the platform with my team hitched outside, ready to take you out to the farm where Catalpa and dear ones will be ready to greet you. Till then, "olive oil," as the sayin' is. Good-by— and God's best and freshest new laid blessing on your soft and flaxen head.

Yours with anticipations and things.

The affair came off in a way that was most gratifying to Nye and to Riley's many other friends, who had long hoped for the poet's metropolitan début.

Chickering Hall was literally littered with literati. The Who's Who of American letters were there. Mark Twain, Howells, Cable, Lowell, and other notables of the first water celebrated the occasion by reading from their best writings. Bill Nye was on hand to inject the sparkle of his wit into the program. At his request, Riley attended him, and after the humorist had spoken his piece, he encored— with Riley.

This was Riley's lifetime opportunity. Few of the audience had seen the Hoosier poet. Many had not heard of his genius. He was little more than a boy in age, and less in appearance. Yet here he was in the presence of the mighty, like Burns at Edinburgh (as Eugene Debs, who has written of this affair, so aptly pointed out). Before this, Riley had received a friendly letter from Longfellow praising one of his poems. And there were a few others among the élite who had discovered him. But his fame had been confined largely to Indiana and to a small group in that State.

Picture this cold and critical audience, a little bored with the thought of indulging the novice. This bouquet of professionals asked to receive into its midst a humble prairie flower. This hard-boiled aggregation already a little weary of a long program of dignified discourse and not a little wary of this exponent of dialect verse.

Now picture Jim Riley at his brilliantest best in his masterpiece, "When the Frost Is on the Punkin." His piece spoken, there was no frost anywhere in Chickering Hall. The house reëchoed with such applause as is heard only when a large audience of sure-footed critics is enthusiastically unanimous in taking a nobody at one fell swoop into full fellowship.

It was on the occasion of this visit to New York that a bit of Nye repartee was uttered, remembered by my cousin Clara Mitchell Millspaugh. Nye and Riley sat late over their Sunday breakfast. Church bells tolled in the distance, reminding them that their tardiness had kept my mother regretfully from her accustomed attendance at church. In the shrill piping voice of an old man, which each was so fond of assuming, Mr. Riley asked:

"Bill, did it ever occur to you that with all the praise and adulation 'at God gits, it never seems to spile him?"

In the same cracked voice, but higher, Bill replied:

"Well, Jim, I sometimes think it's because God's a *self-made* man."

Riley's fresh-laid volume, "Afterwhiles," was doing much to tighten his hold on fame. Among the many who enjoyed this collection, Nye was by no means the least appreciative. On December 21, 1887, he wrote:

Your letter and autographed copy of *Afterwhiles* came duly to hand.

It is surprising what a mad thirst there is here for your poems. You would hardly think that the cold unimpassioned postmaster of New York would care for your work, but he became so enthusiastic that he broke open the package containing your book, devoured every word in it and then charged me 19 cents letter postage extra because the book had writing in it.

Everywhere people are falling over each other in a mad rush for your book, especially if they can get it for nothing. However, your fame is abiding here and you will be able to draw on New York at any time.

I shall appear here a couple of times or more this winter in conjunction or perihelion with other planets; once for the N. Y. Press Club.

We miss Uncle Sidney at our festive board and by the fireside and we miss his stertorous breathing in the parlor where he used to slumber in a desultory way without manuscript, resting on and on and on till his slumberer was footsore.

The glorious Yuletide now coming on apace seems to murmur, "Where in thunder is Uncle Sidney?" The Dying Year turns painfully on its couch and resting its "gooms" on the foot board of the bed seems mutely to wonder what is keeping Uncle Sidney.

Everywhere there is a general demand for you. Write me a good, long letter after the general enthusiasm of Indiana has got back into its banks.

On February 15, 1888, Riley and Nye joined forces at Chicago to boost the Press Club at a benefit. A part of one review, with parenthetical remarks inserted later by Nye, reported:

Nye stole out past the grand piano (upheaval of popular opinion). When he reached the middle of the stage he stopped to remove his eyeglasses and smile (applause while the speaker blushed). "It affords me pleasure," he began, "to play a return engagement for the Chicago Press Club (renewed applause). I have a great reverence for the press. It is a great engine of destruction (demonstration). I often think of what might have been the fate of many great men without the press. Take me for example, or Lydia E. Pinkham for instance (tittering and cackling). I suppose I should have made the opening speech but Mr. Riley kindly relieved me of that onerous duty; so I can get down to business. Poets as you probably know have throughout history been accompanied by their lyres (laughter). Riley appears before you to-night as the poet; I suppose he has his lyre; if not I am with him (redoubled laughter while the speaker caresses the bald spot on his head). I asked a man while riding into a city the other day if he had heard my last lecture. He said he hoped he had (giggling). So I am getting up a new lecture in which I can reel off humor by the yard. Horace Greeley says that a lecture is successful when more remain in the hall than go out. I have talked with some of my friends about it and they suggest that I get a brass band to play half an hour before it and half an hour after. One critic says I would make a hit if the band played through the whole lecture (Gas flickers and rafters shake).

There were a few other engagements near Chicago. After
a repetition of the show at South Bend a local poet was inspired to remark:

> Nye and Riley, Riley and Nye:
> Grin and chuckle, sob and sigh!
> Never had such fun by half,
> Knew not whether to cry or laugh.
>
> Jest and joke and preach and sing,
> They can do most anything—
> Make you laugh or make you cry—
> Dear old Riley! Rare Bill Nye!

The next two letters speak of the Nye-Riley Railway
Guide which was nearing completion:

April 5, 1888.

Your illiterate and obscure note of late date, in which
you said that Harry New had run between a dog and
broke its legs, was duly received. Little did I ever think
that a boy of mine would write such a letter.

I would give a good deal to know why Harry New ran
between a dog and if so how much. Your letter, such
as it is, gave me great pleasure in some respects but it
is too abstruse. You did not say where you would go
from there.

I have nearly completed the *Introduction* for our R. R.
Guide and have been working hard at other business in
the literary line since I got home. I have drod off two
pieces for a paper and they pleased the editor. I think
he will print them. There are several merry thoughts
and two large red bon mots in them. They are disguised
however. Also assumed.

April 18, 1888.

I enclose a letter from the Chicago company which reads very well indeed and virtually accepts the proposition I made them while you were ill here and which you will remember. The royalty is bigger than I thought they would grant us and they accept all suggestions about high grade illustrations, together with good printing.

I saw Miss —— not long ago. She is still wearing a full beard but looked pale, I thought, as if suffering from Loss of Manhood.

The Nye-Riley Railway Guide was a book especially designed for sale to travelers. As they expressed it:

What this country needs, aside from a new Indian policy, is a Railway Guide which will be just as good two years ago as it was next spring—a Railway Guide, if you please, which shall not be cursed by a plethora of facts, or poisoned with information—a Railway Guide that shall be rich with doubts and lighted up with miserable apprehensions. In other Railway Guides, pleasing fancy, poesy and literary beauty have been throttled at the very threshold of success, by a wild incontinence of facts, figures, asterisks and references to meal stations. For this reason a guide has been built at our own shops and on a new plan. It is the literary *pièce de résistance* of the age in which we live. It will not permit information to creep in and mar the reader's enjoyment of the scenery. It contains no railroad map which is grossly inaccurate. It has no time-table in it which has outlived its uselessness. It does not prohibit passengers from riding on the platform while the cars are in motion. It permits every one to do just as he pleases and rather encourages him in taking that course.

The authors of this book have suffered intensely from the

inordinate use of other guides, having been compelled several times to rise at 3 o'clock A. M., in order to catch a car which did not go and which would not have stopped at the station if it had gone.

They have decided, therefore, to issue a guide which will be good for one to read after one has missed one's train

"The authors of this book have suffered intensely from the inordinate use of other guides"

by reason of one's faith in other guides which one may have in one's luggage.

Let it be understood, then, that we are wholly irresponsible, and we are glad of it. We do not care who knows it. We will not even hold ourselves responsible for the pictures in this book, or the hardboiled eggs sold at points marked as meal stations in time tables. We have gone into this thing wholly unpledged, and the man who gets up before he is awake, in order to catch any East bound, West bound,

North bound, South bound, or hide-bound train, named in this book, does himself a great wrong without in any way advancing our own interests.

The authors of this book have made railroad travel a close study. They have discovered that there has been no provision made for the man who erroneously gets into a car which is side-tracked and swept out and scrubbed by people who take in cars to scrub and launder. He is one of the men we are striving at this moment to reach with our little volume. We have each of us been that man. We are yet.

He ought to have something to read that will distract his attention. This book is designed for him. Also for people who would like to travel but cannot get away from home. Of course, people who do travel will find nothing objectionable in the book, but our plan is to issue a book worth about $9, charging only fifty cents for it, and then see to it that no time-tables or maps which will never return after they have been pulled out shall creep in among its pages.

BILL NYE,

JAMES WHITCOMB RILEY.

P.S.—The authors desire to express their thanks to Mr. Riley for the poetry and to Mr. Nye for the prose which have been used in this book.

McDougall being a "World" staff artist, it was necessary to choose another caricaturist to illustrate the Railway Guide. The candidate was Eugene Zimmerman, and he has told the story of his meeting with Bill Nye:

Some time early in the spring of 1888 I had the pleasure of a call from Edgar Wilson Nye. After the preliminaries of making welcome so celebrated a personage, and the exchange of lodge signs and passwords, he began to unfold his reasons for the intrusion. Said he:

"I would like you to consider a bunch of my stuff and hope that you will see fit to enter into a pact with myself and others to flimflam the public out of a few shiners by producing a great work to be known in the future as Nye & Riley's Railway Guide."

The moment he deposited his swanlike form into a receptacle provided for that purpose, and had carefully hung his last year's straw hat on the floor beside him, I exclaimed, to myself:

"There's a funny one!"

I had much correspondence with Mr. Nye, which eventually led me to illustrate his writings in some of the weekly periodicals of that day. Nye's manuscript always supplied me with inspiration and his personal and business letters bubbled with mirth, which goes to show that it simply was in him and had to come out, even if he violated the rules of the Mirth-Provokers' Union.

"We read and forget," but when you read "Bill" Nye you can never forget him.

CHAPTER XV

THE NYE SCHLOSS AT TOMPKINSVILLE

AFTER some months in a rented house at New Brighton my parents discovered a place in Tompkinsville, Staten Island, that was much more to their liking. By May we were almost settled in what my dad called his new Schloss, or rather, "Slosh." A letter to Uncle Mitchell of May 5, 1888, gives an excellent idea of Slipperyelmhurst's successor:

We are now in our Slosh, as we call it in German. It is a large and rangy Slosh with a view. Toward the South one gets a Southern view and toward the North one gets a Northern aspect. Aspects come quite high here. As I write this the tones of the tack hammer may be heard on the floor below, also the muffled thud of the whitewash brush in the basement and the swash of the brush of the man who is greasing the dining room floor. We now live in an atmosphere of varnish and simulated grandeur. I go back into the country a mile or two and practice with a new plug hat every day so that I will not disgrace my Slosh.

Oh, sir, I am trying so very, very hard to lead such a life that future generations will say: "There was a slosher who knew his business. He was a haughty patrician with no hair to speak of, but he always spoke kindly to the poor."

Nature is looking extra well this spring, I think, and

doing some good work. The blossoms are just coming out on the fruit trees, the small goats are beginning to manifest themselves here and there and the nut brown flavor of the burnt boot pervades the air.

Bess goes in to dress Max every morning. Sometimes he is not ready to get up. This morning he said, "Bess, you go wite out o' heah; I aint waked up yet."

He is a little towheaded Yankee from away back. He is also an amoosin little cuss. The baby is as big as ever and draws good houses. The girls are talking German to each other in a superior way which makes their poor old parents, both of whom are kind of self-made parents, feel their inferiority very much. But bong soir, mong cher; bong soir, Mongseer Jacob.

Yours without recourse,
E. WILSON VON NYJ.

Nye had no sooner become a Staten Island taxpayer than he began to fear what came about not many years later, the swallowing up of the island into Greater New York. Naturally he protested:

The proposition to include Brooklyn, Long Island City and Staten Island in the city of New York, thus constituting a town of 2,500,000 people, will no doubt materialize at some time in the future, but there will be strong opposition to it, and especially by the suburban towns referred to. As a resident and taxpayer of Staten Island, I know that I but voice the sentiments of many of my neighbors when I say that we do not wish to have New York annexed to us.

In the first place, most of us removed to Staten Island in order to get out of the city of New York and its temptations, and we do not desire to have the noisy town follow us to our lair with its civilization and its sewer gas. For instance, I am now able to keep a cow, and every night with a wild-onion scented breath she winds slowly o'er the lea. If New York should be annexed to us an Alderman would probably milk her on her way home, and soon also her sweet breath would disappear.

Nye was always an excellent press-agent for any place where he resided. I doubt if Staten Island was ever more in the limelight than for the four years, 1887 to 1891.

Staten Island, where the New York league games will be played this season, is an oblate spheroid where the Democrats, last fall, were flattened at the polls. St. George, which is 25 minutes from New York via the Statue of Liberty, is the point where the disemboweled umpire may be found. St. George is not really a town. It is not even a post office; it is only a name. It has a fine baseball ground, however, a bank, a bright and handsome paper called the Staten Islander, and a telephone.

Staten Island has 19 post offices and a fort. Fort Wadsworth has an excellent site, but there is so little fighting to be done lately and there is such close competition that it is not self-supporting. I am told that if influential friends at Washington did not do something for it every year it would have to be abandoned.

Here we may gather berries in the summer time; also softshell crabs and the mirth-provoking lobsters. Here we may take a straw ride down Jersey Street or catch a swift horse car and see the plaster mill and smell the Standard Oil works.

But in a few years, where now the new milch goat permeates the saline air with his pungent presence—or her presence rather, of course, in this case—and where the bobolink swings to and fro on the boneset bough, a metropolitan museum, open where it will do the least good, will be seen.

So the Staten Islander asks permission to worship the Great Spirit undisturbed and wear flannel shirts after 6 o'clock. And he wants time to get used to the ways of the world a little before he is called upon to dwell in a great city or wear the straight brim derby of Little Fifth avenue.

But the time is coming, and at no distant day, when Staten Island and Manhattan Island will work together more harmoniously, and as business picks up and trade is encouraged, many Staten Island business men will have quiet homes in New York. The feeling of rivalry, though keen and active, is a purely friendly one, and there is no bitterness at all. There is no reason why New York and Tompkinsville should not walk together hand in hand in the great march of progress. Each has her sphere of action, each her allotted task, each her field of work.

Though I live on Staten Island I have not allowed my prejudices to influence me in any way in what I have said. I have tried to be fair and truthful, for I have the kindliest feeling toward New York and always have had, and after a hard and active day in the busy marts of trade at Tompkinsville, nothing rests me or builds me up like an evening's romp on Fifth Avenue.

Once in a great while, on a subject which was close to his heart, Nye indulged himself in a serious essay. His eastern migration made him thoughtful on the subject of transplanted youth:

For many years past, and no doubt for many more to come, the vital question with the young American,

"Where can I do the best and soonest succeed?" has been and will continue to go right on in the vital business. I select the following letter for replying purposes rather than any other in my possession, because it is earnest, personal and pertinent:

Dear Sir: I write to ask your advice as a Western man as to the advisability of a young man of Eastern parentage going West to grow up with the country. Many Western men who crack up the Western country as being the place to live in are continually coming East, investing their surplus or engaging in business with Eastern concerns. If the West offers broad fields for advancement, why then do Western men like you leave such fertile fields for pastures new?

It is true that a great many Western men come East to invest their surplus, but if they had never gone West they would not have had any surplus to invest.

The advantage of the West for the young man consists in this: that he is there given a chance to show his gait and demonstrate his merits. Nobody asks him who his grandfather was, and why he came West. He is tested and indorsed or lynched, according to his merits. He is as good a man with a $5 suit of clothes and a bobtail genealogy as any other man if he be a good citizen and pan out all right. The difference between the East and West is that in the new West less attention is paid to forms and exteriors than in the East. In the West a man may be a millionaire and still be required to behave himself. In the East a millionaire can behave himself days and do as he pleases the rest of the time.

But the chief advantage to a young man who has his way to make in the world consists in this—industry and merit are at once recognized in new countries.

The last question is a more or less personal one, and it shows that the man who wrote it is a philosopher. In replying to it I must not forget that it is a serious and sensible inquiry. My own case is an exceptional one. In the first place, everybody is not allowed to remain in the West. In one way the West is democratic; in another it is exclusive and aristocratic. It is no sign that others may have to move East because I did.

Let me say to the young men who read this that if they are made of the right kind of material they can succeed sooner in the West on less money and with less crest than they can where usages have been long established and where customs are gradually becoming more and more European. In the West *America* sticks out more prominently, and there is a degree of freedom from the petty envies and jealousies which curse the lives of those who live in older countries. I could be poor and come nearer enjoying it in the West than anywhere else. This is not surmise on my part. It is capital to do the best, but what we want is information that will help those who want to know where they can get the most enjoyment out of poverty, where a good citizen is wanted and welcomed.

The main difficulty with New York and Boston boys in new countries is homesickness and disappointment because a good many institutions to which they have been accustomed are not to be found. To succeed in the West a young man must become a part of his adopted country, and loyal to it. He must not act upon the principle that he is still a citizen of New York or Boston, but in good earnest begin to be necessary to the section of country to which he has removed.

And, after all, there is not so great a difference between the East and West. All Western men, with the exception of the Indians, were once Eastern men, and Eastern money makes the West successful. Let no young man from a large Eastern city console himself with the notion that he is conferring favor on the West by removing to that part of the country. The fact that he is there at all is proof that he came there to better his condition, and he cannot conceal it. He who goes West solely to teach the untutored pioneer the elements of refined civilization will not endear himself to his community, for the humble pilgrim who walks into a new town in the Territories and goes to work attending to his own affairs is more apt to return to the East some day in a Pullman car than the man who enters the place preceded by a silver cornet band.

The West, of course, is not now what it used to be, for modern improvements have reached everywhere, and the frontier is pretty well narrowed down, but there is still plenty of amusement, excitement and instruction for the inquiring mind.

I have said seriously what I have said, because this will answer a question that I have been asked often. A good citizen is an ornament and a success, whether he dwell within the shadow of Bunker Hill or the cañons of Colorado, but he would succeed quicker and get the eye of the speaker sooner, perhaps, in Colorado, because the farther a young man can get from the depressing but brilliant record of his grandfather the better off he will be.

I have noticed another thing in the older parts of the country, and more especially in New England, which keeps a young man back. In the town of his nativity he is never considered by the old settlers as a man. He is called Henry or George, or, worse still, "William's boy" or "John's boy" until his teeth begin to fall out, whereas in a new field he would be called Colonel or Judge or Governor on a good salary.

The West wants good, live, self-supporting young men. Whether or not the East can spare them I do not pretend to state. The West will always welcome the sensible young men from the East or from other countries who are equipped for a rough-and-tumble with outrageous fortune. While I would not guarantee success to every-body who goes West to-day, I would certainly under like circumstances go West myself willingly and hopefully. It is no sign that the West is full because once in a while a man who comes from there is in that condition. Neither should young men hesitate about going towards the Occi-dent simply because a few wealthy freaks like the under-signed came East to bedew with their surplus the land of their birth.

I believe the readers of this biography will enjoy a news-paper account of a journey to the home of Bill Nye at Staten Island, unfortunately unsigned, but written by some one who had more than the usual reporter's insight. It is one of the best "interviews" of Nye that have been recorded. And as it gives a sympathetic and intimate picture of the Nye household of that time, I quote from it at some length:

A long, roomy, homelike house, with a cupola, a wealth of broad veranda, and with tall trees waving their sheltering arms above it. A house which looks as though it had been made to live in and to be happy in. It is close to a quiet street which clambers over a high hill above Tompkinsville. It is a house of deep, warm shadows, a house of such an odd, rich, reddish-brown color as you will seldom see, and the windows of big conservatories look out over that trim fence which bounds the owner's domain.

The front door of this hospitable-looking mansion is deep in a double entry. A Swedish serving maid, neater than all the wax in the world, comes to answer the bell.

There is a wide, welcoming hall, with rugs, and a high antique hat-rack, and a solemn old clock. The very gloom is cheerful. As you stand waiting there, a broad smile appears at the parlor door. Then you are conscious of gold-bound spectacles and a bald head which is just a little in advance of a pair of broad shoulders. The shoulders and the stanch body which they overtop are incased in a snug velvet smoking jacket.

"How-de-do! How-de-do! Come right into my play-house here. Pretty bad weather, isn't it?"

Now, there's the house and there's the man. That genial, sharp-faced, athletic-looking fellow, who in slippered feet is ushering you in out of a most miserable day to the light and warmth of a gracious fireside, is Bill Nye.

If his smile were not so youthful that bald head would make him venerable. But if you notice closely you'll see that the fringe of hair which, like the tonsure of a monk, is left to adorn the well-shapen head, is as blond as a boy's. There's not even the shadow of a beard or mustache to cover the fun-lines about those thin lips.

Fond of a sofa is the merry Nye, and fonder of the loungiest, laziest position he can get into. He stretched himself upon the biggest, oldest-fashioned most comfortable sofa you ever saw and talked and gazed out of the window at the leaden sky and across the stretches of snow which a dreary rain was fast clearing away.

"Work and play," said the languid William, puffing away at his corn-cob, "come very close together with me, you see." He pointed with one hand to the pool table. Then he turned towards a roller-top desk in the corner, littered with papers and letters. There are wolf-skins and bear-skins all about the revolving chair upon which Bill Nye is wont to writhe and

hump himself in the throes of composition. These agonies,
Bill says, always take place of a morning, and in spite of
the many windows he has to look out of, he affirms that
he manages to grub away pretty industriously.

If you didn't know Bill Nye well you might think to watch
his easeful ways, and hear his slow, drawlsome speech, that he

A portrait of Bill Nye by Bill Nye

was lazy. Make you no such error. He is like a good printer
who makes no false motions. He works easily, and when work
hours are done he puts work completely out of thought. Life
doesn't wear on him. He just does the next thing—that is,
provided it isn't noon-time. In that case, he puts off the next
thing until to-morrow morning.

"That habit of working mornings," he said, "I reckon I
never shall get rid of, an' I don't know that I care to. I sort

"I go back into the country
a mile or two and practice
with a new plug hat every
day so that I will not disgrace my Slosh."

"We frequently walk abroad into the persimmon
vineyards and ivy-clad gorges of the Blue Ridge."

THE NYE "SLOSH" AT TOMPKINSVILLE, STATEN ISLAND

o' fatten under it. Why, gracious! Three years ago I was lean as a scarecrow. Now, I'm in the neighborhood of 200 pounds. You see, in the first of my newspaper life nearly all my work was done in the morning, and my mind got in a habit of working then and 'laying off' the rest of the day. And for three years I did all my work standing up at a tall desk, like a printer's frame, such desks as you see in old pictures."

"What in the world induced you to do that?"

"Because I had the desk, I suppose."

Nye asked me to excuse him while he opened some mail, and gathering a great heap of letters from the desk he began to break the seals. He went through each epistle carefully and read several of them aloud. There is a wonderful diversity and yet a sameness about Bill Nye's mail. It comes from all sorts and conditions of men, and involves almost every subject under the sun, but every man of them, coal man, ice man, editor, dinner guest, or would-be dinner host, applicant for autographs or photographs—no matter who they are or what they want, they all try to be funny.

As the day darkened into night and Nye still sat gazing out upon the storm, he said: "Do you see those pine trees out there?"

At the back of the house, on the edge of the slope and bordering the orchard, is a row of big, gloomy pines. From the limb of one a long swing dangled, which told of children at summer play. The trees were shadowy now, and were every minute growing blacker in outline against the night sky.

"Do you know," he said, "I always liked a pine, somehow, and that row out there is a regular inspiration. About the best time I can find to write anything sort o' pathetic like, is when the wind gets to blowing through those pine needles. And it's nicest in the summer when you can have the windows open. That carpet of pine needles makes the best kind of a playground for the children, too. This is a great old place here for the children, anyway. Only, you see, they're Western children, and were born and pretty muchly raised in the high altitudes of the mountains. It does n't seem to me this damp air here agrees with 'em."

Just then there came a patter of little feet in the hallway, and two golden heads and chubby faces were at the door. "Aha!" cried Papa Nye, "there are the people." In a moment the two little fellows clad in black velvet had clambered up into Nye's lap. Max, the elder, had come armed with copies of the comic papers—for Nye is a subscriber to them all. The youngster, who has just reached the neighborhood in life when he can talk plainly, put his progenitor through the most trying catechism as to just where the fun came in in this picture and that. My! But the explanations were dismal. At last, tired of making diagrams of other men's jokes, he put the papers all aside. The little fellow's face was glum for a minute. Then some new fun began. The baby, the more tow-headed of the two, seized Papa Nye's smiling face between two chubby hands and looked at it for a long time. At last he seemed to find something very funny there, for he laughed a laugh that seemed to fairly bubble right up out of his little self.

"Papa, take your glasses off, won't you?"

It was a plaintive request. But the paternal genius was curious. "What do you want me to do that for?" he queried.

"I want to see how your eyes look."

Such praiseworthy research must not be hindered. Off came the glasses, and again the little toddler stared long and earnestly into the father's face. It must be there's a lot of humor in Bill Nye's spectacles, for this time the little one did n't laugh nearly so loud as before. But he insisted on having the spectacles put astride of his own little nose, and it was a jolly picture they made Bill and his boy, in the lamp-light there in that big room with its shadowy, far-off corners, and its tall shelves of books.

Not long after Nye came East he signed up to lecture for the Pond Lyceum Bureau. In his book, "Eccentricities of Genius," Major Pond wrote of his relations with my father:

Bill Nye was an editor when I first met him, and as I had been a printer, of course I felt akin to him. I had formed an attachment for him that made me wish to know him, so when I found myself in Laramie, on a return trip from California, I improved the opportunity to make his acquaintance.

I told him people were reading and talking of him all over the country, and that I believed he could make money lecturing. He replied that he had never given the matter a thought, and was trying to earn a living with his pen and through the Laramie postmastership, to which he had just been appointed.

I did not see Nye again until about 1887. I was looking out of my office window in the Everett House in New York, and noticed a tall, straight, slim, fair-haired man, in a slouch hat, whose countenance wore an expression of inquiry.

Bill came in and stared about at the pictures of great men and women on the walls. He told me that he had been engaged on the staff of the New York "World" and was going to move to New York.

After a pleasant chat we dined together at Moretti's. Nye asked if he would be expected to learn to eat spaghetti. This was his first Italian dinner; it was all of great interest to him, all new, and he saw it from the standpoint of an inexperienced youth.

I told him that now he was coming East to live I would make some money for him in the lyceum. He seemed doubtful, but said he would try it.

His first lecture under my auspices was given in Bridgeport, Conn. The Y. M. C. A. in that place seemed to think the name of Bill Nye would draw, and engaged to pay him $150.

Mr. Nye, like every one human who attempts to make a whole evening of fun, found lecturing irksome. The audience would fairly bubble over with laughter until every fun-liking muscle of their faces relaxed and left a somber, wet-blanket expression all over the assembly; and there they had to sit, and the humorist had to proceed to the end of the program without a response. It was the same with Mark Twain until he took a running mate and interspersed pathos by introducing George W. Cable, and by means of a varied program achieved the greatest success ever known in the way of platform entertainment.

After my father had filled several engagements under Pond's management, he suggested to Riley that with Pond running things their team might prosper even more than before. Said Pond:

The result was a combination of humor and pathos for the season of 1888-9. Riley came to New York, and the arrangements were perfected in my office. Nye and I were to be owners of the combination, and Riley, who always declared, "I'm no business man," was to receive $500 a week and his hotel and traveling expenses.

By October 17 plans for the coming lecture trip were well advanced:

Dear Jamesie:

I have turned the program over to Pond for the printer and expressed the identically same wishes as nearly as might be, which you so deftly laid out on paper and drod off with such skill. [Riley had decorated the printed announcement.] I struck out the "carbuncle" and muzzled all my low, coarse but frolicsome nature in order to make that air program worth coming miles to witness.

The "Pipes O'Pan" bids fair to loom up like hell, as Calvin Luther used to say about infant damnation, and I joy with you o'er it.

The aggressive and bloodcurdling Major is jirking frolicsome daylights out of the local committees and has made a most astonishing list of dates covering 20 or more weeks from November 12. He fairly pants in his lecture Bureau Drawers as it were and with two typewriters going at once. *My Godd!!!*

[A pen-drawing of Junius Brutus Pond.]

Pond tells of the Nye-Riley lectures from the manager's viewpoint:

The Nye-Riley combination started in Newark, N. J., November 13, 1888. It was our trial venture. The receipts were light, for both men were of Western fame, and had yet to acquire reputations in the East. The show was a great success "artistically," but the box-office receipts were only fifty-four dollars.

The Actors' Fund had an entertainment in one of the theaters, and I had contributed these "Twins of Genius" as my share of the numerous attractions. They were the success of the occasion, and the newspapers so declared the next day. From that time, applications began to come in from all over the country, East, West, North and South.

Nye's humorous weekly syndicate newspaper articles made him a drawing attraction, and Riley's delightful readings of his dialect poems made the entertainment all that the public desired. I ran the show myself in Boston, securing Tremont Temple for the occasion. "Mark Twain" had come to Boston on purpose to attend the entertainment, as he had never heard this twain. I caught him in the lobby of the Parker House, and told him that he must introduce them. He replied that he believed I was his mortal enemy and determined that he should never have an evening's enjoyment in my presence. He consented, however, and conducted his brother humorist and the Hoosier poet to the platform. Mark's presence was a surprise to the audience, and when they recognized him the demonstration was tremendous. The audience rose in a body, and men and women shouted at the very top of their voices. Handkerchiefs waved, the organist opened every forte key and pedal

The "Twins of Genius" en route

in the great organ, and the noise went on unabated. It took some time for the crowd to get down to listening. As Mark stepped to the front, the silence was as impressive as the noise had been. I had engaged a stenographer to take down the speech, and this is what Mark said:

"I am very glad indeed to introduce these young people to you, and at the same time get acquainted with them myself. I have seen them more than once, for a moment, but have not had the privilege of knowing them as intimately as I wanted to.

"I saw them first, a great many years ago, when Mr. Barnum

had them, and they were just fresh from Siam. The ligature was their best hold then. But literature became their best hold later, when one of them committed an indiscretion, and they had to cut the old bond to accommodate the sheriff.

"In that old former time this one was Chang, that one was Eng. The sympathy existing between the two was most extraordinary; it was so fine, so strong, so subtle, that what the one ate the other digested. When one slept the other snored. If one sold a thing the other scooped the usufruct. This independent and yet dependent action was observable in all the details of their daily life. I mean this quaint and arbitrary distribution of originating cause and resulting effect between the two: between, I may say, this dynamo and this motor.

"Not that I mean that the one was always dynamo and the other always motor—or, in other words, that the one was always the creating force, the other always the utilizing force. No, no, for while it is true that within certain well-defined zones of activity the one was always dynamo and the other always motor, within certain other well-defined zones these positions became exactly reversed.

"For instance, in moral matters Mr. Chang Riley was always dynamo, Mr. Eng Nye was always motor; for while Mr. Chang Riley had a high, in fact an abnormally high and fine, moral sense, he had no machinery to work it; whereas Mr. Eng Nye, who hadn't any moral sense at all and hasn't yet, was equipped with all the necessary plant for putting a noble deed through, if he could only get the inspiration on reasonable terms outside.

"In intellectual matters, on the other hand, Mr. Eng Nye was always dynamo, Mr. Chang Riley was always motor. Mr. Eng Nye had a stately intellect, but couldn't make it go. Mr. Chang Riley had n't, but could. That is to say, that while Mr. Chang Riley could n't think things himself, he had a marvelous natural grace in setting them down and weaving them together when his pal furnished the raw material.

"Thus, working together, they made a strong team. Laboring together, they could do miracles; but break the circuit, and both were impotent. It has remained so to this day. They must travel together, conspire together, beguile together, hoe, and plant, and plow, and reap, and sell their public together, or there's no result.

"I have made this explanation, this analysis, this vivisection, in order that you may enjoy these delightful adventurers understandingly. When Mr. Eng Nye's deep, and broad, and limpid philosophies flow by in front of you, refreshing all the regions round about with their gracious floods, you will remember that it isn't his water. It's the other man's, and he is only working the pump. And when Mr. Chang Riley enchants your ear, and soothes your spirit, and touches your heart with the sweet and genuine music of his poetry—as sweet and as genuine as any that his friends, the birds and the bees, make about his other friends, the woods and the flowers—you will remember, while placing justice where justice is due, that it isn't his music, but the other man's. He is only turning the crank.

"I beseech for these visitors a fair field, a single-minded, one-eyed umpire, and a score bulletin barren of goose-eggs if they earn it—and I judge they will and hope they will. Mr. James Whitcomb Chang Riley will now go to the bat."

It was a carnival of fun in every sense of the word. Bostonians will not have another such treat in this generation. It was Mark's last appearance in Boston.

The '88-'89 season was the most strenuous campaign that Riley and Nye made together, and that memorable tour was the most extensive Major Pond had ever planned. It began in November and was to end in May. It was to extend from Boston to Portland, Oregon, and from Montgomery, Alabama, to Canada, where it was to finish.

On November 15 the two appeared at a benefit for the

Actors' Fund at the Broadway Theater, New York. Booth and Barrett were on the program, Denman Thompson and Mary Anderson in the boxes.

On November 17 they delighted Washington, D. C., with Riley's bear story and Nye's dog story.

Cousin Clara Mitchell (Millspaugh) was almost like one of the children. My mother had lived with the Mitchells after her father's death; and "Aunt Fanny," as Clara called my mother, was much closer to her heart than aunts usually are. Clara was a frequent visitor at our house, and, having a keen sense of humor, a great admiration for my dad, and no mean ability as a writer, their letters back and forth were very amusing. A letter written en route, reveals some of the tribulations of one of Mr. Pond's Exhibits.

Today we made a little fleeting call on the President at Columbus by special invitation of the Porter of his car. He knew us—the porter I mean—and ast us to come in and see His Nibs. We done so. Ben [President Harrison] is as genial as the North side of a Young Men's Christian Association Reading Room in Winnipeg during the month of January. Oh, how his face lighted up as I strolled into his car. Mrs. McKee, known as the mother of Baby McKee and other works, is real nice. I like her first rate. The feeling is not returned I fear however. Tell your Aunt [Mrs. Nye] this. We hobnobbed with the Prest for quite a while and basked in the smile of Lige Halford, author of Halford's Sauce and other treatises.

Today I wrote a real mean letter to Jay Bird Pond, the great Tabasco Sauce Repositor of 18th St. and only living exponent of Mr. Beecher—and his illness. I am quite hot at Junius Brutus Pond, for he has lied, oh, so much, in order to get us into Schenectady on Xmas day. I do not see how we can avoid it. He made the date and then "advised" with me about. He is doing his thinking with warm water and Tabasco Sauce.

I can say no more. Your gentle efforts in the interests of progress and refinement in the Nye family are most thoroughly appreciated by the writer of these lines, aside from your personal qualities of mind and heart. If Max be severe on the surface remember that, none the less, he is concealing his good and tender heart. I honestly believe this for he is very much like my father, who is better beloved as we look back and see how he feared to give way to any untoward expression of his genuine affection. He was just exactly what J. B. P. *is not*, a man of the strongest affection who scorned to slop over.

With love to all and a kiss for my sweetheart née Fanny Smith—also the children, I will say good-by.

In December Nye and Riley filled a return engagement at the poet's home town, after a week in Ohio. President-elect Harrison was among the most appreciative of a large audience at the Grand Opera House.

By April the lecturers were in Missouri on their way to the Rocky Mountains and the west coast. There the journey ended abruptly as the result of an occurrence at Staten Island. The episode is related by Riley himself:

Perverse fate denied to Nye and his wife a wedding journey. He was poor, but of a sanguine temperament, and at the time of his marriage good-naturedly informed his bride fully of his circumstances. She probably foresaw the force of the man and his coming recognition; at any rate she had great faith in him, and cheerfully accepted the situation. Their wedding journey was deferred from one cause and another for years;

so long that they came to refer to it as to be taken upon the marriage of their eldest child, when the two couples could take the journey together.

In the spring of '89 California had been prescribed for him and we had made a line of engagements toward the Pacific slope after the regular season.

It had been arranged that Mrs. Nye was to meet us in Kansas City, and the trip from there to the coast was to be the long-deferred wedding journey. He had built great hopes upon this prospect, and in the pleasure of anticipation had devised a dozen little schemes for the surprise and entertainment of his wife, who had already left their home, on Staten Island, to join us. She had left their four children, in care of her niece, and was on her way to Kansas City when we arrived there. Nye had expected to find her there, but instead he was confronted with a telegram from his Staten Island physician stating that all four children had been stricken with scarlet fever. During the few hours prior to Mrs. Nye's arrival, and in all agony of apprehension, Mr. Nye busied himself with canceling future lecture dates. When Mrs. Nye finally arrived he broke to her the painful news. Arriving home after that terrible journey, they found the children so ill that they could not be told of the arrival of the father and mother; and Nye, with his heart breaking, sat downstairs and wrote to the children he was not permitted to see, long and happy letters from "California," telling them what jolly times their mother and father were having in the land of flowers.

CHAPTER XVI

EXPOSING THE PARIS EXPOSITION

By June 1 we children were practically well, the last nurse had gone, and my father was scheduled to sail on the North German Lloyd Steamship *Elbe* on June 8 for Europe to report the Paris Exposition for the "World." I understand he was paid a thousand dollars a week and all expenses.

Arrested in Paris

This, Nye's first visit to Europe, was full of interest and adventure. He had the distinction of being arrested in Paris and was charmed with the courtesy of the French police.

Arrested under all circumstances and in many lands, I can place my hand on my heart and say that I would go hundreds of miles to be arrested by a John Darm.

In a letter to my sister Bessie he gives the inside story of the arrest:

Place Vendôme, Paris.
July 15, '89, 5 P. M.

You will see where I live by the picture on this letter. The Vendôme Column is of bronze and much larger than it looks here. It has a winding stair and a statue of Napoleon on the top. As I write I can see him. He is holding out a torch or a banana or something till I should think his arm would ache. I have just been out for three hours looking in the shop windows all the way from the Place Vendôme to the Louvre and back. It makes me tired to see so many things I want.

I think you see more beautiful things in the Paris stores than you do in New York, for the French have such excellent taste especially in dress and art. They wear what looks best on them whether it is a blue pair of overalls or a pair of silk tights.

I was arrested last evening, but don't tell anybody, for it came out all right. You know yesterday was a great national *fête* day like the Fourth of July and the city was very crowded so as I passed along our street I heard a glass crash and looked back where a little café table stood on the sidewalk. It was a wine glass and I had gone 30 feet away before I heard it. However, a waiter followed me—also the proprietor, and demanded pay for the glass. The crowd gathered and a policeman dressed like a general told me I would have to go with him. But a young Italian, Count de Passano, who knew me, came along and made the gendarme let me go. Wasn't that funny?

In a letter to the "World" dated July 5, 1889, he said:

I saw Senator Sherman and wife, also Buffalo Bill; also many other Americans. Miss Eames was on the program and sang charmingly. Mr. and Mrs. Jim Hill and daughter were there. Mr. Hill is the President of the St. Paul, Minneapolis and Manitoba Railway. The Misses Hill are noted for their agreeable manners and exceedingly graceful way of conversing on all subjects. I might also add that, by way of relief, they are something interesting to meet. One never hears either of the Misses Hill referring to the amount of money pa has spent on cabs and tips since they came abroad. Among others were Mrs. Helen Dauvray Ward and Charles Rheinhart, John Hay and wife, Mr. and Mrs. Henry E. Abbey, and Theodore Tilton. The band, after three weeks' rehearsal, played "Yankee Doodle" and "Hail Columbia." The fountains squirted and the pink spinal columns of the feminine contingent gleamed in the soft, voluptuous light along with the bald heads of eminent men.

By the way, the American Minister cannot poke fun at me much longer on the dome business, for he has a good-sized skating rink on the back of his head which the cartoonists ought to utilize. We compared think-tanks last evening, and although I do not claim anything in that line, he is getting, as I say, quite arid on top. However, Mr. and Mrs. Reid are ably and luxuriously representing the United States and hold up the national fabric in good shape, a thing which in former years we have not had too much of in our foreign ministers. Our ministers have been, in many instances, a disgrace to the pulpit.

Frenchmen, old ones, I mean, have a way of brushing their hair forward when they get bald, which I am going to adopt. They part the hair in the neighborhood of the shoulder blades and work it all forward. It looks real cute.

I dined in the tall tower the other day, and, while the green grass lay far below in little squares and the plan of Paris was laid out beneath my eye, I ate the loftiest dinner I have ever become the proprietor of. I would not live always—if I had to board in the Eiffel Tower. You see the restaurants have to pay 25 per cent of their receipts for the privilege of being there. Then they have to haul the provender up so far. There is no competition, and, altogether, I am glad I do not have to take my meals there. But the sight as one sits at the table, peering down over the parapet or up toward the top of the hill, and eats his choice juicy garçon or tells the pecon to bring in another pickled bête noire is one never to be forgotten.

Below you the Seine winds itself in and out among little farms and rich vineyards, and far away you see the ocean. The mighty hippodrome looks like a pig in clover. Think of going up over a show 1000 feet and thus saving your admission fee! Already the tower is one big autograph album. If you want a chance to write your name on the tower, you will have to be here inside of two weeks. There will be no room after that, unless you telegraph. Such great names as those of Peleg Hitchcock of Lower Sandusky, and Lulu Merkins of Dead Horse, are here, also Miss Vivian Bull of Shake Rag, Ill.

One reason I did not speak of the United States exhibit before was that I had not been able to find it. I happened to see it today because it was a very clear day, and I had a powerful glass with me. The truth is sometimes disagreeable, but what I like about it is that when mashed to earth it will invariably rear up again upon its hind feet and assert itself. The United States are poorly, cheaply, meanly, and meagerly represented.

As I write this my feet are sore from the weary march over the great exhibition, and yet I have not seen a fraction of it. A bright young American correspondent told me on my arrival to visit the concert and dance of the Algerians, and I did so. It is one of the most unique things of the show. It costs a franc, but it is worth more than that. After drinking two cups of powerful coffee of the Tunis variety, costing 15 centimes, I paid my money and visited the concert and stomach dance of Algeria. The can-can of the continent is not knee high to this great exhibit. It is barbaric. It is heathenish. It is unique. There are about twenty people on the program, including the orchestra. They are all shades of color, from the charcoal to the olive tinted dancers, and the figures they cut would attract attention and startle the eye of the entire Union. With good advertising and lithographs, they would offset the continued success of Buffalo Bill.

A very pretty girl in Turkish trousers with small hands and feet dances a colic dance, which meets with much applause. It is different from anything I have seen at the Patriarchs' ball in New York. She is attired in a cool white costume of mosquito netting and a Marseilles quilt, which she lays aside when she begins. She also wears gold anklets when the weather is cool and a silk scarf in

ALICE'S

ADVENTURES IN WONDERLAND.

INTERIOR DECORATIONS BY JAMES WHITCOMB RILEY

each hand as she proceeds with the dance, allowing joy to be entirely unconfined. Her corset bill is very small. She wears what would be called a health costume, and when she dances she does so with great vigor. Several people from America went away while she danced, but a Frenchman and I remained. I stayed because as a newspaper reporter I have become accustomed to sights which would shock other people, and the Frenchman remained because he was a Frenchman.

I hardly know how to describe the dance in such a way as to get the account printed, but it had a certain element of voluptuous cucumber regret about it which I do not expect to see again. I never have seen the human form jostled about so heartlessly. The girl was as pretty as a poem by Lord Byron, but the style of the dance itself made me blush more than I have for years. In the midst of antics she looked at me askance. There ought to be some way to put a stop to this. An international exhibition ought to be something to point to with pride in after years. I immediately walked out of the room and strolled to the top of the Eiffel Tower to cool my brow.

I hurt myself at the hotel where I first stopped by getting in the first evening at 10:30 o'clock. The concierge was a violet-eyed French girl. She gave me the key and the one-franc candle with which I intensified the gloom of my D-width boy's size room. She looked at me reproachfully. She was pained to see a man with such a noble mien and such a scope of brow go to bed at 10:30 at night. She mentioned it in pure English to me and I could see that I had lost a good friend. I could only promise her that it should not occur again. And now whenever I am tempted to retire early I can see those blue reproachful eyes, and my solemn promise made to that simple, gentle girl while the hot candle grease ran down over my arm comes back to me, and I smother the wish and scorn the temptation.

I will now pause in my literary career to go and get shaved again. What I like about the French barber is this: if you do not like his lather you can spit it out.

P.S.—Before mailing this I learn that the beautiful Algerian girls who dance the stomach dance or gastric calisthenics referred to above are natives of Paris and live on the Rue de Rinktum.

Did the bright-eyed reader ever send a cable message from this side? If not, there is an experience in store for him. I got anxious as the days went by and no letters came from home. The old green stamp that I had cussed at home repeatedly in round and rubicund terms did not show itself in my mail. The soft colors of the French stamp and the English stamp and the German stamp were to be seen frequently, but never the old bust of the American on the pale green medallion. So I decided to find out if all was well at my slosh by the sea.

I hunted up a cable office at the Grand Hôtel—the Caisse Télégraphique—and asked for the man who speaks English and who, like the editor, is not in. I did the deaf and dumb asylum act, and after a long time the able man at the window gave me a blank. I gave him several— under my breath. The blank he gave me looked like the form of a warrantee deed or the abstracted title to a home in New York, and it was in French. It had conditions on the back like a pass or a porous plaster, and I could see that I would probably get myself in jail if I signed it, but I wrote my message and the foreigner counted the words, also the letters and figures, including the date and the address and the signature and the conditions on the back and the blots and the punctuation and made three words of Tompkinsville. Then I paid for it at the rate of $40 a thought and went away.

That was a week ago and I have heard nothing from it. You may cast your bread upon the waters and they say that after many days, somewhat disfigured, it will return. But a cable message sent from France by a man who speaks French with a Staten Island flavor is lost in the capacious bosom of the moaning sea.

The place to receive good treatment, if nowhere else, is at the banks and especially the large banks. I go to the Credit Lyonnaise and get money just as I would from my wife without identification and with the utmost courtesy. An English-speaking young man shows me a big luxurious department, where I sit down. He brings me a lot of American papers, then he goes to the vault and gets me a quantity of funds, says we are having rather an open winter, and in every way he treats me as his equal. I actually yielded to the impulse and gave him two francs. This is as true as that I sit here and hope safely to reach America. Did anybody ever dare to tip an American cashier? Never! The American cashier may incidentally tip himself, but the customer would hardly dare to offer him 40 cents for being courteous. But in this case, although my brow flushed delicately with shame at the moment, there was no cause for it. He at once invited me to visit Versailles with him on Sunday, so that we could become better acquainted.

Upon my arrival I was quite ill, owing to the heat and change of climate. I was afraid I was going to die, but then I learned that it would be expensive to die and so I

rallied.   It costs $1000 for a stranger to die in Paris at
a hotel, to say nothing of the funeral.

I go to the Morgue whenever I feel depressed.   There
is peace.   Even the Frenchmen are quiet.   It is not so
shocking as you might think.   The sad harvest from the
river lies inside a glass inclosure in a low kind of "doby"
building back of Notre Dame.   This Morgue is said to
be the most successful in the world.   Bodies may be kept
on exhibition for identification a month or more; but I
wouldn't care to appear in public so long.   Profoundly
thankful for the demonstrations, I would ask to be excused from an appearance extending beyond a week.

I can realize slightly the sorrows of the man without a
country.   Think of living out a life without a home newspaper!   We cuss the press from time to time when we
are at home, but when we no longer hear our own tongue
and we blindly eat and drink things that we do not know
the names of and try to make people understand by speaking very slowly and distinctly, or grope about yearning
for things and unable to get them (except as we combine
the back part of the spelling book with the deaf-and-
dumb alphabet), we welcome papers which at home we
would scorn to read.   We buy old back numbers.   I even
bought my own paper, printed the day before I sailed,
just because I thought there might be something in it
that I had not read, and, moreover, because it looked so
all-fired good.   Even the time-tables and crop reports
looked better, and I regarded with actual affection the
well-satisfied features of Lydia Pinkham and the modest
little wood violet that makes the three-dollar shoe.

The Exposition is having an enormous success.   I
would like the gate receipts for a week if I could appeal
strongly enough to the management.   But it would be

useless—they would not understand me. Nobody under-
stands me. If I were to die to-morrow I could safely say
that I went down to my cold, clammy grave wholly mis-
understood.

I met a young man from America a few days ago.
He sympathized with me, for he had trouble of his own.
He had tried to hire the carriage which belonged to the
Sheriff of Paris or the City Marshal or something of
that kind. Possibly it was a deputy. (It's a great town
for Deputies. They have a Chamber of them not far
from my boarding place.) Well, he failed in that. He
said to me in a town where the police and mail-carriers
looked like Major-Generals he had supposed that hacks
were built on the same scale. He did not learn wisdom
by that, however, and the next thing he did was to mail a
letter to his loved one in Brooklyn with a French revenue
stamp on it. I followed him around over the city just
to see him do things that are absolutely absurd to one who
has been here some time, as I have, and who knows Paris
like a book.

Paris is quite an old town. It is older and wickeder
than Cheyenne, I think, but I may be prejudiced against
the place. It is warm here this summer, and there are a
good many odors that I don't know the names of. It is a
great national congress of rare imported smells. I have
detected and catalogued 1350 out of a possible 1400.

From Paris Nye went to London where he was promptly
interviewed.

"And what do you think of Paris?"

"Paris is remarkable to me for its noiseless style of doing
so much. There seems to be so little jar and worry, and
yet what a ponderous amount of business is done! The

beautiful and smooth streets help very much, and the care
generally taken to do everything exactly and decently helps
also."

"What are your plans for this season?"

"I expect to sail on the *City of Chicago* on the thirty-
first of July, and begin a lecturing tour in California, with
James Whitcomb Riley, the funny poet. I am hoping,
however, that the tour will be postponed until November,
in which event I shall remain abroad longer. I want to pay
my respects to the queen, the shah, and Gladstone, if I
have time."

In due time he found the opportunity to pay his respects
to the British metropolis:

While enjoying to the utmost the hospitality of London and wishing that I could get 26 hours into a day,
I could not help thinking how easily the matter of entertaining was attended to here. I would have to borrow
dishes and put two more leaves in the dining-table before
I could begin to return the kindness. The children would
have to eat at the second table and be kept out of sight
during the meal so that they would not announce the
menu in advance. One of the dining-chairs would have
to be reglued, and the cigars I smoke would not do at all.

You go into the Savage Club and eat and talk and
smoke as you would have gone into your mother's pantry
when a boy, after you had been fishing all day. There is
no more formality about it than there used to be when you
tore out the end of a loaf of bread and put jam on it to
your heart's content, sucked your fingers and went to
bed. It is great. And yet the Savage Club is a place
where you will meet men who say things which they
thought of themselves.

A fair young girl playfully undertook to pat me in a bantering way the other evening as I trudged gayly home in the opaque gloaming. She struck a bunch of keys which I had in my pistol pocket and went sadly away wringing her hands. I felt sorry for her, but at the same time could not afford to stop and pity her, so I gave a piercing shriek and darted away like a frightened deer. Many of those girls stay out until a late hour at night conversing freely with comparative strangers, thus giving the public ample opportunity to gossip about them and to misjudge their motives. A girl in London cannot be too careful about conversing with strangers that way. One of those pleasant and piquant maids admired my umbrella very much, and taking it gently from me with a winning smile, spreading it and holding it over us, took my arm and trudged blithely along with me until I told her that here our ways seemed to diverge and our paths to fork, as it were. Reluctantly I took the umbrella, and telling her to run along home before it rained, I passed on toward my inn.

London is too large a place for me. I go out for a five minutes' walk and come home late at night, hopelessly lost in the labyrinth of her streets. The cabman is my salvation. I get lost purposely, so that I can surprise myself at one and six by getting back in two minutes.

I would not do London on the guide-book plan, or by program, but by strolling about, studying people more than places, and getting into the usual number of scrapes. I saw the House of Commons in session for the first time, and listened to several eminent gentlemen who spoke ferninst the royal grants. I can do it myself now. It is quite easy. You say something, and then look up and

say "ah," until you can think of something else to say.
Other gentlemen with their hats on sit around and slumber, but spectators are not allowed to wear their hats.
Only members can wear their hats and snore above a certain key.

Mr. Gladstone, better known as the Grand Old Man,
sat on the front seat. He is very bald, indeed, and his
throat whiskers are white. He is much smaller than I
had thought. He wears low shoes and red woolen socks.
When he works down so as to sit on his shoulder blades,
his trousers gradually ascend his limbs until you can look
over the tops of his cute little red socks with perfect impunity. He is the author of his own thoughts, and I
hear him spoken of in high terms, especially by his friends.

Mr. Robert Lincoln's last reception was brightened up
briefly by a pleasant call from me. Many Americans
were present and drank the tea of the minister as administered by his bright young daughter. Without wishing
to express political opinion in any way, I must say that
the general sentiment of the American contingent is that
both in France and in England we need not be ashamed
of our ministers or our consuls general. Mr. Reid and
General Rathbone seem to be beautifully representing us
in Paris. General John C. New says that I have ruined
his reputation in the Old World by referring to him as a
poker player and so I hereby apologize. He is not a
poker player. He plays bean-bag, however, with great
skill, and lawn tennis in a way that arouses the astonishment and admiration of the effete monarchies.

For his triumphant return from Europe, Nye (so he
solemnly states) had arranged an ovation. He had always
wanted an ovation, and as the idea had never occurred to

his friends, he undertook it himself.   He had hired a tug
to meet him, accompanied by a band and a glee-club.   A
neat little speech was all prepared and ready for delivery.
He hoped the proposed ovation would not interfere with the
captain and his plans for landing.   But there was a slip
of some kind.   His arrival found the tug dumping garbage
far out at sea, and the result is thus described:

> When I got home to Staten Island feeling that I had
> been away a hundred years, and thinking I would hardly
> be remembered even by my family, I found that nobody
> knew I had been away.   I can now see for the first time
> how the world squeezes along so well when a great man
> dies.

Mr. Pulitzer, however, was pleased with the Paris letters,
for he presented to Nye a beautiful scarf pin in appreciation of the good work done; a cornucopia in design, sur-
mounted by five diamonds.

CHAPTER XVII

A MAN ABOUT TOWN

NYE was making new friends in New York, many of them among the distinguished. With one of these he went fishing:

It is a mistake of the average angler that he squanders too much time in angling and not enough in getting ready to go. Why should we put in a whole day consigning an unknown worm to a watery grave and only an hour to preparation, when the pleasure is not in fishing but in getting ready to fish?

I did not know much about angling, except in a desultory way, until I met Guy Carlton. It was really pitiful. I was liable at any time to go fishing for striped bass with a silver-bass reel or to angle all day for an Illinois sucker with a Virginia reel.

I did not know the first thing about angling as she is angled.

I didn't know any better than to fish for landlocked salmon with a night-key. I was about the most obtuse angler at large.

Once I fished all day for striped bass with a Scotch plaid fly.

Guy and I went out yesterday to catch a few striped bass for the restaurants. I carried the beer-jug and he carried the tackle.

We went up the Hudson River several miles and angled off the clinker-built coast near the iron works.

But we did not secure the crinkled seersucker bass we went after. He was not there. He was extremely elsewhere.

We only succeeded in securing a tomcod, a fish that rises to the angle-worm and dies perfectly reconciled.

He grows to about the size of the sardine, but is more blasé. He rises to the surface like a slice of liver, gasps two times and then looks as though he had been dead all summer.

Nobody eats the tommy, even while suffering the pangs of hunger, and this is a wise provision of Nature, for he is absolutely unable to defend himself.

I caught one myself. The tomcod hasn't the force of character generally assumed by the common cod. Neither has he the same winning smile.

We did not succed in getting any worms for some time, but finally bought a dozen at five cents apiece. You will find people who claim that living in New York is expensive, and yet within an hour's ride of the City Hall you can get twelve angle-worms for 60 cents.

Some day I am going out again after game fish. We are going to catch some shad roe and some Maltese catfish and some navy blue fish and some low-neck clams.

If Nye was disappointed in the virility of the fish provided by Mr. Carlton, it was not long before he had his revenge, according, at least, to an item that appeared in a New York paper:

Henry Guy Carlton, who is an epicure as well as an author, gave a dinner to Bill Nye, in which the leading dish was a large pompano, brought by rail from New Orleans. Through some mistake the ice gave out on the journey and the fish arrived in New York in a very bad condition. The cook was a stranger to the Southern delicacy and imagining it was a game fish in both senses cooked and served it. Each guest took one bite and became horribly silent. Carlton, who had not tasted it, asked the company:

"How do you think that was brought on here?" intending to explain the refrigerator service between the gulf and the metropolis.

Nye looked up very solemnly and answered: "I think you brought it in a hearse!"

Taking the "World" artist with me in order to know fully what I was talking about, I visited the Academy of Design a day or two ago for the purpose of witnessing some of the pictures from Paris which are now on exhibition there. Many of these pictures are large and beautiful, while others are small and ornery.

No. 123, "Diana Surprised," is no doubt the best picture in the whole collection. The tall and beautiful figure of Diana in the middle distance in the act of being surprised, is well calculated to appeal to any one with a tender heart or a few extra clothes. Diana has just been in swimming with her entire *corps de ballet* and on coming out of the water is surprised to find that some one has stolen her clothes. The artist has very happily caught the attitude and expression at the moment when she is about to offer a reward for them. The picture is so true to life that I instinctively stammered "Excuse me," and got behind the artist who was with me. The figures are life size and the attitudes are easy and graceful in the extreme. One very beautiful young woman in the middle foreground, about seven and one-half inches north of the frame of the picture, with her back to the spectator, crouches at Diana's feet. She has done her beautiful and abundant hair up in a graceful coil at the back of her head, but has gone no further with her toilet when the surprise takes place. The idea is lofty and the treatment beneficial. I do not know that I am using these terms as I should, but I am doing the best I can.

We often hear our friends regret that their portraits, dressed in clothing that has long since become obsolete, are still in existence, and though the features are correctly reproduced, the costume is now so ridiculous as to impair the *de trop* of the picture and mar its aplomb.

Jules Lefebvre has overcome this great obstacle in a marvelous manner, and gives us Diana and her entire staff surrounded by an atmosphere that time cannot cloud with contumely or obscure with ridicule. Had the artist seen fit to paint Diana wearing a Garibaldi waist and very full skirt with wide hoops, and her hair wrapped around two or three large "rats," he might have been true to the customs and costumes of a certain period in the history of art, but it would not have stood the test of time. As it is he has wisely chosen to throw about her a certain air of hauteur which will look just as well in a hundred years as it does now.

The picture has a massive frame and would brighten up one end of a dining-room very much. I was deeply mortified and disappointed to learn that it was not for sale.

I give a letter of Bill Nye to his grandmother, written on October 15, 1889, when he learned that she had fallen and broken a few of her well used but old and brittle bones.

It seems pretty tough to get such a jolt when you thought that you had already had your share, doesn't it?

Your grit, however, is the best feature of the case, and that will do for you what youth and a consistent Christian life might not do.

I believe that God loveth the gritty toiler in his vineyard fully as well as He doth the flatulent author of a rip snorting prayer.

Your life has been one long, eloquent prayer, not for exhibition purposes, but for the comfort and pleasure of those nearest to you. And so now I am hurrahing for you, Grandmom, and betting on your victory over this little accident.

The next thing to hazing seems to be the reception given a maiden speech at a Clover Club dinner. Bill Nye crossed voices with other, louder, and ruder orators on the occasion of the Clover Club's sixth annual repast.

Here is his version of the dinner:

It is now an historical fact, established by means of research, acrostics and cryptograms, that when Demosthenes went to the beach and practiced with his mouth full of pebbles, striving to outbellow the billows and patiently clinging to the thread of his discourse, even while the loud boom of the breakers caught up his shrill remarks and hurled them into space, he was not preparing to make an impression upon the history of his time, as we have been taught. He was simply rehearsing a speech which he hoped to deliver at the Clover Club, of Philadelphia.

People who have formed the idea that Philadelphia is not given to sociability and a cheerful interchange of thought are unfamiliar with the methods of the Clover Club, especially under the administration of Moses Purnell Handy.

For the information of those who may read this piece, yet have not had the pleasure of addressing this successful organization, let me say that it is a custom of the club to invite eminent statesmen, poets, judges, humorists and other freaks to come to its annual dinners and make speeches. The club assists in the delivery of these speeches, adding thoughts of its own as the orator proceeds, and also making inquiries regarding the personal characteristics of the speaker, which are calculated to divert his attention from what he was about to say.

The only way to speak successfully at a Clover Club dinner, I believe, is to avoid saying what you were about to say.

I had the pleasure of holding a conversation with the Clover Club on the occasion of its annual meeting. I had been led to believe that the air of refinement which people notice about me wherever I go would entitle me to the respect and kind consideration of the club. Even should that fail, however, I thought that no one could help admiring my unwavering confidence in myself, a confidence which is all the more praiseworthy on my part because it has not been shared by the general public.

But the Clover Club is not constructed with a view to the building up and fostering of rhetorical industries. It is built upon the moral theory that a man who speaks publicly does so for the edification of the audience. This is a quaint and extremely eccentric idea. Generally it is otherwise. Public speakers arise and enjoy themselves, while the audience, though largely in the majority, has to suffer. If the members of the Clover Club do not like the tendencies of a speech, they suggest to the speaker some other line of thought.

I did not know that. I had always before selfishly

reveled in the wonderful cadence of my own melodious Skowhegan voice, forgetting that the audience had rights.

I enjoyed it very much, for I was down at the foot of the table having fun with Dr. Bedloe, and I knew that at this rate, with a hundred guests to be gently scared half to death in that way, I would not be reached before Friday, and I thought that I could get away before that time. It was at this supreme moment, when saturated with a soothing sense of security and congratulating myself on the wonderful way in which Mr. Maltby's dress suit fitted me, that the president of the club, observing that I had my mouth full of ice which I did not know what to do with, introduced me to the brilliant assemblage.

I felt embarrassed and was about to say so, I believe, when ex-Governor Bunn, who was appointed and received the portfolio as governor of Idaho solely by reason of his great powers as a conversationist, said something to me which did not bear upon what I was about to say myself.

While I was thinking of a bon mot which would wipe Governor Bunn from the face of the earth, such as a reference to him as Bunny, Mr. Jerome, a gentleman from New York, who is sixty-nine years of age, said something which was highly enjoyable, but which, with running comment by Colonel Thomas P. Ochiltree, Colonel McCaull and Colonel McClure, seemed to open up an entirely new line of thought from what I had intended to follow.

I was about to administer a tart rebuke to Mr. Jerome, when I happened to remember his greater age and resolved not to do so. My attention was also at this time attracted by the sounds of music. It was a Tyrolean air, and referred to the Derby Ram, which seems to have a wild fascination for the gentlemen of the club. And when such voices as those of Wayne MacVeagh and General Horace Porter join in the refrain it is well worth going to Philadelphia and sitting up till long after 9 o'clock to hear.

So I decided not to speak while these well known vocalists were engaged in song. As they were encored, they obliged by singing "Maryland, My Maryland," with improvisations by the great impresario, Mr. Jerome.

I then stood on the other leg awhile and tried to recall what I had said, which had reminded the auditors of these songs, but I could not. In all my remarks so far, although I had been on my feet twenty minutes or so, I had carefully avoided saying anything that would call forth an attack of this kind. I had used no language which would naturally provoke such men as Colonel Taylor or Colonel McClure to song. People afterward spoke of my impressive manner and said I also used first rate discretion in avoiding so many unpleasant features which are apt to stir up ill feeling at such a time.

They named whole columns of things which I had thus evaded, and every one said that if I had erred at all it was in the direction of conservatism. All the members of the club who expressed any opinion about it said that they were in favor of printing my remarks with a rubber stamp.

There can be no more comfortable sensation, I fancy, than to be a guest at one of these annual dinners, with the personal recognizance of the president in your pocket binding himself not to call upon you for a speech and certifying that you have previously had a fair and impartial trial on the charge that you were a good after dinner speaker and that you have proved an alibi.

In his written account, unfortunately, Nye does not explain by what means he extricated himself from this difficult situation.   But others, who were there, say that he came out on top.   According to one witness he got the floor at last, and before he sat down the Clover Club had to admit that they had been outdone.

The thin edge of the wedge by which Nye finally got the attention of the roisterers was a remark that the audience reminded him of a crowd his Republican brother Frank had once addressed at Erin Prairie, Wisconsin.   The members of the Clover Club scented possibilities in a situation involving a Republican political address in a town with so Democratic a name, and they listened.

Wiser and older politicians had sidestepped the engagement, but the Nyes have always been hopeful and my brother fell into that trap, just as I have slipped into this one.

Practically the only Republican in that town was the chairman of the meeting.   But there was nothing going on in Erin Prairie to amuse the voters save morning, noon and night, so quite a crowd turned out.

The reception of my brother and his red hot Republicanism was as cordial as could be expected; that is to say, the audience listened with all the courtesy, with all the consideration that distinguishes, for example, the Clover Club.

In other words, they didn't listen at all.   In fact, they booed him in a manner that would have inspired you gentlemen to new triumphs, could you but have been there to observe their advanced technique in heckling.

But there was one kind-hearted Irishman in the crowd —the man who swept up.   When the others had gone and

my crestfallen young brother prepared to shake the dust
of that inhospitable town from his shoes, the old janitor
comfortingly remarked:

"Niver mind, Mr. Nye. This aggregation wasn't ripri-
sintitive of Erin Prairie. They was nothin' but the rag
tag and bob tail of the town, they was. *Ivry man who
had a damned bit of sinse shtayed to home.*"

Wherever Nye went and whatever happened there was
something amusing to be seen through his funny glasses.

Wandering about the other day and waiting for Otero
to come forth and dance at the Eden Musée, the manager
said, all of a sudden, as he noticed that I was being mistaken for a new wax figure, and that I seemed embarrassed
by the way people were feeling of me and wondering if I
were hollow: "Come up stairs with me. I want to show
you something. Did you ever go into the work room
where wax figures are made?"

"No."

"Well, take the elevator with me; Otero will not dance
for an hour and you can see the whole business, studio
and work shop, in that time. You will enjoy it just as
much as you would remaining here with that vacant and
guileless look, being constantly taken for Henry Irving
or the deathbed of Napoleon."

So I said, yes, we would go. I had never watched the
process, and very few people, as I understood it, were
permitted to go into the mysterious chambers where great
men were made and unmade even quicker than the newspapers could do it. The principal works—wax works,
I may say, or tableau foundry—would seem to be facing
Twenty-third Street, one floor above the entrance. Quite
a number of people are busy there all the time adding

new figures and tableaux to the great collection in the
halls below.   Every time a monarch croaks and a new
president is elected the genius of the wax sculptor up
there is called into use, and before you know it the head
of the new republic, in a neat fitting suit of clothes, is
inserting his nice pink hand into the bosom of his frock
coat and trying to look far away, while people are watching him earnestly in the great group of potentates.

The sculptors were working on a group of Christopher
Columbus.   The artist had seized upon the happy moment when Columbus is about to discover America, and
he is debating in his own mind whether or not there is
anything in it.   One can see readily by his deep, earnest
look that it is a problem in his brain which he has not
yet settled whether it will pay him to discover a country
which will introduce the use of plug tobacco and freedom.

The head and face of the figures are made first in clay,
as a sculptor would do it.   It is fun.   I made one.   It
was pleasing, but the man it resembled I had never met.
He was a stranger to me.

Wax people are noted for their dignity and repose.
They have no brains, but they never forget to be dignified.   I hate dignified people.   I never tried to be dignified
but once, and that was two weeks ago.   I wore a handsome
new frock coat and a new, shining silk hat, to drive my
family over the Finger Bowl Road on Staten Island and
on to South Beach.   I was proud and haughty, dressed
up, serene and mentally vacant in order to look dignified.
People who saw us driving thus afterward paid me a high
compliment by telling my wife what a dignified and thoroughly clerical looking coachman she had.

Since that I have not tried to look dignified.

Some of Nye's "interviews" were by means of absent treatment. Doubtless his readers thought his chat with the Duke of Marlborough a figment of his imagination. Not so. He did meet the duke, and to omit his one-sided tête-à-tête would be an oversight indeed:

I have just terminated a pleasant call upon the Duke of Marbro at his lodgings. I write his name Marbro because that is the way we pronounce it here at Newport. In the language of my ostensible colored friend, Mr. Rankin, the amateur pronouncer would call it Marl-bor-ough, with three grunts, while in fact Marbro, the correct pronunciation of the name, is executed with but one grunt.

The duke is suffering from a slight cold, which he contracted for during the early part of the week. It resulted from his ignorance of our changeable and freckle-minded climate. On Tuesday he took a long stroll, and while several miles from his lodgings and wearing his light summer cane, he was overtaken by a severe and sudden change in the temperature.

The duke rose languidly as I entered, and, taking a reef in his pajamas, looked at me in an inquiring way which betokened that, though of lineage high, he was not entirely at ease in my presence.

"Duke," said I, standing my umbrella up in the corner to show my childlike confidence in him, "how's your conduct?"

Five minutes afterwards I would have given worlds if I could have recalled my rash words. I did not mean anything more than to utter a piece of pleasantry, for I am passionately fond of pleasantry even in society; but

Marbro seemed to take it to heart and to feel distressed. He made a low, guttural sound, but his reply died away in the mansard roof of his mouth.

To hide his embarrassment, Marbro "rosined" his eye and put a glass paper weight in it. He then regarded me with some amazement through this piece of bric-à-brac, while I poured out a grown person's dose of Rectified Ruin which stood on the escritoire and drank it with keen relish. Everything I did was done to make Marbro feel at his ease.

I told him I had known the Marbros in Maine ever since I was a boy; that we didn't feel above them then, and it would not do to begin at my time of life to look down on people just because I now wrote pieces for the paper, many of which were afterwards printed. We always thought that the Marbros, or Marlboroughs, of Maine, got their name from burrowing in the marl along the Piscataquis, I said.

Thus I chatted on with him for an hour or two without seeming to chirk him up at all. "Duke," said I at last, "I know what the matter must be with you—you are socially ostracized. I knew it as soon as I came into the room. You cannot disguise it from me. You are suffering from social ostracism, and it is breaking you down. The social demands made by America upon an imported social wreck do not give said wreck time to eat his meals and obtain a necessary amount of rest. I suppose there is nowhere in the world a climate that is so trying on a person suffering from social ostracism as that of my native land. In other climes they give a social outcast rest, but here he gets absolutely no rest whatever."

I then drifted into society chat in a graceful and naïve way which has never failed to melt the stoniest heart. I told him that I had understood, since I came to Newport, that the demands of society here were so unrelenting that they had kept Mr. and Mrs. Mayonnaise dressing all the time.

A long pause ensued here, during which I could hear Marbro's reason tottering on its throne. After waiting three-quarters of an hour, by my watch, and failing to see that my remark had shed even a ray of sunshine, I gave him my address and told him that if, in the future, he derived any beneficial effects from the above joke, I would be glad to have him communicate with me. And even if I were to die before he could truly say that he had been benefited by this joke and grappled with its keen, incisive nub, my grandchildren would be tickled almost to death to know that he had taken it to pieces and put it together again and found out how it was built and laughed at its ingenious mechanism.

I then let myself out of the house with an adjustable passkey and hastened away. Shortly after I got back to my own lodgings, sometimes called a 7⅛ room, a lackey from the duke, wearing a liver-colored livery, handed me a note from Marbro, in which he said he hoped that in case I used this interview for publication I would be careful to give his exact language.

In my poor, weak way, I think I have done so.

Bill Nye wrote such a great number of stories for the "World" containing autobiographical references that I have to practice the severest restraint in including so few. But this must be a one-volume biography. And I shall have to omit all except brief bits of some of his choicest tales. There was, for example, his visit to Ludlow Street Jail. Said he:

We are stopping quietly here, taking our meals in our rooms mostly, and *going out very little indeed*.

You can get to Ludlow Street Jail by taking the Second Avenue Elevated train to Grand Street, and then going east two blocks, or you can fire a shotgun into a Sabbath-school.

Here the burglars go to bed at the hour that the rest of us do. We all retire at the same time, and a murderer cannot sit up any later at night than a pickpocket can.

The structure has 100 foot frontage, and a court, which is sometimes called the court of last resort. The guest can climb out of this court by ascending a polished brick wall about 100 feet high, and then letting himself down in a similar way on the Ludlow Street side. That one thing is doing a great deal towards keeping quite a number of people here who would otherwise go away.

The clerk does not seem to care whether you have any baggage or not. You can stay here for days, even if you don't have any. All you need is a kind word and a mittimus from the court.

Heavy iron bars keep the mosquitoes out, and at night the house is brilliantly lighted by incandescent lights of one candle-power each. Still, of course, we miss the sea breeze.

We retire at 7:30 o'clock at night and arise at 6:30 in the morning, so as to get an early start. A man who has five or ten years to stay in a place like this naturally likes to get at it as soon as possible each day, and so he gets up at 6:30.

My family suggests that I include the information that my father's visit to the jail was purely voluntary.

Of the seashore near New York he wrote:

Long Branch looks bright and smiling this season, and along the ocean drive many new faces are seen. By being economical I frequently save up enough during the winter to stop over at Long Branch between boats.

Bathing in a hired chemiloon with red braid on it does not give me that sense of thorough ablution that I felt when in childhood I defied the police and, clothed in nothing but conscious rectitude and a little bag of asafœtida which I wore around my neck to keep off the prairie mange and other plagues incident to a thorough education, I plunged like a long buff streak into the bosom of the mill-pond.

I hear some complaint this summer at the bathing places regarding lack of proper care at the bath-houses, and the crying need for more cleanliness. One lady at Coney Island, whose home is on the east side of New York, and whose husband made his money by a judicious system of sanitary plumbing and unsanitary charges for same, told me that her eldest daughter, Elfrida, came home after utilizing one of those public bath-houses and her clothing was just literally covered with *ermine*.

Here are a few remarks by Bill Nye in denying his candidacy for the presidency:

In an interview which I have just had with myself, I have positively stated, and now repeat, that at neither convention will my name be presented as a candidate.

But my health is good.

I think my voice is better than it was either four, eight, twelve, or sixteen years ago, and it does not tire me so much to think of things to say from the tail gate of a train as it did when I first began to refrain from presenting my name to conventions.

According to my notion, our candidate should be a plain man, a magnetic, but hairless patriot, who should be suddenly thought of by a majority of the convention and nominated by acclamation. He should not be a hide-bound politician, but on the contrary should be

"In an interview which I have just had with myself, I have positively stated that at neither convention will my name be presented."

greatly startled, while down cellar sprouting potatoes, to learn that he has been nominated.

In going down my cellar stairs the committee will do well to avoid stepping on a large and venomous dog who sleeps on the top stair. Or I will tie him in the barn if I can be informed when I am liable to be startled.

To those who have prospered during the past twenty years let me say they owe it to the perpetuation of the principles and institutions toward the establishment and maintenance of which I have given the best energies of my life. To those who have been unfortunate, let me say frankly that they owe it to themselves.

He was not so reticent with regard to the New York postmastership. His open letter to Postmaster-General John Wanamaker, ordering a suit of clothes and suggesting himself to handle the New York mails, referred to another suit he had bought while postmaster at Laramie:

I wore this suit through my entire administration, also through the places where it came most in contact with foreign substances. I now apply to you once more for a suit that shall be durable and plain, and yet fix the eye of a stranger at once and compel him to say: "There is a thorough gentleman. There is a man worthy of any office in the gift of the Federal Government."

So if you will be kind enough to send me some samples of your goods, with rules for self-measurement, also stating at the time what, if anything, has been done about the Post-office at New York, you will do me a favor and you will not do yourself any harm.

I would want a plain business suit that would also look well for Sundays. I generally fix up for Sundays and spend the day in self-communion and silent admiration of my past life.

My home now is not far from the Post-office in New York and I pay taxes there. I also have writing to do for the "World" newspaper, directly across the street. Writing these pieces does not take all my time, and so I thought that we might help each other. I could help you to introduce your goods among our best people in New York, with whom I am very thick.

A dark shade of goods with an invisible check in the pocket of the vest would suit me very well. I wear a tail coat and a very long lithe pant. In post-office work I dress plainly but neatly.

Remember me to the Administration and say that while unusually busy this season I have not allowed prosperity to crowd the Administration out of my memory.

I was quite sorry not to have seen you when last I was in Philadelphia, for I know that we would have pleased each other. I am a frank, open-faced man who forgot to order sufficient hair while putting up the job. I am easy to get acquainted with and hard to shake off.

In speaking to President Harrison about this matter you might say that I was the first man to suggest his name for the Presidency. This is not so, but anything I can do for you in a similar way I will cheerfully do.

While traveling Nye spent four days in the company of the original Jack Dempsey, the famous boxer, known as the Nonpareil.

I never felt so free to say anything I wanted to—to other passengers—as I did at that time. I wish I could afford to take at least one pugilist with me always.

Mr. Dempsey's great force as a debater is less, perhaps, in the matter than in the manner. Striking in appearance, aggressive in his nature, and happy in his gestures, he is certain to attract the attention of the police, and he cannot fail to rivet the eye of his adversary. I saw one of his adversaries, not long ago, whose eye had been successfully riveted in that way.

Some one called Bill Nye a "Mexican hairless humorist" and was promptly challenged to mortal combat. In his letter to his antagonist Nye wrote:

I forward this by the hands of a slow messenger boy, who will bring me your answer as soon as he gets thoroughly rested.

I hope, sir, that you will excuse anything that may seem brutal in this challenge, for I desire to take your life without giving you any offense. May I ask that you will name a quiet place, as free from malaria as possible, where we may kill each other undisturbed?

I have consulted several friends about the prospect of our meeting in a duel at no distant day, and all of them seem to be highly gratified. If you would prefer to wait a few weeks, till the weather is cooler, so that you can lie in state longer, I will try to muzzle my wrath.

My second will no doubt inform you that I am an expert and deadly swordsman and will try to convince you that it will be best not to name the sword. Do not be too proud to heed his advice. It may save your life —and mine also.

I hope you will not treat this challenge lightly, sir, and try still further to heap ridicule upon an old and mildewed name by suggesting soft gloves or watermelons as weapons. Let us meet as gentlemen, sir—fire and fall down, stagger to our feet, lean heavily against a tree, mutter a few words in a hoarse voice, gasp two times in rapid succession, put on our coats and go home.

Of a fox hunt Nye said:

We did not see the fox, but we saw almost everything else. I remember, among other things, of riding through a hothouse, and how I enjoyed it. A morning scamper through a conservatory when the syringas and jonquils, and jackroses lie cuddled up together in their little beds, is a thing to remember and look back to and pay for.

To stand knee-deep in glass and gladiolas, to smell the mashed and mussed up mignonette and the last fragrant sigh of the scrunched heliotrope beneath the hoof of your horse, while far away the deep-mouthed baying of the hoarse hounds, hotly hugging the reeking trail of the anise-seed bag calls on the gorgeously caparisoned hills to give back their merry music or fork it over to other answering hills, is joy to the huntsman's heart.

As an athlete Nye was willing but not convincing:

I swang the Indian clubs last year. It benefited me a great deal. Formerly I had operated a scroll saw and had made a lot of fayence and things, among which were a hollywood clock, with a wealth of holes in it, and other little articles of vertu, including a bas relief—bass wood —of myself. In swinging the clubs I obliterated these things, especially the clock; and so I regard the Indian club as one of the most beneficial things, in proper hands, of which we are at present informed. I also have a set of dumbbells, which I use to keep the door open in summer time, thus giving a free circulation of fresh air. In this way the dumbbell is a great boon.

Nye tried other sports and reported his injuries:

I got a very large wheel, because I run somewhat to legs and could propel an enormous vehicle, if I could once maintain a good poise. It had a little flat oil can and an alarm on the withers, which could be rung in case I should be crossing a railroad at night and desired the engineer of an approaching train to save himself by instant flight.

This bicycle I gave to the physician who set my leg

for me. He did it so well that I gave him the instrument, together with the wrench I had received while falling from it.

My new machine looks well. It is what we wheelmen call a full nickel machine. I have had my photograph taken with it. That is, in company with it. It is a beautiful picture. You can easily tell which is the bicycle.

Although called a genius, Nye had little use for the temperamental egotist, and he took a crack at a certain one who had just crossed his path:

You have seen such a genius. He walks over the prostrate bodies of his friends and regards his wife as a misguided being who has been mercifully permitted to stand around and admire him and reach up under his vest for a stray suspender that he cannot get hold of. He does not hold himself amenable to the laws which govern other people. Being a genius, he takes three pieces of pie and then expects the family to sit up all night and hold his head for him.

His soul's all aglow with sunshine when things go his way, but when they do not it is aglow with a red reflection from the great coke works where the fire department is an ignominious failure. I would not advise a tender, trusting girl to marry a genius like that. Marry a plain, open-faced mechanic who is willing to submit to the laws which govern humanity in general, rather than the spoiled pet of a pelt-hunting public which adores at a distance and despises at short range. Select one who is willing to give blow for blow, smile for smile, and dollar for dollar wherever he goes; a man who does not live in the artificial warmth of a silly adoration, who is not perpetually yearning for another curtain call, whose morbid and boundless appetite for praise takes at a gulp the simple devotion of a wife and children and howls for more and more.

Genius is a good thing, but if it should break out in my family I think I would call in the doctor before it got much of a start. The history of genius has been clouded by ingratitude, domestic infelicity and cruelty. Let us each and every one, as we crouch around our own firesides to eat the popcorn and Spitzbergen apples of mediocrity, remember that there is a sweet and beautiful flavor to a square and yet uneventful life which the pampered children of abnormal and over-grown talent never know.

Nye visited the studio of a faith-healer for relief from clam melancholic:

The room was plainly furnished with a dark-browed door-mat and an umbrella. The mat had a number and street engraved on it that belonged up near Harlem. Nothing is sadder to me than the sight of a door-mat with no home, driven from door to door. People ought to throw such influences around a door-mat as to make it spend its evenings at home instead of wandering away to seek out the delusive joys of a life among strangers. One of the best restraining influences I know of consists of a small brass chain with a padlock on it. Moral suasion does not work well on a door-mat.

We are told of many strange and almost miraculous cures by this new method. Patients who have been supported by charity and one crutch have risen and gone forth reconstructed; and in one instance a new eyeball sprouted and grew an old socket full of optic. Large classes are formed to receive instructions in the faith cure, and if they succeed in believing the above statements they are graduated.

The healer said that as a general rule the cure was effected by the influence of her own mind over the mind of her patient, but that in my case it would be the influence of mind over matter. So I sat there and watched the unequal contest between my simple faith and thirteen Little Neck clams.

I attributed the failure of this treatment in my case to the fact that ever since I was sixteen years of age I have had a slight impediment in my faith, brought on by trying, during a hot day, to believe that I could detect a certain card out of a possible three, arranged with their faces down, by a man in whom I had perfect confidence.

During a visit to the navy-yard Nye formed a high opinion of our floating forces:

The Navy has been thoroughly refitted and refurnished throughout, and is as pleasant a navy as one would see in a day's journey.

I had the pleasure of boarding the man-of-war *Richmond* under a flag of truce and the *Atlantic* under a suspension of the rules.

The yard is inclosed by means of a large brick wall, so that in case there should be a local disturbance in Brooklyn the rioters could not break through and bite the Navy.

The feeling against arduous spirits in the United States Navy is certainly on the increase, and the day is not far distant when alcohol in a free state will only be used in the arts, sciences, music, literature and the drama.

Modern guns are made with breeches, which may be easily removed during a fight and replaced when visitors come on board.

CHAPTER XVIII

THE LAST SEASON WITH RILEY

WHEN the telegram announcing four cases of scarlet fever in the Nye household at Staten Island ended the Nye-Riley lecture season of 1888-89, both poet and humorist were thoroughly fagged. The writing of each had suffered as a result of the strenuous itinerary, and in a sense it was a relief to them to be able to cancel their further engagements.

But the season had been a financial success, and from all parts of the country came requests for their entertainment. Major Pond spurred them on to undertake a thirty weeks' trip beginning the following October. The first stand was at Stamford, Connecticut, but the route soon turned westward. Newspaper critics were liberal in their praise. At Detroit and Pittsburgh the notices were especially complimentary. To his repertoire Nye added a commencement day poem entitled, "The Autumn Leaves Is Falling":

> Lo! the autumn leaves is falling,
>   Falling here and there—
> Falling in the atmosphere
>   And likewise in the air.

with other verses for encores.

This poem was read, in the style of the sweet girl graduate, from a quire of foolscap paper secured by a wide, pale-blue satin ribbon. Nye wore the largest and loosest white cotton gloves he could find and made a picture of callow yet pretentious awkwardness.

About this time Eli Perkins (Melville D. Landon) published a large red book, "Kings of the Platform and Pulpit." According to him, "The most unique, humorous lecture of the century is being delivered by Mr. Nye and James Whitcomb Riley, the Hoosier poet." Mr. Landon took the trouble to get one complete lecture verbatim. I shall not take the space for it here but will try to give my readers an outline.

Nye opens the lecture with solemn and didactic mien. Says he:

> The earth is that body in the solar system which most of my hearers now reside upon, and which some of you, I regret to say, modestly desire to own and control, forgetting that the earth is the Lord's and the fullness thereof. Some men do not care who owns the world as long as they get the fullness.

Never for one moment deviating from his scientific manner, Nye proceeds for about fifteen minutes to give forth dry geographical and astronomical facts, interspersed just often enough with brilliant but apparently unconscious flashes of the utterly ridiculous.

About the time that the sides of his hearers begin to ache, the speech is brought to a climax, and Nye withdraws to make way for Riley.

The poet's first number is a familiar dialect poem, "Long Afore I Knowed Who Santy Claus Wuz." This he renders so exquisitely that his hearers' tears of laughter have become tinctured with softer sentiment, refreshing them in preparation for Nye's next sally.

The humorist has now exchanged the professor's stodgy manner for the school-boy's high voice and clumsy ways, as he tells the melodramatic story of little George Oswald, a tale such as we seldom encounter outside of McGuffey's school readers:

> One day, as George Oswald was going to his tasks, and while passing through the wood, he spied a tall man approaching in an opposite direction along the highway.
>
> "Ah," thought George, in a low mellow tone of voice, "whom have we here?"

The tall man of course turns out to be George's long lost father, who unclasping his shawl strap, presents the worthy youth with a large forty-cent watermelon, whereupon George, in gratitude, exclaims:

"Ah, this is indeed a glad surprise. Albeit, how can I ever repay you?"

Riley in his second selection presses the pathos stop a little harder in the poem of consumptive Jim, who "could git ever'thing but his breath."

Nye's next is not in character. He simply describes an incident in a Wisconsin sawmill in which the buzz-saw takes a chew of tobacco from a plug the sawyer carries in his pistol pocket and then begins on him. Nye doesn't know whether it was the nervous shock that killed him or the concussion of cold steel against his liver, but he allows that the moral of the tale is that if one must lean against something let it not be a buzz-saw when it moveth itself aright.

Now comes Riley with his sprightly "Me and Mary."

And then Nye tells his story of the boy who has carved the school desk, shames his father into paying the dollar's damage to avoid a flogging, takes the flogging, and keeps the dollar, later remarking that he favors a fine of five dollars instead of one dollar.

Riley's next is a short Civil War poem, and Nye's last

selection is the narrative of his cyclone experience. Riley
closes the show with "Good-bye, er Howdy-do."

Many were the tales Riley told in after years of the
happy happenings of his tours with Bill Nye. Would that
we could stop for more than two or three.

Nye's method of "stringing" people was entertaining always,
but never earned him the resentment of the people who were
the victims of it. One of the most artistic cases of this sort
I recall was the way he got revenge on a Chicago tailor. The
tailor did not know him when he went to order his suit, but he
did know from his style that he was from the country. He
told Mr. Nye just what kind of a suit he wanted, selected the
cloth and measured him with the assurance that this was a
beautiful fast color and would wear like iron. When Nye
paid him for the suit and asked that it be shipped to a way
station in Iowa the tailor was sure that he was right in the
mental measurement he had taken of his customer.

The suit arrived, neatly lined with farmer's satin. Day by
day its bright blue grew lighter and lighter, until, when we
arrived in Chicago six weeks later, it was a dingy dun color.
Nye remarked as the train pulled in that his first duty in that
city would be to go around and interview the merchant-liar.
He ambled back to the rear end of the shop, where he found
the man who sold him the garments. He shook hands with
him cordially, said he was glad to renew the pleasant acquaintance and asked if he knew what had caused the suit to change
its beautiful color, at the same time turning up the lapel of
the coat and showing the striking contrast between the original
and the present tint of the cloth.

"Why, man!" cried the tailor, bristling with defensive in-
dignation, "what in the world have you been doing to that
suit?"

"Well," replied Nye, in a tone of the meekest apology, "you
did not warn me, and I suppose it was my fault, and I ought to

have known better. But, since you insist, I'll tell you frankly what I did—I put it on and wore it right out in the sun!" The tailor saw the point and insisted upon making another suit.

Mr. Nye's sudden comments made in the midst of a lecture were often the means of bringing the house to its feet. He knew better than anybody his lack of physical ability to fill a large hall with his voice, and he strained every nerve to meet it. Any extraordinary commotion in the hall often disconcerted him, and he would wait until it subsided. I remember one occasion when we had a remarkably large hall, crowded to the walls. The entrance was at the further end, opposite the platform. Mr. Nye had barely started when the doors opened and a great fellow, about six feet two inches, entered and immediately fell into an altercation with an usher about his seats. Nye paused, and the altercation could be heard all over the house, this fellow arraigning the usher in a loud voice.

Nye replied with great composure. "In view of the great size of the hall," said he, "I must congratulate the audience upon the foresight of the managers in securing a speaker for each end."

Mr. Nye was a fatalist—not a complaining one, but a fatalist no less. He was pursued by a spirit of the perverse. Unexpected, trying things were always happening that seemed especially to test his patience. Indeed, I was sometimes jealous of him, for these things seemed to occur with greater force and persistence to him than to me. I had frequently remarked upon the recurrence of the number thirteen with me during one of our trips in the South, but this was one superstition at which Nye scoffed. He told me that at the next hotel we struck if I objected to being "incarcerated" in No. 13, he would risk it once.

Not long after I found myself registered for that fatal number; whereupon I promptly informed Mr. Nye that I should hold him to his promise. Nye declared he wanted to size up the room he had been assigned to, and went on down the hall with the landlord. He soon returned with the remark that he

could not lose much and walked into the thirteen room and set
his grip down, returning to where I waited in the hall outside.
He had not more than got out of the door when the heavy trans-
som fell to the floor with a crash.

Some years ago I visited Columbus, Ohio, where I met
Mr. Opha Moore, then secretary to the governor and long
a political factor in Ohio. Mr. Moore entertained me with
several anecdotes of my father's visits to that city.

Once when McKinley was chief executive of the State,
Nye, while sitting in the lobby of the Chittenden talking to
Moore, noticed a distinguished-looking gentleman come out
of the elevator, speak to Mr. Moore, and walk toward the
door. Nye asked Moore who his friend was. Moore told
him and, thinking Nye would like to meet McKinley, hurried after the governor and brought him back. There were
some Nyes in Washington County, more or less prominent
in politics, and as Moore introduced his friend simply as
"Mr. Nye," the governor, after a casual "Glad to know
you," turned and walked away.

Mr. McKinley's lack of interest evidently made an impression on Nye, for soon after, in a Sunday newspaper
article, he gently roasted the honorable governor. Here is
exactly what he wrote, if you'd like to have it first-hand:

> I shook hands with Governor McKinley at Columbus
> the other day and added him to my handsome and grow-
> ing list of eminent acquaintances. He looks more like a
> statesman than any other American I have been at all
> intimate with since the untimely death of Daniel Webster.
> Governor McKinley is an ideal statesman in appearance
> and bearing. His head is well shaped, his carriage is
> dignified and easy and his manner comfortable and re-
> fined. Gentleness and repose constitute the two great

> primary elements of the gentleman, and Governor Mc-
> Kinley has these.
>
>   The true gentleman does not like to make anybody feel
> uncomfortable. We did not talk long, as I am a very
> busy man and cannot pause in the great battle of life to
> visit with the various governors with whom I am thrown
> in contact, so we merely passed the time of day, and when
> I had taken in a good full breath to explain this to the
> governor I discovered that he had gone.

Moore called the governor's attention to the dig, forgetting for the moment McKinley's meager sense of humor.
Moore told me that the governor seemed rather hurt by the
reproof.

Columbus was an enthusiastic Nye town. A performance early in the season had been so successful that a return
engagement had been arranged. Nye, by way of introduction, was explaining that as this was the second show in the
same season, he would vary the program as much as possible. A late and perhaps convivial arrival proceeded to
make his declaration of independence down front over some
fancied wrong in the seating arrangements. Nye remained
perfectly quiet for several minutes while Mr. Newcomer
held the floor. When quiet was restored Nye announced:

"As I was saying, the program will be changed as much
as possible and one or two little novelties introduced."

Another time at Columbus the lecture was held at the
First Congregational Church. For some reason the church
was slow in opening, and a large part of the audience, as
well as Nye and Riley, were waiting outside when the janitor
finally unbolted one of the doors.

The pastor introduced the speakers and called attention
to the beautiful new edifice, especially announcing:

BILL NYE AND HIS MUSICAL "SUPPORT" OF 1890

Frank Downey, pianist; Ollie Torbett, violinist, and Gustave Thalberg, singer.

"When leaving the building you will find five commodious exits at the rear."

Nye saw his opening, and no sooner did he have the floor than he related how he and Riley, missing connections, had chartered a special train to Columbus so as not to disappoint their customers, had hurried into their glad rags without supper and rushed over to the church, only to be detained for some time in the street; and then, to cap the climax, the reverend doctor had said that whereas there was but one door by which to enter, there were five through which to escape.

When Nye and Riley came to a certain city in Pennsylvania my father was feeling low, and the chairman of the entertainment committee thought to cheer him up by saying:

"You will find this an unusually healthful city. The death-rate is only one a day."

Nye took the committeeman by the arm and hurriedly asked:

"Is he dead?"

"Dead!" ejaculated the committeeman. "Who dead?"

"Why, the man for to-day."

The committeeman stared.

"Isn't there a clerk or register or coroner, or something like that, of whom you could find out whether a man for to-day has died?" Nye continued.

"Why, yes, I suppose so," replied the committeeman.

"Would you be so good, then, as to find out, before I commence the lecture, whether the man is dead? If he is dead I am all right, for we are to leave the city early to-morrow morning; but if he is not dead, I cannot but feel uneasy about myself; I am not well to-night."

The naïve committeeman hurried away to get the information.

When Nye and Riley were in their room that night a bell-boy told Nye that a gentleman wished to see him. He went down into the parlor of the hotel and there met the committeeman.

"I am sorry to disturb you, Mr. Nye," he said, "but I could not find the information any earlier. It is all right. The death-rate I spoke of was only an average, and a man died this morning."

Augustus Thomas, while discussing the prevailing emptiness of New York theaters a few seasons ago, recalled a trip which Bill Nye and Riley made through Illinois. Nye's companion, looking through the peep-hole of a village theater curtain one night, remarked:

"Bill, the house is just about empty."

"I don't see why," replied Nye. "We've never been here before."

From their first appearance together in February, 1886, until January, 1890, the Nye-Riley combination, with interruptions due mostly to ill health, had marched steadily to bigger time, greater prosperity, and more enthusiastic audiences. Nye, who retained his Yankee shrewdness in making lecture contracts, was pulling down as high as a thousand dollars a week. And the tour was a mint for Major Pond. But the blessings were by no means unmixed. Nye knew that he was putting too great a strain upon his physique; and Riley, in the midst of plenty, became disheartened over the fact that in two lecture seasons he had written only two poems that satisfied him. Furthermore he had made a five-year contract in 1885 with another lecture agency at a time when he expected little from lecture receipts, and this agency was riding along on the contract, taking a large part of his earnings.

To add to his injured sensibilities this contract had been

turned over to Pond for a consideration, and Riley felt that he had been sold into slavery. These things depressed him greatly, and his depression and rebellion took the form of indulgence in his weakness, drink. Amos Walker had traveled much in the company of Riley, and his chief duty was to stand between Riley and the alluring demon. My father had been ill and had on several occasions been required to give the show alone. On one occasion, after leaving Riley at the hotel, he had come to the hall and was just explaining that his partner was indisposed and unable to participate when the audience broke into loud laughter. Nye turned around, and there was Riley making a heroic effort to look composed.

The climax came at Louisville, one night in January. The next day it was apparent that Riley would not be in condition to resume his speaking for a day or so, and Nye thought it best to terminate the tour and cancel all engagements. Riley surprised everyone by pulling himself together, and though he could not quite manage his evening-clothes he did appear that evening at the Masonic Temple in street dress.

In an interview Nye showed characteristic kindliness and forbearance. He voiced no resentment and spoke in praise of Riley's splendid qualities.

The Nye-Riley friendship lived on, but the Nye-Riley lecture combination was at an end, though in later years Riley gave ample evidence of his ability to come back. And Nye, in the six lecture seasons that remained to him, never found another team-mate who came near filling the place of the gentle Hoosier.

Many of the disappointed applicants for the Nye-Riley lecture wanted Nye even if Riley was not to be had, and so it was arranged to piece out the season with musical sup-

port instead of poetry, and the unfinished tour was resumed.
On February 14, 1890, Nye wrote his mother:

> I go tomorrow again to finish out my trip supported
> by a violinist, tenor and pianist, and hope to get through
> all right this time.

Perhaps you will be interested in a short notice from a
Winnipeg paper:

Edgar Wilson Nye, alias Bill Nye, made his début in Winnipeg last evening. His appearance at the Princess Opera House
was one of the most notable successes ever witnessed in Winnipeg. The program, which is brief, spicy, and sparkling, opened
with a piano solo by Mr. Frank Downey, a member of Mr. Nye's
capable company. Ollie Torbett exhibits skill on the violin.
The other member of the company—barring the "old man"
himself—is Mr. Gustave Thelberg, a Swedish gentleman, whose
clear, bell-toned voice will be remembered here for many long
days to come. Bill Nye's reception, as he appeared on the
stage to "interfere with an anecdote," was the signal for loud
applause. Before he had talked two minutes the only person
who was not laughing was Bill Nye.

From Winnipeg, in a letter to Bessie, he says:

> We seem quite near home now we have been so far
> away. We can get St. Paul papers only one day old
> so it is quite like getting back. I am tired of seeing "Bill
> Nye" in big red letters everywhere. It hurts my feel-
> ings actually to see it on the walls, it looks so much like
> "Eat H O" and "Use Castoria for the Breath."

Writing his mother on March 4, 1890, he said:

> Our new show goes very well, but I do not think I will
> do any more show business after this year. I hate it for

many reasons and want to stay at home more. Shall go through this year if I can and then quit.

Had a great ovation at Laramie and Cheyenne. Band out to meet me. Legislature adjourned and a reception at both places. It was very gratifying indeed.

To Cousin Clare he wrote:

I got a letter this A. M. from the Hoosier Poet [James Whitcomb Riley]. It was slightly dilatory in getting here but breathed the right spirit after all. He said all he "hed" was mine.

As the "we wifey" has wrote you no doubt, Sam Clemens, who used to write pieces for the paper, is coming over in a few days to stay some little time, also Joe Goodman, his old employer Joe has spent a few evenings in the joint company of A. Ward and Mark, and came on from California to see *me* and Mark together for a séance. I expect to take them along with Rastus to the Inn for a cold bite and a ride by diligence to the Woods of Arden and back again.

I am now getting up an Almanac for 1891 when the weather is not too by jolly hot. I think of making some pictures for it also and besides make some money out of it at the same time. Just got a letter from a San Francisco manager asking, nay begging, for 50 nights on the coast. He will no doubt come over to see me whilst East, and if I do negotiate with him, it will be with a view toward making a spring tour in 1891 along with Frances. I still hope to travel with her in some way, though the fates have been agin it so far. If I go, I will get a typewriter and make up a lecture of mere thoughts which I will read to one and all.

It is now time for the play entitled "A Midsummer

Night's Dream" with Miss Winnie Nye in the blood-curdling character of Bottom, and so I wipe my pen in my abundant hair and hastily jumping into me dress clothes I go to applaud and prespire.

That you may rapidly grow well and frolicsome and that you may have a green old age like your untootered Uncle is my prayer. We go to Church now most every Sabbath, in a carriage at my womern's expense and I am really getting so's I can address the Throne of Grace near enough like Bro Johnson [the rector] to fool most anybody.

Here is a letter from Mark Twain referring to the get-together with Nye:

Hartford, Apr. 17/90.

Dear William:

I am just your man! I expect Joe Goodman East before many weeks, & when he comes, we'll foregather, you & Riley & Joe & I, & just have an elegant time—a time that will beggar description, if that is the right literary phrase & sufficiently un-hackneyed; & if it ain't, we'll substitute a time that will cast a gloom over the whole community.   Yours ever,

MARK.

Bill Nye's Almanac for 1891 was a pamphlet of about thirty-two pages, published to sell for twenty-five cents. It contained a wealth of short remarks by the author, who was also the illustrator and the publisher. I regret that the experiment was not repeated. Here are a few samples of the contents:

You can be a good Christian with much less fatigue if you will take regular exercise, breathe through the nose and confess nobody's sins but your own. People who take in repentance and attend to it by the dozen for the neighborhood are apt to break down before they get round to their own.

Let us not despise them that hate us, for they neglect their own job in order that they may apprise us of our faults.

I hate to speak disrespectfully of a relative, but for a man with the chance he had, Adam seems to have won immediate recognition as the most gifted ass of his time.

On hearing that Uncle Mitchell was coming East in August my father wrote him:

Why do you so carefully and methodically select a time to come East when we will all be away from home? Do you do this because, as you state, your clothes are de trop, or is the true reason that you desire to evade me and my folks?

I have solemnly agreed with my absent wife and present daughters to go up on the West Shore R. R. on Saturday morning to join their mother, who is now 40 years of age and yet takes a strong interest in life, walks her little old mile a day and can thread her own needle without glasses.

In another month I shall be 40 years of age. Soon we will go into the tottering industry, will we not? Oh, let us then improve every moment given us this side of eternity to fit ourselves for that bright but slightly drafty home beyond the skies. Let us do all the good we can to to each and all, no matter how much we may hate it. Let us try to become more serious and dignified so that we may fit ourselves for the society of those pure, pious snivelers who claim to have filed on the most desirable real estate in the New Jerusalem and to practically own the town.

Let us avoid having any fun here so that finally when
we are called away to pick onto our harp, and also onto
those which got left and have to wail in hell indefinitely
because they didn't take the papers, we can give our
whole attention to it. Oh, what a sad and solemn enjoyment it will be to take our dinners and go out and sit on
the battlements and let our feet hang over whilst we
crochet a large tidy for the Throne of Grace and ever
and anon catch the odor of a singed unbeliever, or listen
to the muffled snort of some unsanctified gentleman who
has thoughtlessly sat down on Satan's punishment works.
The baby [Neddie] has been very sick indeed but though
not well yet is much better, so Fanny writes.

Yours as here 2. 4.

WM. VANDERBILT NYE.

A few days later my father wrote to his mother:

I have only time to write very briefly that Neddie died
yesterday morning at half past one. He grew steadily
worse for the last three or four days, suffering a good
deal, poor little fellow, but died very peacefully, worn
out by the disease. He looked toward the last much like
father and now as he lies in his little casket still reminds
us both of him. I believe they are together now, and
it is a comfort, just a drop of comfort, at this terrible
time to think it. It is no use to write more. I could not.
Neddie died from the results of grip and teething, together with the fact that he never had the proper nour-
ishment to make him able to resist disease.

Six months after the Louisville fiasco Riley had a strange
psychical experience. In the words of Edmund Eitel, his
nephew and literary executor, "It was at night; Riley could

not sleep and he arose with a feeling that he must write—
that he must express, in some way, the sympathy that he
felt for he knew not whom. And so the poem was written,
and, as was very unusual, set down quite rapidly, the entire
composition requiring less than half an hour. A few days
afterward news came that the child of his comrade, Edgar
Wilson Nye, was dead. Riley at once addressed the poem
to the bereaved parents, believing that he understood what
had prompted him to write it."

And here is what Riley wrote at the passing of little
Neddie (Edgar Winthrop Nye):

> Let me come in where you sit weeping, ay,
> Let me who have not any child to die
>   Weep with you for the little one, whose love
>   I have known nothing of.
>
> The little arms that slowly, slowly loosed
> Their pressure round your neck—the arms that used
>   To kiss—such arms, such hands, I never knew.
>   May I not weep with you?
>
> Fain would I be of service, say something
> Between the tears, that would be comforting.
>   But oh! So sadder than yourselves am I
>   Who have no child to die.

During the last five years that Nye lived he saw Riley
infrequently. They wrote to each other occasionally, their
letters giving evidence of the comradeship of other days.
But they lived a thousand miles apart and so had less to
say to one another.

As I near the close of this chapter in the life of Bill Nye,
and there passes in review the fellowship between him and

Riley, my eyes dim at the contemplation of their attachment.

Great was the fund of qualities they had in common, and greater still their dissimilarity. Both men were self-made and mainly self-educated products of the prairies; Riley in Indiana, Nye in Wisconsin. The open-sesame of each was his unlost touch, elbow to elbow, shoulder to shoulder, with nineteenth-century America. No other place or time could have produced either. Social ambition would have wrecked their democracy.

Only the keenest sensitiveness enabled them to grasp and delineate the subtle trivialities which they immortalized. Little of what they wrote was beyond the comprehension and delight of the humble. Others could see what they described after it was done, and could laugh or sigh with relish. But who else has set down, or can record, the homely little things in just the manner of their penning?

With all their unfeigned diffidence, they battled on against odds of health and temperament, spurred ever to wrestle with the world, by that unconquerable urge to write their piece and speak it. Here were manly spirits fighting a courageous fight. Occasionally they faltered, but only to regain their breath that they might press on.

For four years, through hundreds of performances and tens of thousands of miles of travel and travail, they remained fast friends, unenvious, admiring, brotherly. And when their parting had to come, they separated without bitterness or fault-finding, too big not to understand, too kind not to forgive, too steel-true not to go right on with the same old-time affection for each other.

Verily Mark Twain found happy similes in the Siamese Twins, in dynamo and motor. Nye's mental processes took in an extraordinary area. His association of ideas covered the widest range. A suggestion to him brought thoughts of many things—some logical, a few grotesque, and therefore mirth-provoking. He was encouraged to pursue incongruous ideas. His ingenuity, always within easy reach, became second nature. He hated monotony. He spurned second-hand thoughts.

Riley's art lay more in the sympathetic interpretation of what a keen observer saw. Riley's poems were retouched photographs with delicate decorations. Nye's "articles" were word cartoons. Riley's verse stands near the top of our country's poetry for the many qualities that make it individual. His writings will live long.

What Nye wrote was Bill Nye's own, differing from the product of all other pens. What Riley painted with his pen or pencil was nineteenth-century Indiana set to music. When Bill Nye spoke there was nothing reminiscent of any one else. Right or wrong, pleasing or otherwise, Nye was Nye. He never became anything but Nye; while Riley, consummate actor that he was, forgot himself to live any one of the parts in which he cast himself.

They are both gone. Will the place of Bill Nye ever be filled? For thirty years the arrival of his successor has been awaited. Even were Bill Nye to live again in the twentieth century, he would not be Bill Nye but some one else. No less is true of Riley. With Riley has passed the Indiana of Little Orphan Annie and the Raggedy Man. The Little Mammoth Lecture Stand is a fading memory. But the world will not soon forget that these two kindly, tender-hearted boys, in loving their fellows, loved each other and lived a partnership that will be an inspiration to all who value friends and wish to keep them.

On February 10, 1891, Nye wrote to his mother:

> This P. M. we go to the Wiman wedding [Erastus
> Wiman was a friend and neighbor] at Christ Church,
> and this evening I am the guest of the Alumni of N. Y.
> University Medical Department at Delmonico's. Speech.
> Have got so I can do it all very comfortably with no in-
> digestion, worry or head the next day.
>
> We shall be glad to leave this raw coast for a time at
> least. Business is good, and if nothing happens we will
> have a better balance at the end of our next year than the
> past one.

With the coming of 1891 my parents made up their minds
that the New York climate was not good for the children.
Neddie's death and other cases of illness had cast shadows
of gloom over the otherwise happy household. The management of the "World" was approached, and arrangements for syndicating his writings were made, giving Nye
entire freedom in the matter of his residence, so long as
he continued to do his stuff once a week. So what more
natural than to engage a cottage near Asheville?

In a letter of February 3, 1891, Edgar tells his mother
the news and for once points with pride to the growing
signs of his recognition:

> We shall hope to get South by the 5th of March, the
> family going to Skyland Springs and I to Texas and
> so on to do my lecture month.
>
> Have been rather "doing" New York this season, as I
> shall very likely never have a winter here entire, again.
> I've attended a number of dinners, especially of the big
> official kind, at the Lotos Club and Delmonico's, making

the acquaintance of men of whom I have long heard. Wasn't it singular that I should never have met Mr. Windom till the night of his tragic death? I had a long and pleasant chat with him just before he went into his last dinner. This sounds, I know, like the expression Uncle Steve used to make about being there when the first horse was hitched on.

The picture is forever photographed on my mind; the beautiful decorations, the quiet banquet hall, the waltz of the orchestra between courses and speeches, the intellect of the Union, both Republican and Democratic, 250 well known financiers, together worth a billion or more, the impressive speech and elegant voice of the speaker, the rumble of applause, the smile of triumph, followed by the stare and pallor of Death.

Two evenings later in the same room we dined Stanley and I sat at the fatal table, being one of the speakers. I made quite a hit, to be modest about it, and this moment got a very enthusiastic letter from Mr. Gilder, Editor of the "Century," who was present, asking me for the speech if it had not already been engaged. How's that for *the* acknowledged literary authority of the "Century"? He in a recent speech referred to me as one of the pronounced literary successes of the time and *got applauded* for saying it too.

I have an article in a coming number of the "Century" called "The Autobiography of a Justice of the Peace."

I go this P. M. to Wilmington, Del., for a show along with my Musical Co. which I had in Minneapolis. Glad Frank starts off so bully under the new dispensation and *know* he will never care to monkey with politics again unless it's when he is fat and old and rich and goes to the U. S. Senate.

Early in March, 1891, the last things were packed, and the Nye family, after coming East in two jumps from Wyoming, and staying a few years in both Wisconsin and New York, had turned south to spend five short but happy years together in the Land of the Sky.

BOOK FIVE

CHAPTER XIX

WHEN NYELAND WAS SKYLAND: 1891

WHILE my mother was settling five-sixths of the Nye family at Skyland, the other and very important sixth was completing another lecture swing, this time under the management of H. B. Thearle of Chicago. His new companion was Alfred P. Burbank, whom Thearle termed "The Foremost Entertainer." Under his picture on the circular was the legend: "The beams of song, the blaze of eloquence." This was in the heyday of *elocution*. In the present blasé era it is amusing to look back and read the showman's blurb descriptive of Professor Burbank.

My father must have had a quiet smile when he read of the "difficulties of elocution as a science" and saw his partner referred to as the "Shakespeare of vocal expression." Nevertheless the almost uniformly enthusiastic press-notices show that Burbank was much more than a foil and counter-irritant for Nye.

Like Nye's caricatures, Burbank was spare and bald, while Nye had put on considerable weight since McDougall had first trade-marked his face and figure in the newspaper drawings. As Burbank broke the ice, it was not uncommon for audiences to mistake him for Nye. On such occasions, Burbank modestly disclaimed the applause which greeted him and explained:

"I am not Mr. Nye. I'm the other fellow."

Nye could hardly wait for his lecturing to be over so that

he could join the family in Skyland. On May 6 he had
filled his last engagement and was en route home, and writing to his mother he said:

> In an hour I start for North Carolina but will stop off
> at Lexington, Ky., to look at a team which I have heard
> tell of as a bargain. We cannot have much fun at Sky-
> land except to be out of doors. Riding will have to be
> our principal dissipation. I have heard of a good
> matched team that is afraid of nothing at all. If I am
> not deceived, they are what we need. I dread fooling
> with the matter though, for I am *not* a hoss man.
>
> Mr. Burbank and I closed with glory and reasonable
> financial success at Detroit on Monday evening, he going
> direct to England. I went out with him on an agreed
> price which made it safer and even more profitable than
> my arrangement with Pond.
>
> I have an offer for next year of twenty weeks at the
> same or a little better rate. I will talk it over with the
> family and decide next week.
>
> Have just bought at Columbus a yaller surrey and set
> of russet harness for the country-side. It looks real swell
> and I am hoping that there will be no runaway with it.
> [There had been an accident of this kind at Staten
> Island.] Bess rides splendidly. So does Max.

Skyland is a station on the Southern Railway about seven
miles south of Asheville. My first recollections of North
Carolina center about a cottage near Bonnycrest Inn, where
we spent the spring and summer of 1891. I can well understand why my parents were so happy when my dad's chores
could be arranged so that we might live in the Land of the
Sky. The improvement in the health of the whole family
was immediate.

Thirty-five years ago the Land of the Sky had just begun to attract general notice. Last summer I visited it again after an absence of twenty-seven years to find that a facetious prophecy of my father's, made in 1891, had been fulfilled almost literally:

> The time is coming when every hill in Buncombe County will have a hotel on it, and lots may be bought as far back as Sandy Mush.

Nye's best description of Skyland is contained in a letter to the "World" written on one of those rare June days:

> Buncombe County—which may also properly be spelled Bunkum—is a large and beautiful county on the French Broad and Swananoa Rivers, with Asheville as the county seat. The name itself first gave rise to the expression "Talking for Buncombe," which is now a classic.
>
> Buncombe County has an all-purpose climate that cannot be beaten in the world.
>
> Skyland is a small but growing place, containing thirty-seven inhabitants and eight head of horses. It is quiet here at present, owing to shrinkage in values at the large money centers, but this, it is thought by our best minds down at the store, cannot last long.
>
> My house is rather a heavy set cottage and is made from the trees which grew where the house now stands. It faces towards a little brawling stream called Croup Creek. I call my place the Skyland Thought Works. Skyland has an inexhaustible water supply, consisting of Croup Creek and a couple of patent wooden pails on which bonds have been issued bearing a low rate of interest.
>
> George Vanderbilt's extensive grounds command a

fine view of my place. I was over there yesterday to see
how the work on his new home was progressing. From
the foundations of his prospective mansion one can see
for miles up the beautiful French Broad River, and the
smoky tops of the soft, blue mountains make a magnificent picture of gentleness and repose.

It is a pleasant sight to drive over there on a quiet
morning, when the thrush is singing in the persimmon
branches, to see Mr. Vanderbilt, with a little leather boot-
leg bag of shingle nails tied around his waist, laying
shingles on an outbuilding which he proposes to use as a
chicken-house; or possibly, wearing a pair of lime-spat-
tered boots and finishing out a chimney as he cheerily calls
for "More mort." He likes to be busy, he says. "Duty
done is the soul's fireside," he remarked to me yesterday,
as he put a lot of nice fresh liniment on his thumb and
showed me where a pretty little pink nail was sprouting
over the ruins of the other one.

Mr. Vanderbilt will have one of the most extensive and
beautiful homes in the world. One reason I have not finished my place is that I want to see what George does,
and thus get the advantage of his experience. He does
not mind that, he says.

A railroad running from Biltmore, on the main line, to
Mr. Vanderbilt's place is owned by him, and is used solely
for conveying building material and salaries to the men.
It is called the Vanderbilt system. And yet my grounds,
especially on Monday, present, I think, a more cheerful
appearance than his'n. I often tell him that when our
folks are rinsing out their white clothes in the second
water, and placing my new parboiled shirts on the lawn
to bleach, I know of no landscape gardener who can begin
to get such effects as we do.

On June 4 Nye wrote A. J. Mitchell of the joys of Skyland and of a shake-up on the "World":

> Dear Brother-in-Lor:
> I am now sitting on the porch and the pure breeze is tossing my locks about and toying with them in a lascivious manner. The sky is clear and blue, the birds are twittering in the contiguous trees, far away we can see the blue dome of Pisgah and the velvety slopes of Busbee.
> Berries are a burden now at 5 cents per quart—real quarts. We measure them ourselves, and they are picked over and hulled and are so sweet and wild and sylvan and slick and the price suits us so well that we are almost happy. We got half a lamb the other day for $1.12, which makes the Staten Island meat bills look like the Andes in the distance. Of course, humanity is slow, and poor, and shiftless, and very aggravating, but good natured and fairly honest too.
> Cockerill wrote me yesterday that he now owns the "Commercial-Advertiser" and the plant of the "Star," which was afterward the "Continent." He wants my Sunday letter and I am inclined to transfer it to him. I have written him today what I will do and believe that I can help Cockerill and help myself too by taking in the "Brooklyn Eagle," Cockerill's paper and the "Post Despatch," where now the "World" has the monopoly. McDougall, the artist, is going to leave.

The Fourth of July had always been a major holiday in the Nye household. We were in the South now, where ordinarily Independence day is not so noisily observed. But my father imported some fireworks and celebrated the Glorious Fourth in his accustomed style. This letter written on July 5, 1891, gives the harrowing details:

We live in the bosom of nature here, so I thought it would be a good scheme to celebrate the Fourth in an abstemious, yet highly luminous manner. Ignoring the sparkling domestic wines of the hill country, made from the large early yellow dent corn grown upon the suspensory farms of Buncombe County, I decided to purchase a few choice fireworks direct from the factory. After touching lightly on the beauties of American freedom, reading the Declaration of Independence and an opening prayer, in which the national policy for the coming year might be briefly laid before the Throne of Grace, I allowed to set off at eventide about eight dollars worth of pyrotechnics, which would furnish a fitting close to the day's celebration.

It was generally understood as far away as Upper Hominy and Sandy Mush that on the evening of the Fourth I would let off over 200 pieces of pyrotechny, including a part of my thumb.

It was a gala day for Skyland. The fireworks had come, and some friends from Asheville brought a lemon with them. We spread the buffalo robe on the grass, and a table was brought out for the speaker. For convenience I divided up the exercises of the day into two parts, viz.: Part I, morning exercises at the grove; Part II, evening exercises, also at the grove.

In speaking of the grove I do so more for devilment than anything else, for this end of the State is all grove, being a virgin wilderness against which the tongue of scandal has never breathed the breath of the deadly upas tree, nor bigot forged a chain.

The morning exercises consisted of the usual selections—"America" on the organette, accompanied by child

voices; reading of the Declaration of Independence and
a few selections from the proceedings of the Tennessee
Legislature; complimentary prayer by the chaplain;
singing of "Red, White and Blue" by a man from States-
ville; piece on the melodeon, entitled "Pee-Wee Bird
Waltz," by a young woman from a distance who is visiting
North Carolina, and who was left at Busbee Station by
the train while gathering golden rod; address by me
touching on "The Growth, Progress and Final Plunk
of Nations."

There is hardly room here for more than a résumé of
the address, for it was long, covering, as it did, the history of man and the evolution of Government from the
feudal ages, and even back of that, extending through
barbaric centuries, and so on down to the present time,
when National and State government becomes not only
a duty but a pleasure.

The speaker touched with great power and feeling upon
our duty as citizens, owing it as we do, he went on to say,
to ourselves and our posterity to suitably prepare minds
and hearts by early education and association for the
great duties of citizenship, and both by our precept and
our practice so to live that we may safely leave the mere
act of voting to other heads. The speaker said also that
to the newly arrived citizen voting is a new and thrilling
experience. Why not allow him more of it to do, while
we who have the taxes to pay, and who therefore need
rest and change of scene, may safely take much needed
relaxation on election day, and if we do not like the result
we can write a piece for the paper signed "Taxpayer,"
and marked on the top "(communicated)."

This was followed by applause, which, on being looked

up, turned out to come from the wife of the speaker, who had been huckleberrying, and, hearing a noise in the direction of the speaker's stand, had drifted around that way and, having met the audience before, shook hands with him and sat down to hear the address.

We opened the evening with song. I sang a selection from "Il Trovatore," accompanying myself on the xylophone, that pleading and almost human instrument. I touched off a bunch of firecrackers in order to seat the audience, and then let off a Roman candle, the breech-pin of which blew out, sending eight beautiful variegated balls up my sleeves.

I next sang a song entitled "Sparkling and bright in its liquid light is the water in our glasses. 'Twill give you health, 'twill give you wealth, ye lads and rosy lasses."

After this came a mine which the catalogue said would spout gold and silver showers, interspersed with red, blue, yellow and green meteors. This mine was a non-dividend declaring mine, like one that I partly owned in Wyoming. If I had owned it entirely I would have been a poor man to-day, but I only owned a little of it, and so I have no reason to complain.

The pyrotechnic mine, however, acted as it might if it had got wet in some way, so we dried it out near the stove this morning.

It did not look so well when it went off as it would if it had been at night, but it lit up the little plain kitchen, and made it look almost like a fairy palace.

We then had some more Roman candles. I can readily see that the Romans as a people could not have enjoyed reading much by candlelight if these things sputtered then as they do now, and I can see why the Roman nation

thus got behind and lost their power. The Greeks, also,
were not practical. Who could enjoy an evening clustered about a Greek fireside?

The summer of 1891 was employed in strenuous resting
and loafing and included much exploration of back roads
and mountain streams. The Skyland cottage was a temporary resting-place, and Nye was beginning to think of a
home built to his order, a place with a view of the mountains and a house big enough to be always open to relatives and friends; every one in fact who felt sufficiently
drawn to exchange the inconveniences of travel for a visit
with the Nyes.

The neighbors were friendly and congenial, and their
Southern hospitality and hearty welcome to all of us had not
a little to do with the growing conviction in the mind of each
Nye that we were here for keeps. At last Edgar had found
that land of peace and plenty, in search of which his father
and mother had set out forty years before.

The prospect of the new home gave Nye additional in-
centive to sign up for another lecture season with Burbank,
that he might lay aside the necessary means for defraying
the cost. There was an excellent school for my sisters at
Asheville, and Mrs. Glaser conducted a "select boarding
place for paying guests" in the near-by city called Mountain
Cottage, which would answer for my mother and the boys
during the winter.

"The Village Postmaster," Nye's play, which had languished in the small towns of Illinois several years before,
and in due time had been buried, was being disinterred by
Nye's friend, Stuart Robson, and was to be produced under
the name of "The Cadi" at the Union Square Theater in
New York in September. Thomas Q. Seabrook was cast

for the Bill Nye part. A few days before the opening my
father wrote from the Hotel Imperial, New York City:

My Dear Family:

We are all 'stablished here at this nice new tavern
where gas is burning in well nigh every room in the house.
We like it real well. Our meals are cooked for us whilst
we wait and we can have most anything that we can pay
for.

Times seem to be good in New York and there is a
good deal of gaiety. I could hear people talking and
setting up till after 11 o'clock last night. It is noisier
than what Fletchers is. We found Mr. Floyd, [manager
of "The Cadi"], wife and baby here, and Mr. Robson
just came a little while ago.

Prospects are good so far as we know for the play,
though I am quite unnerved as I may say.

Be good children and do not fool with the wrong end
of the Donkey.

PAPA NYE.

P.S.—There is not much here that is really good 'cept
my play.

Last evening I made a *Hit!!!* at the Fellowcraft Club.
I spoke along with Thos. C. Platt and Bourke Cochran
and the prest., Chester I. Lord, said I made the speech
of the evening.

Today I sent in the second article for the 35 Century
Magazine.

I got off a good joke this morning—kind of comical I
thought. Speaking of Gould bursting into tears as he
did the other day at a Board Meeting I said kind of
careless like and—dry. I says, "Strikes me it's only a
new way he's got of watering his talk"—see?

Kind of comical I thought! Wasn't it?

Kiss the dear ones each and all. Bless their delightful little hearts and gizzards, how I would like to lay hold of them.

Your proud and old Reliable
UNCLE.

Nye warned the public of the coming production of "The Cadi":

I take pleasure in announcing that on the 21st of September, at the Union Square Theater in this city, "The Cadi," a play, will be produced with a disregard for expense, which would be perfectly appalling to me if I had to furnish the money for it myself.

The play is practically a chapter from my own experience as a Justice of the Peace on the frontier, and will therefore be of great interest to those who feel a great interest in things of that kind.

Yours truly,
BILL NYE.

P.S. (confidential)—I wrote the piece myself.

B. N.

The program was not without its Nyesque touches:

The interior decorations of the woolsack used in this piece are supplied by Messrs. Spangel & Wetherby, ranchers and sheep growers of Power Creek, Wyoming.

The watermelon used in Act III is from the farm of Mr. Joseph Jefferson in Louisiana. It was also arranged and adapted for this play by Mr. Jefferson.

The quarrel scene in the second act was submitted to Mr. Booth, who says that it does not in any way encroach upon the rights of Mr. Shakespeare.

The mailbags used in the second and third acts were furnished by Mr. John Wanamaker, author of the "Red Figure Sale."

The noise in the third act is furnished by the Manhattan Elevated Company, who created the part.

The piano used is from the well-established house of Weber & Co. It was brought to the theater by Mr. Claude McGuire of Avenue A, who moves pianos, bric-à-brac, mirrors, previous questions, china, glassware and adjournments.

On the whole the critics were kind. Nym Crinkle's review was encouraging, both to Nye and Seabrooke. And so was his editor, who placed at the head of the column:

Triumph of "The Cadi"

After all is said, Mr. Bill Nye has unwittingly achieved one of the most remarkable stage triumphs that I have seen. He has put Bill Nye upon the boards without plot, passion, story or dramatic interest, and he has stayed there by virtue of the uniqueness and quaintness of Bill Nye. Two or three times I have sauntered into the Union Square Theater and sat there, feeling a warm glow of humor spreading through me that disarmed my judgment and melted my critical mood like wax. It did not take me long to find out who and what it was had saved Mr. Nye.

It was Mr. Seabrooke.

His is the personality and his is the talent that have got into the heart of the quaintness and made it radiate itself through three acts of colloquial and undramatic pleasantry.

"The Cadi" ran for 125 nights at the Union Square Theater and then went on the road. Its success was not startling but encouraged Nye to try his hand again four years later.

There were more lecture engagements with Burbank to be kept that fall. November found the two men in St. Louis. On the twenty-second Nye wrote Cousin Clara Mitchell:

All unwittingly you have helped me to draw off a piece for the paper to-day, for a page of your letter was gently but firmly appropriated whilst yet your back was turned.

The Eternal Verities gave me a chance and so I sort of hitched up your prancing thinker even as Gustav [the coachman] would have done with the spirited and high bred Kentucky brutes, and they sailed away, yours and mine, into the great "pahster" of Thought—.

Gosh but it is a funny letter! I don't know when I have pointed to myself with such pardonable pride.

Sol Smith Russel (Dog on that pen) just came. He is the same sweet old lady with the mellow voice and says, "You're going to have a good night for yer tinktum, ain't ye?" That's what he calls our show. Poor Billy Flounce who served the public so nobly and so well, and who had more *good* solid friends than most anybody, was it not sad for him to die in a hotel in America while his wife lived at another in London? That is what it is to be the hired man of that jealous and unmerciful mistress the Public! Damn the public, curse it, I say, a plague upon its approval and its disapproval!

I hope this finds you well and happy as you deserve to be. Continue to love your parents and your Uncle and his folks, and your life will be a song—a prelude to the great chorus that sings and flaps its great 9-foot wings around the throne accompanied by the New Jerusalem String Band! Won't it be nice?

Your proud and complaisant
UNCLE.

One of the newspaper critics compared Nye and Sol Smith Russell. Said he:

In each the gift of humor is so evident that they have only to walk awkwardly down to the footlights, smile ever so little or not at all, and say a word or two, to make a reserved audience good-natured and an impulsive one hilarious.

Nye's jinx hadn't smitten him for quite a spell. The cyclones had passed him by, runaways had not mussed him up, and he was about due for another encounter with unkind fate. It happened at Yazoo City, Mississippi, on November 28. The next day he dictated a letter to Mr. Burbank for my mother:

My Dear Wife:

I have just wired you a few words regarding the accident last evening. I did this in the fear that reports might creep into the press somewhere which would alarm you.

The circumstances were about as follows. While Mr. Burbank was opening the program I went to the back door of the dressing room expecting to step outside on the landing and stairs, both of which it seems had been recently removed. As a result I fell like the author of "Beautiful Snow," only that I lit harder on a pile of scantling studded with rusty nails. I suppose that I was unconscious for a few moments; then I groped my way back to the front of the Opera House or Rink, and Mr. Conable notified Mr. Burbank, who announced the accident from the stage in a highly artistic and pathetic manner.

A physician of the saddle-bag variety was summoned

from the audience. He found no fracture, though he said that the wrist was severely sprained.

We traveled all night in order to get better medical advice, and a thoroughly competent New Orleans physician found at once that both bones of the right arm were broken near the wrist. To-day they have been set, however, and we hope to finish our trip as planned. I am as comfortable as I could be under the circumstances and very fortunate in having considerate friends about, one of whom is now acting as my "Private Secretary."

Yours "Yost de sem."

EDGAR.

The "opera house" where the accident happened had been advertised as a "New and Improved Skating Rink." The first thing Nye said after recovering his speech was, "This rink is not improved *enough*." The following Monday Nye appeared in New Orleans. Explaining to the audience the accident to his upper anatomy, and making a wide sweeping movement with his right toe, he said, "Under the circumstances I shall confine my gestures to my feet."

Of course his weekly letters had to be kept up. And, by the way, through sickness and health, accidents and shipwreck, he never disappointed his publishers or the public. His last article, written before his final illness, appeared just after his death.

By keeping five or six weeks ahead of the printer he had a margin of safety. While his right arm was in splints the surplus stock was exhausted, and he got down to his last manuscript, but managed to train his left arm for writing just in time to meet the emergency. His managers, both editors and showmen, knew that Bill Nye could be counted

on to his physical limit, and far beyond the physical limi-
tations of many performers.   He could and did take a great
deal of punishment.   There is not a doubt that he short-
ened his life by the hot pace he set himself.

The accident that followed was not serious, but it created
an amusing situation:

I got up at 2:30 A.M. yesterday.   Early rising and an
illy lighted (this word I got at a fall opening in Chicago)
stairway threw me at Benton Harbor and injured my
ankle so that I could not get to the depot without assistance.   At that hour it was impossible to get a horse, for
the city was yet young, like the newborn day itself.   The
clerk tried to rouse every or any livery stable in town,
but he could not.

Meanwhile I lay moaning in the arms of an attendant.
The train would be due in eight minutes.   What to do?
Anon I heard a dull thud as the clerk broke in the door
of a blacksmith shop and pulled out a piano box buggy
valued at $18.50.

Hastily placing me in this with the aid of my attendant
and valet, he started on a run for the station, neighing
joyously as he met a team that he recognized.   In a trice,
or possibly a trice and a half, we were there.   I was taken
out and placed in a berth, where I moaned the balance
of the night away; but I cannot be too grateful to the
clerk of the hotel at Benton Harbor, where this melan-
choly accident occurred, for he showed tact, ability and
kindness, to say nothing of the fact that I found him to
be thoroughly gentle and a good roadster.

As he left us I wrang his hand two times (for ice water),
and, turning away my head so that he could not see my
tears, I presented him with my autograph.   When I get

| home I shall send him a nice new red fly net for next summer. |

Four days after Christmas, 1891, a banquet was tendered to Asheville's new son by thirty of her leading citizens. In part the affair was reported by the "Asheville Citizen" as follows:

Regular Bill Nye climate. The discomforts of the blustering gale and nipping sleet were at once dispelled by the cheery welcome that prevailed within.

The arrival of the guest of the evening was supplemented by the appearance of another widely known humorist, "Our Zeb," the talented Senator Vance.

The committee soon had these worthies on terms of neighborly intercourse.

My. Nye spoke of the various kinds of humor, referring to the close relationship between American humor and pathos. "There is only the finest kind of a line separating them," said he.

Mr. Nye's speech was made up almost exclusively of stories, told in his inimitable way, and the audience wept with laughter.

Senator Vance said that he was glad to welcome Mr. Nye to Western North Carolina, and hoped he would be received into fellowship—not like the servant girl, who joined the church, and when asked by her mistress if she had joined replied, "Not plumb jined—they just tuck me in on suspicion." He hoped Mr. Nye would not be taken in on suspicion, but that the people would get all his money they could, drink all his liquor that was offered, give him all the advice possible, and say to him, "I told you so," if he should make a mistake—this was the ordinary way in which humanity received their fellows.

CHAPTER XX

BILL NYE TROOPS WITH BURBANK AND BUILDS
BUCK SHOALS: 1892

No one can read much of Nye in the late eighties and early nineties without realizing what an incubus the lecture grind had become. His family had exhausted its vocabulary trying to persuade him to give up public appearances. His doctors had forbidden him to continue. He had never recovered from his first attack of cerebrospinal meningitis, and the wonder was that he had regained sufficient strength for sustained effort. But the uncertainty of his health was the very reason for his working so hard.

During the latter years, my father's chief object in life was to provide adequately for the family so that after he had gone we should not suffer. He had been warned repeatedly that he was traveling on his nerve and that a collapse could be expected any moment. It came, in part, in 1892. He had given up hope of again being robust or of freeing himself from the excruciating headaches which were attacking him with increasing frequency and violence. Time after time he was only able to keep lecture engagements by calling upon local doctors for emergency aid. Bromide was used frequently, and morphine was prescribed. Nye had a horror of becoming a morphine addict and usually refused to yield, even when it was prescribed by the doctor. Contrary to the impression given by his own writings, Nye was not easy-going, lazy, or self-indulgent. The high principles of his parents, his New England background, the severe discipline of his boyhood on the farm, and his own inborn strength of will—all of these influences combined to combat the slackness and Bohemianism which his literary pursuits and itinerant life held out to him.

Nye wrote a great deal about drinking. Even in preprohibition days a reference to liquor was usually good for a laugh. My father was not a total abstainer, save occasionally when the family doctor banned the stuff for the time being. Neither was he a heavy drinker. He enjoyed an occasional or several occasional glasses with his friends, rarely alone. The most imbibing indulged in by him was just before he left Staten Island. His friends in New York were numerous and their entertainments frequent and convivial. He found it difficult to avoid many private and public dinners which he would have preferred to forego. And on such occasions he felt called upon to be a "good fellow." The whole subject was summed up by Nye when he said: "I positively refuse to fill a drunkard's grave. If drunkards want their graves filled they will have to do it themselves."

My father was wise enough to know that even Staten Island was too near to temptation; temptation not alone to eat and drink more than was good for him, but to spend his time and energy in unproductive social doings. There were too many persuasive hosts who wanted the magnetism of his presence at their tables. These thoughts, as well as the family's health were in his mind when the move to North Carolina was undertaken.

The summer at Skyland had afforded opportunity to pick the site for the new Nye home. The country-side had been combed for the ideal spot. Buck Shoals was finally chosen, and a farm of about one hundred acres was purchased on the east side of the French Broad River near

Fanning's Bridge. Above this point the historic river had been made navigable for several miles. The farm, purchased from a good friend and neighbor, Dr. Fletcher, was within a bend of the river, with Buck Shoals roaring in the distance. The site chosen for the house was near the top of a hill a scant half-mile from the river and commanding a magnificent view down the valley and of the mountain range in the west. The eye had to scrutinize the landscape with care to pick up any habitation of man. There were numerous trees upon the hill, many of which were cut down to make room for a large frame house.

This spot was nearly four miles from the main road connecting Asheville and Hendersonville, now an excellent concrete highway and one of the most heavily traveled in the South. In 1892 this turnpike was paved with good intentions and bright red clay, which in the rainy season had the consistency of underdone molasses candy. A considerable length of private road had to be built to connect Buck Shoals with the main road via a back road which entered the highway near the Arden station. There was a small cottage at the foot of Buck Shoals Hill. Here J. T. Mize, with his wife "Eller," was established to help with the construction of the roads, the clearing of woods and underbrush, and the cultivation of Nye's red clay "upright farm." J. B. Lance and Sam Fraidy assisted with this work, and later Jim Pinner was installed as gardener. More of them later.

The house was designed by an Asheville architect named Wills, perhaps too actively assisted by my mother. It was a large clapboard and shingle structure with a tower, porte-cochère, several porches, balconies and other impedimenta. The main floor included a large entrance hall, a drawing-room, dining-room and library. The second floor had a nursery, my mother's room, father's room and three guest-chambers.

While waiting for the completion of the house, we rented what was known as the Fanny Blake place near the main road at Fletchers, Fletchers or Fletcher being the station south of Arden on the Southern Railway.

Before close attention could be given to the work going forward at Buck Shoals there was another circuit of lecturing to be rounded with Burbank. It was at about this time that my father had an encounter with Herrmann the Great. This is the way Nye told the story:

> I met Herrmann in Tiffin, O. We played against each other. We stopped at the same hotel. He asked me to sit at his table. I said I did not mind doing so if he would not play any tricks on me. He said he would not. Before we got half through the meal he begged my pardon—he is a very polite man—and said there was some foreign substance in my lettuce. I said doubtless. There always is foreign substance in lettuce, but I could not ignore the fact that there was indeed a diamond ring. I looked it over with a sigh and gave it to the waiter girl. Everything that one finds that way he should return. If I were to go to that house again I would get two pieces of pie and a hearty welcome.

Herrmann admitted later that he had considerable difficulty reclaiming the diamond ring.

On February 5 Nye wrote to his mother, and of his new ranch he said:

> It is an oblique farm with a fender on the lower edge to keep the potatoes from falling into George Vanderbilt's farm, which is below me on the French Broad River.

Nicknames were plentiful in the Nye household. He who only had two or three to bless himself with was ill provided. We usually called the Governor "Papa," with the accent on the first syllable. "Tod" and "Todsie" were frequently resorted to. My mother was "Mama," "Mollie," "Catalpa," or "Mumchie." Bessie answered to "Bess," "Becky," "Fet," and "Robbie Burstyourbuttons Shinkatank." You will notice the variety of salutations (and for that matter, of signatures) employed by my father in writing to Uncle Mitchell: "Jake," "Birdie Grubb," and others too numerous to mention. You may have observed that some of my dad's most amusing letters were written to Uncle Mitchell. The two had much in common beside having married sisters. Both were Middle-Westerners of New England origin. Uncle Mitchell had a twinkle in his keen old eyes that invited wit. He was a rare listener, and when he spoke he made you think of Mark Twain. In Nye's letter of February 13, 1892, to Uncle Mitchell he couldn't conceal his eagerness to "jump the bars of the lecture field."

My Dear Jackson:

Sometimes I almost wish I was once more again busted but pure. Wealth brings its cares, I find. Gould tells me it is so with him. His victuals don't always agree with him, he says, and he almost wished he was surveying again up in Delaware County.

We go along at a big rate and play to the capacity of the houses. Last week was our biggest one, and this one crowds it. Got a telegram yesterday from my first womern. All well. Got a new coachman (colored). Gustaf got too able and ran over some more people. He then wept and went away. Fanny likes the new boy first rate.

Presume it is the beginning of a Senegambian invasion of our peaceful home.

Six more weeks and my shiney and overworked swallow-tail will go into camphor and my bright little *bon mots* will be vermifuged for the summer. Oh, it is then I will kick up my chilblained heels and with a glad whinny jump the bars of the lecture field to browse on the sassafras beds of Buncombe County till the cows come home.

Before Nye could turn South again he crossed the border to buck the Canadian winter for a few days.

In Canada without a crime.

Once more I have evaded the customs of a neighboring country and the etiquette of a mighty dominion. I have never been the slave to the customs of my own country; why should I submit to those of a province?

I have just rearranged my trunk and tucked carefully back into it the thrilling narrative of a rich slumber robe which fluttered in the Canadian breeze all the way from Windsor to London.

Came the ides of March. My mother was in Chicago to meet the hard-working head of the family and to visit the Mitchells. We children were being chaperoned by "cousin," who received this letter under date of March 15:

My Dear Child:

A letter from Major Pond is here. He writes to all his friends sobbingly referring to the death of Ozias [his brother], enclosing circular of coming attractions for next year. His happy union of pathos and box office is always a wonder to me.

We are all well. Fanny bounded into my arms at 6
A.M. today with a glad cry, and happy tears and suspender buttons fell with a low plunk on the pavement.

Alas, you do not know what it is to strain a loved one
to your breast till his eyes pop, do you, cousin?

How long is this to continue? Feel free to come and tell
me about how long you think it will be. I will not tell any
one but the Englewood "Eye" and so it will remain a secret
betwixt *us* three.

I was real glad to see your Aunt. She looks awfully
nice *to me*, I bet you. Better'n anybody else in the whole
world. Her new clothes are out of sight. No, not that of
course—but they are real sweet.

We have talked long and fast about the new house—
talked it up and down two or three times.

Aunt sends her love and says do not *starve* yourselves.
Eat sassafras freely and say begone, dull care. That's
what I say.

One day, at the Fanny Blake house not long after the
lecture season closed, my father had a light stroke. I remember it well. I was frightened of course, but he seemed
to recover quickly, and I little realized the significance of
this warning signal of the tragedy to come. It was such
a seizure as brought his lecturing career to a close at Paterson, New Jersey, three and a half years later. The stroke
was the "accident" to which my father referred in this letter to Uncle Mitchell:

Dear Birdie Grubb:

Your note enclosing statement that I had "fell on the
edge of a cuspidor and injured myself whilst rashly con-
templating a bath" is just received.

NYE'S "SHATTO" AT BUCK SHOALS, N. C.

JAMES WHITCOMB RILEY WITH MAX AND JIM NYE AT BUCK SHOALS

It is not so!

Frances and I just returned from Asheville, where we drank lime juice to excess and quarreled under its influence, but as Gustaf is not with us any more, no one of our set was arrested.

We now have Darkest Africa doing our chores both in and out of doors. We also have a Miss B—— (formerly having saw better days) who is waited on by Max and Jim. She is quite nice, quiet and willing to smother her pride, sah, and wipe noses at an agreed price per month.

I've got a new saddle hoss called Dandy from the blue grass country, 5 years old but kind and versatile as to the gaits. The girls and I ride him indiscriminately and I have a pair of melodramatic riding boots from N. Y. which make me look like Simon Legree—also a pair of corduroy riding panties which I am practicing with—after dusk.

Jim has pizened himself and looks like a bob tail flush, but is most well again. As I write, Max is running on No. 9's time on the piazzer and supplying his own noise. He also imitates the air brake and other sad whistles and noises.

My physician has cut off my cigars, and my wife has cut off tea and coffee, and as I some time ago cut off my grog and have not said Gosh since Easter, I shall hope to be confirmed by cool weather in low neck and short sleeves.

Tell Clara that Mr. Paine, the Fall of Pompeii man, has sent me via Thearle 160 lbs. of fire works prepaid, and before that we had ordered $15 worth from Boston, including flags of all nations, and 1 gross of comic masks for the children, so that we are going to make tyranny tremble on the Nation's natal day.

Max just comes in to state as follows, "When we get down to Buck Shoals we are going to have a nice big frog place, ain't we, Pop?" He has his utensils already now, including a red flannel covered hook.

Burbank and wife are at the Battery Park, and I regret to say he is not gaining strength very fast. His voice is feeble. He is in a sad plight.

Yourn,

Lydia E. Pinkham.

P.S.—Have a cash offer for a new book of old stuff, which sum will build new barn.

Nye's Buck Shoals well became famous. For a long time the vein tapped in the owner's mind was much more prolific than the stream of water encountered by the digger.

Those who are interested in the subject of wells will be glad to know that workmen on this well known structure of mine struck water on the evening of the 8th inst., and were compelled to get out with great haste to avoid being drowned. Two feet and ten inches were reported by my well superintendent, who tapped me for another assessment and went home to obtain a much needed rest. I thought that two feet would hardly be sufficient for our family, several members of which use water exclusively as a tonic, so I got another man to put in a final blast.

This blast was ill advised, as it cracked open the bottom of the well and let out the two feet and ten inches of water which had been put there on the night of the 7th inst. It is low enough to salt a gold mine, but the man who will carry water from the "branch" all night to salt the well of a kind hearted northern invalid who is willing to let bygones be bygones and let the dead past do its own undertaking is not going to encourage cobwebs on the mouths of your cannon the way I feel like doing.

In a newspaper letter Nye recalls a conversation with Chauncey Depew regarding the fatal results of humor on statesmanship:

He told me that Garfield said to him that early in life he learned the fact that if he wished to advance as a statesman he must not allow himself to be humorous, so he throttled every desire to make a joke in order to be president, "And," says Mr. Depew, "he warned me to beware of humor as fatal to political preferment. What do you think about it?"

I said about as follows: "If you really want to put yourself where Mr. Garfield is—*viz.*, in the bottom of a dark grave, two or three miles from town and far from postal facilities, in order that your vignette may be printed on the face of a five dollar bill which lies at the bottom of the ill ventilated sock—now is your time to throttle the heaven born smile and the light hearted *bon mot.* I will answer your dinner invitations for you so long as old Colonel Gastric can lift his arm to his head or the tired Follicle rise to greet the frosted cake.

My parents were making delightful and loyal friends among our new neighbors, but my father missed his old-time cronies. He urged his brother Frank and Cousin Solon to visit us in the summer of 1892, and, as this letter shows, his disappointment was keen when he received word that press of business would prevent their coming.

Fletcher, N. C.
August 9.

My dear Solon:
Your brief but all too extensive letter got here a day or two ago. It would be tautological to say again that your

welcome here would have been something to stand off and admire at a distance.

I have never been so full of hospitality and other chemicals; never had so much leisure or freedom, or a more burning desire to monkey with those I love, than this summer. And so when both you and Frank wrote me you could not come, I was more disappointed than you can wot of. Yet I am not after all a damned fool. I know that there is a good reason or it would not be so. Time and experience have not been utterly thrown away on me, and every time I have had the bark knocked off of me I have tried to make it teach me something. So when a man comes to me and honestly explains a matter that has given me pain and bitter disappointment, I bow to the will of a Higher Power and acknowledge that there is One who is wiser than I am, and Who, doubtless, if the worst came to the worst, could write better pieces for the paper, perhaps—not at first very likely, but after awhile.

Referring again to the Higher Power spoken of in exhibit "A," I am quite unsettled regarding the future, not being able to pry into the future aforesaid and Mrs. E. [a medium] being so far away, and so I cannot see in my horoscope, aside from a little sugar and a fly with a jag on himself, anything that is especially pleasing. I too have to work, and though I am often told it is better to wear out than to rust out, I should like to try the latter with board for a year or two. All send love, even the large girls and tanned boys, the stripling Fanny and myself. God bless you and keep an eye on you and at last bring you to North Carolina, where Rest reigns eternal, and the Industrious Man is regarded with curiosity not unmixed with surprise.

One of the vivid recollections of my boyhood is the journey to Cæsar's Head. Recently I came across my father's narrative, which I include:

"I am quite unsettled, not being able to pry into the future"

We have just completed a trip to Cæsar's Head. It is one of the most delightful and soul renovating trips one can imagine. Cæsar's Head is situated at the summit of Cæsar's Head mountain, an outlying spur of the Blue Ridge in Greenville county, S. C., and is 4600 feet above the level of Arietta Street, Tompkinsville, Staten Island.

In leaving New York for Cæsar's Head you cross the Cortlandt Street ferry and take the first right-hand road. Cæsar's Head is so called because of a peculiar shaped rock at the summit of the mountain which bears a striking resemblance to nothing that has ever been seen before in the history of the world, either sacred or profane.

I took my own team and added a phaeton attached to a

saddle horse, but would not advise this course for others. The team is designed more for ornamental driving down the mall at Ticktown, and after thirty miles up a mountain road these glossy steeds have not life enough to even stab feebly at a fly with their deformed tails. Also the saddle horse Dandy loped in the phaeton a good deal of the way and tried to follow a pack of hounds at Buck Forest. Nothing can be less dignified than a saddle horse hitched to a phaeton riding to hounds.

The road from Calhoun is said to be very wild and beautiful. We traversed most of it after dark and in the midst of a terrific mountain storm, so it struck me at the time as rather monotonous. And "hit-a-raining." Half the time one would have to pause and say, "Mr. Speaker, where was I at?"

We traveled by diligence up the Jones Gap road in the darkness and terror incident to a mountain tempest and with no knowledge of the road, while on the left a bottomless canyon sent up a never ending thunder from a white and angry torrent concealed somewhere in its bosom. I was clothed in outing flannels which had caught the golden sunset coloring of the red clay and been soaked with the gummiest of mud. Searching for the right way, yet prone to wander into by and forbidden paths or fall over a brink or chasm, it was a solemn moment.

We were told that in two miles we would encounter a signboard, and there we must turn to the right. We were also told that the signboard was eight miles away and that we must turn to the left. One kind man said it was eleven miles and that the main bridge was washed away. He would keep us for the night, however, if we could put up with his humble fare and rather pronounced views regarding the existence of a "literary hell." We afterward learned that he was not a man of his word. The bridge was not in bad repair. Also, there is no bridge.

The Jones Gap road is a marvel of engineering. It was laid out by Solomon Jones, who is still living. His method of laying out a mountain road was to employ a large sow in winter time. By driving her gently down the hill, she would naturally select, through the snow, the gentlest descent and the easiest grade. As a result of this method, the Jones Gap road is well planned and the descent from Cæsar's Head as gradual as it is from Queen Victoria to the Prince of Wales.

As the thunder boomed louder and the torrents of rain beat in upon us and injured our costly and beautiful clothing, a signboard of some kind glimmered in the uncertain flash of lightning that split the drenched and inky world. I got out into the pelting storm, and with the icy torrent running down my frappéd spine I climbed the post and waited for another flash. I tried to light a match, but the place where I generally strike a match was all wet, so I gave it up.

The lightning did not make any remarks for a long time, but remained where it was, looking roguishly down on me as I clung trembling to the guide-post, wiping my spectacles on the tail of my coat. Finally a glare of intense light tore open the somber robes of night and lighted up the silent guide-post. It went on to say: "Facial blemishes, warts, eczema and superfluous hair removed without publicity at your own homes. Also, cash paid for hides, pelts and furs."

A letter to Uncle Mitchell evidently written right after my father's birthday (August 25):

We dined at the Westfeldts last evening. The horses have their tails bobbed and the negro "coshay," as we say in Paree, is as stiff and dignified as a ramrod. God knows it may be wrong, but I love to tell a funny story while out riding and make him cover his face with his large but neatly gloved hand to conceal his emotion.

Got a call to come via Philadelphia and hold a secret meeting with the editor of Lippincott's Magazine. Can it be the offer of a job?

Some of the charm of my father's personal letters must be lost by those who do not know the personalities referred to and the peculiar fitness of the humorous references. Nevertheless I include a number of such remarks, asking my readers to draw upon their imaginations to fill in the missing background, which if furnished would make this book too voluminous. The following letter to Cousin Clara is typical of what I mean:

Fletcher, N. C.
September 21, 1892.

My Dear Clara Isabel:

You will doubtless be surprised to receive a letter so soon from one whom you will remember to have seen casually but who is yet a great admirer and constant reader.

This letter is partly to say that you are never to write to me when you would rather take off your shoes and cast yourself upon your couch for an hour of soul refreshing rest or even to read or do anything else. Realizing as I do how a "conscientious" person may be overburdened with correspondence, and a real blessing turned into what's called an incubus, I hasten to say that you need not feel in honor bound to keep up a red hot correspondence with the whole Nye family.

Possibly I could do as well to write to as a representative of the family as any one of the outfit, yet even I will not be unreasonable, knowing how busy you are.

The rain which has not shown up for a good while is now coming down in grateful showers and making everything look fresh even to Miss A——, the fungi gatherer of the Blue Ridge.

Blank has a new derby hat but still wears the old string tie; also the same iron gray hedge down the middle of his upper lip.

Miss X—— had gained over half a pound this summer but lost it again in August. We saw her in evening dress at Arden at about that time. The articulation of the scapula with the humerus was very noticeable, and when she swallowed I got a clearer idea, I think, of how this great act is accomplished than ever before.

By the way, the E——s were here with us last week, and fell over the rugs again. Just as we were plunged in despair and trying to train a new colored waitress, against whom the finger of scorn and scandal has been eight times leveled in rapid succession, here came Henry and the great Cape Cod tumbler and water colorist from Asheville.

Fanny was cool and reticent. I was silent and sarcastic, but it wound up by sending their horse around to the barn, and in less than fifteen minutes our large red rooster was bounding headless across the area and spattering his hot blood against the sour-wood tree.

She sat next me while I carved, and I resolved that if she dictated as to platter gravy I would run the carver through her corset and revolve it rapidly to and fro while Henry looked on with his wet eye and husky voice.

Curse them! I say.

Dr. S—— [oculist] asked hungrily about you as if he would like to get another whack at your eyes. My own are better than I had hoped they would be, and they both may be frequently detected regarding the same object at the same time with much interest. They don't hurt so much eyether.

With love to one and all, as John L. Sullivan says, and hoping that you will not be too quick to take me at my word in the letter line—for I already regret my rashness—I am your Uncle—at all times.

EDGAR W. NYE.

In a letter of about this vintage my father recalled an incident of my baptism. He explains that I threw my feet into the air and showed more original sin than any child he ever saw baptized. Then a long embarrassing lull struck the company. No one could think of anything to say. My brother Max, about a year and a half old, was present. The baptismal vessel to him was reminiscent of our silver service. So he softly and solemnly called across the room:

"Please pass the pream."

And this brought up another story:

Children are not born with such great veneration for sacred subjects as they might be, and yet they sometimes surprise us with their reasoning.

I have a little son called Jim—just Jim Nye, that's all—and one day when he was only 5 years old I requested him to do some slight thing or other, but he kept on playing and humming a little song about the "sand man." I spoke to him again more firmly, for as a general thing my children regarded me more as a source of amusement than anything else, and as he did not stir I gave him a gentle spank with the dictionary. It did not hurt him, and he rather enjoyed it until he looked at my face and saw that I was in earnest, and then his heart broke with a loud report.

At dinner he said nothing and ate very little, and when it was over and we were just about to leave the table he got up in his mother's lap and said:

"Mamma, I wish that you had mawied Jesus. He loved little children!"

This episode did not make me feel so frightfully proud of myself, but I was glad that the child at least regarded his mother as a very worthy woman.

CHAPTER XXI

ABROAD AGAIN: 1893

THE thank-you letter to Cousin Clara which follows, reminds me of the Christmas that had just been celebrated, our first at Buck Shoals. In the mind of every child there is one Christmas that stands out above all others. To me, that Christmas was the Yule-tide of 1892. The new house shone in its pristine splendor. The waxed floors mirrored the crackling log fires. The fragrance of burning oak, hickory, and fat pine filled our nostrils. An enormous holly-tree (it seemed so to the boy of five) stood at one end of what we called our "drawering" room. Mistletoe and galax leaves, growing plentifully on the farm, garnished the house. My father had come home laden with mysterious packages and eyes a-twinkle with mischief and good cheer. To add to the delight Max and I had anticipated the festivities by discovering the closet in which Santa Claus had parked a part of his heavy pack. In the attic we thoroughly rehearsed elaborate sets of building-blocks and other pleasant surprises. By combining these block structures with octagon soap and bricks of maple-sugar, the latter bestowed upon us by one of my father's Vermont admirers, our art embraced not only architecture but likewise landscape-gardening and engineering projects of great scope; to which we should have pointed with pardonable pride, had we not realized that to do so would have detracted from the holiday pleasure of our parents. Max and I were very thoughtful in that way. At times we were downright indulgent of

our parents. Perhaps we spoiled them a little. But knowing that they had both endured hardships during their
youth, we sought to make it up to them in their later
years.

There were the jolliest festivities about the tree on Christmas eve. Every one on the place was invited. The farmer
Mize and his unprepossessing "Eller" were there with bells,
and the colored servants grinned and chortled in the background.

My father had prepared surprises and delights of many
kinds for us. I shall give one example. Max and I had
received enormous but light paper parcels of about the
same bulk. We were encouraged to enter an unwrapping
race to see who should be the first to uncover the mysterious contents. We untied string, unwrapped and tore
paper madly in our scramble to reach the true inwardness
of those parcels. This was not an easy matter. Hours
must have been spent preparing the joke. It took us a good
many minutes to reach the core. Meanwhile the bundles
diminished in size until a strong doubt arose in our minds
whether there was any core. Suspecting that the winner
of the race would be the butt of a conspicuous hoax, our
efforts began to lag, and toward the last we gave an imita-
tion in slow motion of a Scotchman paying a street-car fare.
But our persistence was finally rewarded with tiny gold
cuff-links.

The children slept that night feeling that there had never
been such a Christmas before. It did not occur to us that
more was to follow. But sure enough, the early morning
found our stockings well filled and the pieces of greatest
resistance grouped about them on the hearth. Did ever
kids have such a Santa Claus and such a happy childhood?
And now the letter:

I think I can put my hand on my heart and say that what I got was also just what I wanted and I thank you and all hands—all those who thought of me so sort of spontaneously and so "sweetly," I was going to say.

I suppose that with the various letters that have went out from here "to you ward," as the Apostle Paul puts it, you have long since heard how our folk celebrated and the big holly tree and the mistletoe bough hanging from dangerous places, where I had two or three opportunities to attack Mrs. Mize but did not, for I fear the hot Southern blood of a man like Mize. Mize comes from Georgia and has a little strain of malaria and the Oglethorpes in his blood. So "Eller" is safe.

This is one of those days that I would not be ashamed to show anybody. It is like a pleasant recollection. The haze on the hills is blue and sort of pansy-like and the river kind of purrs where the shoals is at. The sun shines bright on the old Carliny home—one might say.

We stood the blizzard very comfortably, and the new clock arouses a devotional spirit when she chimes. Mr. W. saw it and said "they 'ad one like it at 'ome." Yes I can almost see it a-sittin' there.

Everything we have reminds him of what he has had. When I broke my arm last winter it reminded him that he had fractured *all* his limbs at 'ome. He has had everything, as Jerome says, but "house-maid's knee"—whatever that is.

Fan [Mrs. Nye] and Nan [Miss Mines] have went to "Assville," as Gustav called it. They went last evening with Bess and Win to school, and so the boys and I are having fun here at 'ome. They mostly take care of themselves, and I love to watch them wash the center of their faces, and fight shy of their chapped wrists. They are rosy and well, Max being taller and taller and toothless, while Jim seems to be busting his clothes at every point. He still eats heartily.

We have a new nigger named Charlie who has got more mirth in him than anybody. He attends to fires and does a miscellaneous business besides having a low liquid laugh that spurs me up all the time to do things that I never attempted before. You know Dixon was always a little too dignified for me? I've made him put his big red glove over his mouth several times, but I cannot say that I've really conquered him, for his is not an emotional nature. I never feel that I can live up to Dixon as I ought, for he was Colonel Rice's coachman for twelve years in Charleston, S. C. But Charlie I can play on as one would on a xylophone. Wish you could be here and listen at him.

——has a new suit of clothes. We have not yet discovered who wears his shirts while they are clean.

Just before leaving North Caroline for the second leg of what Mr. Thearle called "Bill Nye's Transcontinental Tour," my father found time to pen a few lines to Uncle Mitchell:

I will send herewith a French critique of myself and the Wm.-Lloyd-Garrison-at-eighty picture that goes with it. I cannot read the critique but do not mind that. To some are given the gift of tongues, to others baldness or biliousness.

Jim and Max are tough, sir, tough, and devilish sly. They put on rubber boots and are out all day. When they come in they are chapped and ruddy and hungry and well. We pay nothing for physic as the English say

but use the money paying the poor for work they imagine
they have done.

Jim yesterday did the kind of thing that they do most
every day. His mother found in the tin heating oven a
cigar box which did not belong there, so she examined
it and found a dead rat that Jim was trying to revive.
He has one of the most prosperous cemeteries in the
country but does not like to bury the meanest of God's
creatures till all modes of resuscitation have been tried.

Max is half a head taller now but Jim can knock a
nigger down with his clenched fist.

I go Monday from Baltimore to the Golden Gate.

The new lecture swing was two days old when there followed a short letter to "Cousin":

Hearing that our train is late, I grasp the opportunity and a large trenchant pen to write you a line to
say that once more Burbie and I are at large, talking
freely to great numbers of interested and delighted people who have not heard before that "Karnal is out with
twenty (20) men, to raise the border side." We are
conveying that news to them from time to time.

We spoke in Baltimore in a blizzard and had to borrow chairs. We spoke under the auspices of the Young
Hebrews' Association. I did not know before that they
had auspices but they have. Last night we spoke under
some more auspices; viz., the Bicycle Club of this place.
We had a packed house. Should we keep on this way
we will be able to keep Remenyi and some other attractions of Mr. Thearle's from stranding.

We are quite well. Burbie has two grips full of drugs,
paints, oils, home remedies, two gallons of cod liver oil,
demijohn of Scott's Emulsion, large inhaling pillow,

BILL NYE'S BROTHER, HON FRANK MELLEN NYE, OF MINNEAPOLIS
"We were nearly of an age, and up to the spring of 1876 were scarcely separated
for a single month at any one time."

smelling like the opening of a Swedish bedroom in Pompeii. Also two inhalers, nose douches for Lent, Easter and great Church festivities as well as secular cubebs to smoke, puff ball inhalers and a thing to spray his throat in the morning. I saw him do it once as his throat was reflected in a mirror.

Gettysburg of course was horrible, but I would be prepared for it now, I think.

In a letter written during the spring season Nye set down some observations upon lecturing as an indoor sport:

The lecturer has two or three great obstacles to overcome which the actor has not; *viz.*, he has no scenery, he has to occupy the entire evening alone, and there is no division into three or four acts with a chance for the audience to rest and run down the show. And yet the lecturer often starts out fearlessly without training, or with training that is far worse than none, and on the reputation he has made in some totally different art he fearlessly rushes in where angels would naturally hang back.

At the expense of the public he thus, if persistent and brave, at last learns to be natural—if he didn't foolishly get his originality and individuality trained out of him by a journeyman elocutionist on the start—and is then considered a professional. He can think of other more interesting topics, than his speech, as he seats himself by the roadside of life, at times, to calmly remove the thorns and brambles from his tired feet.

From Kentucky, on January 20, Nye wrote Uncle Mitchell:

I was never made for unusual winters. These polar
waves go for me and my heart only beats a little during
meal time. I try to battle agin it, and though the spirit
is willing—the goose-flesh is weak.

I do not know whether Sister Ann is freezing to death
at home or in Buck Shoals. Have not yet heard. We
are fighting the cold here the best we can, but we do not
look attractive. Burbank most gave out last night with
the icy air between the hotel and station. We had to walk
at 2:50 A. M. over the Kanawha in a high breeze and we
did almost perish.

A few days later this letter to "Cousin" was written.
[As I quote so frequently from his letters to Clara
Mitchell—now Mrs. Charles Frederick Milspaugh of Chicago—I cannot but be reminded of the profound debt I owe
to this cousin, who not only saved all these letters carefully
and has lent them to me generously, but who by her witty
and sympathetic rejoinders stimulated my father to come
back early and often in his best vein] :

Your letter, full of Soul and things like that, came
some days ago and one from my other niece with the
sunny hair. Both of them were real good and I swelled
around for quite a while refusing to see a number of people who sent up printed cards. I now refuse to see people
with printed cards no matter who they are.

Your uncle now has a sort of mellow distance that
works well with undesirable people and after he has said
"Yes?" to them a few times they open their great coarse
watches and go away to secure repose and talk with
people who respond.

My child, we are just sending people away. Ask
Harry Thearle. Burbank delights those who like "cur-

"I swelled around for quite a while, refusing to see people who sent up printed cards"

few shall *not* ring tonight," and I feed the mind. People go away with mental colic and sit up all night. I amuse and instruct. My Sunday letter now is being syndicaled in the English papers, and soon these germs of thought which I give out so merrily will begin to sparkle wherever the sun shines. Isn't it gladsome to know that the sun never sets on your Uncle's simple greatness? Oh, I sometimes think how ungrateful we are that we do not show more gratitude! Isn't it?

Riley came to Evansville and put in the day and night with us. He was like himself and real funny. We laughed and said merry things all day on a prohibition basis. I offered him some of my Apollinaris, but he said no; he had been, of course, unjust to his stomach but never cold and cruel.

I will now close, however, as I cannot think of any more thoughts to write. Whenever that occurs I close even if I have half a page left useless. So good-by with my best wishes and love of a high order as when you really lived in our family instead of going away to seek your fortune in "the west."

I hope that Winifred is well again and that you are all
likewise and happy, even Jake, the merry blade, with his
side whiskers, upon which he used to subsist, swept away,
and his round pippin cheeks glowing in the cold.   Even
to him.

Nye wrote humorously but appreciatively of California.
Would that I could include a bit of his description.   He
summed up his opinion in this short paragraph:

There is something about California that I like, and it
does not depend on isothermal lines or mean temperature.   It is the word "Welcome" written on every hearth-
stone and over the Oakland entrance as well as the Golden
Gate.   California and I understand each other pretty
well.   She is a good fellow.

Eastward-bound Nye wrote Solon Perrin from Helena,
Montana, on April 15:

Come to Minneapolis on the 29th, as I propose giving
a *tea* to the boys.   Hope to have Carroll, Frank Perrin,
Doc Woodworth, Burbank and possibly one or two others.
Nothing immoral will occur.
Our trip has been the biggest winner of all. . . .
                        Your cousin on your mother's side,
                        EDGAR.

P.S.—Please report at Fargo (25th) so's I shall know
how many nut cakes to order.
The tea will occur at eleven P.M. after the show.

The tour with Burbank, ending in the Twin Cities, was
his last with "Burbie."   Three years had not passed before both the game fighters against invalidism had been

forced to give up the fight and accept eternal rest. Burbank
was the first to go, and his partner did not tarry long.

Back at Buck Shoals, "Uncle Edgar" writes the news
to his "nice niece":

We are all counting on you and Win for the summer,
and I bet we will have some plain fun grown on the place.

The city will be far away, and we will eat steaks in the
morning tide, steaks that we can cut with acids.

Aunt Fanny is dieting now, and it is already affecting
me. Often I think that souls truly wedded that way and
eating the same bran croquettes day after day "fall off"
in a similar manner.

Max and Jim are waxing brown and toothless. Poor
Jim has a ghastly looking mouth, but the flavor of it is
as of yore. They are just starting off with me to Long
Shoals to see a colored baptizing of some importance.
William, our *garçon*, has experienced religion, such as it
is, and last Sabbath was immersed in the vast rain hole
looking east from Beale's. We will now have to watch
him. Dixon, the *coacher*, has had religion a long time
and asks blessing at table. He asks a good blessing and
is about as square as the average professing Christian
with whom I have dealt.

We have a Shakepeare Club. Frances belongs to it.
She is also trying to live on 5 cents a day. I do not mind
that except that it involves the rest of the family. It
will be mostly over when you come and bacon will once
more enter the *menu*.

Jake Huff, a colored man who works for me and is almost like a brother, has lost one wife and another has
runned away since you left. He cannot account for the
flight of the last one but will be glad to hear from her
dead or alive. She has a big "wend" on her neck and is

sort of spindlin'. Yesterday he said that near Greenville, N. C., 9 children, 2 wives, and a big red tumor, done taken out of his side, all slept in one grave. He is cast down now and says that this is the first time for over thirty years that he has been plumb out of wives.

This season at Buck Shoals Nye's chief chore was his "Comic History of the United States," probably his best known book. His other books had been collections of short stories previously published. Lippincott was to publish the history, and Fred B. Opper was to illustrate it. It was to be much better printed and bound than the other books, and Nye was proud to be engaged in such a work.

Late in the summer he wrote Uncle Mitchell:

The drowth is done busted and we have started in on forty days of shower.

We got our oats in just in time. Max and Jim hauled four loads with their donkey, fifty bundles per load. It was a amusin' sight.

Crops look well for this country and are worth something too. The market is always good here, for the State never raised enough of anything for a supply, 'cept only hell.

I'm too industrious to have much fun this summer. Also have literary bearing down pains all the time. Hope to be out by September 1st, when, if I do not slip up on it, I will get out on the bosom of the old easy-riding ocean and associate with people who give Industry no encouragement.

Winifred Mitchell plays graciously for the just and the unjust, and we are getting soaked full of good music. Both girls are one of us. They are so much so that J—— rather suffers by the contrast, for she looks far away and

WASHINGTON'S INAUGURATION

BUNKER HILL

COLUMBUS DISCOVERING AMERICA

Bill Nye's HISTORY OF THE UNITED STATES

only interests herself in her new clothes and feed-time and letters from O——.   O—— is her prospective husband. O——, Attorney and Counsellor at Lor.   Some day I am going to visit O—— and take my trunk with me.   He comes of a good family; possibly he is a Bontecue [a proud name in the genealogy of the sisters Smith, whom these two cronies had married].   He's all the time throwing up his family to us as if we could help it.   Where people belong to a very old family it is their own misfortune, and others cannot help them.   His family tree is old and wormy, I understand.   But his wife starts in with no past, no genealogy.   She is an acorn.   Her history is only a pamphlet now.

Excuse this penmanship.   I am writing with a rusty old steel pen, and the ink in this bottle has evaporated down to the charnel house, where the flies lie dead with their little gray swollen stomachs turned sadly upward. Occasionally I get a nice formal letter done, and sign it with a dead beetle as big as a mud turtle.

In spite of Bill Nye's reflections upon the English sense of humor, his popularity was growing in Britain.   And certainly there was no more pleasing way of proving Nye's opinion wrong than for the English to admire his wit.   For years his writings had been reprinted on the other side. Now they were being syndicated there.   His books sold well in London, and he had urgent invitations to make another journey across the ocean.   He took passage on the *Umbia*, sailing September 15.   I give a hasty note to my mother written just before his departure:

I just received your telegram and have to go aboard *tonight*, as the boat goes at 6 A.M., so I cannot see any

> more people here. Of those I *have* saw, I will say more
> when I return.
>
> I have made verbal contract with the American Press
> Association for two years more at the old price, $8320
> per year, and $2600 with the "World" to *January 1st*,
> $10,920, in all, with the hope of *more*, but at least I go
> cheerfully away.
>
> If you need $$ tell me care of my address. I will try
> to meet you here by October 20.
>
> Gosh! how I've hustled to get six weeks ahead and fit
> to go aboard ship!
>
> Pray for me, all of you.

The reference to the new contract with the American
Press Association needs explanation. When my father left
Staten Island he had contracted with this syndicate for the
rights to his weekly letters outside of the metropolitan dis-
trict, continuing the "World" in New York. In this way
Nye had more freedom and more income, and he cost the
"World" less than before.

I give part of another letter to my mother, written a
few days later:

> There is little to write about since leaving New York,
> and I did not get through with what I wanted to do
> there. The "World" I continued with at $50 under
> Major Smith's [president of the association] advice, as
> he said that changing papers in New York was hazardous.
> When I went back to the "World" I should have made a
> written contract with it. Yet that of course would ex-
> pire, and a new editor might have new and wild ideas of
> economy. However I made another two-year contract
> with the American Press Association at the old figure,

and so shall not have that to worry over. Mr. Bennett
of the "Herald" is still confined to his bed from the injury
he received some weeks ago or I would run over to Paris
and talk with him.

The American Press wants me to take a deliberate trip
around the world *at its expense,* mind you; say about a
year from January. That would exactly fit my plans
of closing the lecture business this winter of '93-'94.

Here's a letter to Uncle Mitchell written on the high seas:

I have not seen the papers lately so cannot discuss silver
or anything of that kind but just write a line regarding
life on the ocean wave and a home on the rolling deep. I
trust you will not criticize my penmanship, for the road
is not so smooth right here as it was four years ago. I
forgot also to rozzun the chair before I sat down and
it is very hard to hold on.

We live on music and gravy. Everything has gravy
to it, sometimes two kinds, and you take your choice.
Even pie has gravy to it.

I cannot understand much German but enough to convince me that America is not a success at all. Chicago is
being constantly compared with Berlin and Leberwurst
and Smearkase and other German towns. Sometimes I
wish I was dead. America is so savage. Of course I was
born in captivity myself and have had Bible privileges,
and even now on this damp Sunday morning I know that
by sin, death came into the world.

Although Nye had gained six weeks on the printer before he left the States his pen was not idle in London. He
had been there but a few days when he paid his respects to
Brown's Hotel:

When I left America, to bring refinement and the light of the Gospel into Great Britain and Ireland, I was told to go to a hotel first and lodgings afterwards. A friend told me to go to Brown's Hotel, in the Strand. In landing at Waterloo station, which is handy to the postoffice and courthouse, I took a four-wheeler and had my nice new tin trunk put on the top.

We drove to Brown's Hotel, on Dover street, and I was soon assigned to the room which seemed to match my steerage trunk and Ellis Island bag. It was nine shillings per day, but that did not include amount brought forward, attendance, use of electric light, bath, use of poker and fire-shovel, use of fire-escape, breakfast, dinner, tea and coffee, sugar, milk, use of sugar tongs, desserts, ices, suppers, wear and tear of napkin, board of valet, corkage, use of corkscrew, use of nutcracker, liquors, spirits (of just men rectified, I presume), ale and stout, aerated waters, cigars, sundries and breakage.

The lion and unicorn may be seen over half the shop entrances in London, with the announcement that the merchant or tradesman there is, by special appointment, fishmonger or plumber to Her Most Gracious Majesty.

One tradesman on Old Bond Street deals in nothing but elephant guns, and announces that he is by special appointment elephant gunmaker to Her Most Gracious Majesty the Queen of Great Britain and Empress of India, by the Grace of God.

Another man, a tailor, who makes nothing but fine trousers, has the audacity—but we will let that pass.

The "London Sketch" for October 1, 1893, had an illustrated story of Bill Nye. The interviewer's angle is typically British:

Mr. Edgar Wilson Nye, whom a nation impregnated with
Bret Harte persists in calling Bill Nye, though he is not attired in top-boots, or a bowie knife, or a red Crimean shirt, is
in London. He does not wear the mark of Cain, for a milder-
mannered-looking person, at first sight, than this clean-shaven,
bland, brown-eyed, bespectacled, bald-headed man it is not easy
to conceive. All his caricatures, and they may be numbered
by the hundred, depict him with a baby face, a hydrocephalous
head, and goggles. If you look a little deeper, you will read
a great deal of quiet determination in the man—no man who
hadn't grit could travel as Mr. Nye has done. For many
years he has been the most popular lecturer on the road in the
United States.

He is equally in request among the clubs of New York and
Boston and Philadelphia on "Storytellers' Nights." The moment his tall figure, with its dry Yankee face, rises, there is an
unusual hush, even for the well-behaved American audiences;
every one knows that something good is coming. Mr. Nye's
jokes have points, and he has a habit of remembering what
jokes he has told before in a place. Mr. Nye has become
a power in the land; the President himself is not more caricatured. His sayings are quoted everywhere. There is hardly
a town with a Sunday newspaper that does not print his latest
column.

Though Mr. Nye goes about as little as he can, he is a very
familiar figure in New York literary clubs, such as the Authors',
the Aldine, the Fellowcrafts. Those who had the pleasure of
hearing him when he was taken completely by surprise at the
Zola Dinner of our English Authors' Club last week will easily
understand this.

At the Zola dinner, on September 28, there were about
ninety guests. Nye sat at the table with Emile Zola,
Thomas Hardy, G. Du Maurier, Henry Arthur Jones, W.
W. Astor and Frank Harris. Other distinguished guests

were Gilbert Parker, Arthur à Beckett, Jerome K. Jerome, Fred Villiers, A. E. Jones, Henry Harland, J. Todhunter, and Douglas Sladen.

On the way back, on October 22, Edgar wrote his mother:

> Steamer *Aller*, Half way across.
>
> It's a quiet Sunday here in Stateroom 323. I have not been down town this morning but remained quietly at home sometimes on my head and then again turned the other way—for we are in a "cross sea" as they call it.
>
> I have had a "corking" time in London and glad of the rest and soothing purr of the ocean after it all. To jump from the quiet of North Carolina into the mighty nightmare of London was a sudden plunge, but I soon got used to its noise, its hours and its varied aggregation of frolic and hurrah.
>
> It has sort of shaken the cobwebs out of my mind for a year or so and joggled up my lonesome ideas.
>
> We shall, if we land at all, land in New York Thursday P. M., and when you get this letter, you'll know I'm safe ashore, for New York is just now my nearest post-office over 1600 miles of slushy wet road.

On December 4 Nye is despatching his Christmas letter and gifts to his mother:

> I send you today a check for $50. I send too an enamel and gold knot pin which I got when away and which is really better than it looks. All this vast holiday package goes with a wish for a Merry Christmas and a Happy New Year.
>
> The hard times have given me a couple of whacks and may give me a couple more. How much it will foot up

in the year I cannot tell yet. So long as we have enough and are well, I do not lie awake nights over it.

The proofs are read, and today the last went into the publisher's for the new History of the United States. We shall have to wait a while for the artist, which makes me mad, for I was done with my work over three months ago.

We start out January 15 on our lecture tour, Mr. William Hawley Smith and I. Mr. Burbank is out of the race, I fear, for the rest of his life. Mr. Smith is a good man, upright and entertaining too.

Let me close the year 1893 by including one more letter to Clara Mitchell:

Uncle James [mother's brother] has written us a letter and given us a few ideas about bringing up our children in the nurture and admonition of the Lord, and I feel *stronger*. I can beat Max most every evening now at backgammon, even on Sunday evenings, which I could not at first. Lately he, of his own accord, has suggested that we should not play backgammon except on week days. So mayhap he will accept the better way on his own hook. James is no doubt, however, as good a man as ever "laid out doors." I have sent him a pale green check to put in his sock for Christmas, but his methods of bringing up the children that have been captured by other people are not in demand.

Just a month from today I take up my cross and start out once more on the rostrum. I am the guest of the Philadelphia Art Club one month from tonight and on the 15th open in Washington. Thence three weeks— the East and New England and Canada and West and South, closing in the Southwest. The Art Club is a big and beauteous corporation, and I have rooms there while in the City.

We like Winnie [Smith, another cousin] very much, as I knew we should. She is young yet but about as real as a two-year-old colt. Max is more mature and is bringing her out. It is fine to see the three "little ones" in a heap at evening, Winnie reading in that syrupy voice while the little striplings fold their dusty primary-school corduroys about her and listen with bated breath. Speaking of the primary school and its atmosphere, I ran upon Dickens' picture of the Dotheboys school the other day, the vacant room with its hint of half eaten apple and the odor of old slate sponges. It is very graphic, but them days is gone. I'm glad of it. Going to school now must be a real pastime up to 15.

CHAPTER XXII

NYE AND WILLIAM HAWLEY SMITH: 1894

BURBANK had made a game fight and had lectured long after his health warranted. Now he was dying. He did not survive the first half of 1894. Nye himself would have done well to stop work. But the same stern necessity to provide means which spurred Burbank to travel made his partner feel that he must press his good fortune while his public smiled. For the first three months of 1894 Mr. Thearle provided a contrasting type of entertainer, who, like Riley and Burbank, wore the mask with the mouth that drooped at the corners. The new foil was William Hawley Smith of Peoria. And the lecture season, shorter than usual, opened in New England in the middle of January, closing in Texas on April 13. A paper at Ottawa, Illinois, reviewed the show thus:

There was a full house at the Nye-Smith entertainment at the Grand Opera House last evening. Mr. William Hawley Smith commenced proceedings by some humorous remarks as to the pictures round town of himself and Mr. Nye. They had created a difference between himself and Mr. Nye, he said, as to the way they parted their hair. Mr. Smith explained that it had been arranged amicably. Mr. Nye took all the parting, he took the hair.

After a very spirited recitation of "Shamus O'Brien" from Mr. Smith, Mr. Nye appeared and complained of Mr. Smith's introductory remarks.

The cruel allusion to his baldness seemed to hurt him. He had only to say that some men were bald, like himself, on the outside of their heads, others—and here the audience anticipated the hit.

Then came fun, fast and furious; with Nye perverting our vocabulary to his own uses and Smith perverting his voice and face into every dialect and every expression—preaching a sermon in broad country English—reciting as small boys, girls, and elocutionary professors recite—mingling fun with pathos, and pathos with fun; with Nye walking in casually and telling stories that he alone was able not to laugh at, and looking all the while as if he really meant no harm, and Smith aiding and abetting—what was the happy audience to do but clap and encore until the innocent and innocuous Nye was compelled to explain to them that he was "usually in bed at this time."

The last of January found my father in his native State, Maine, from which he writes a letter to my brother, aged eight.

Your letter just came here over a thousand miles and made me feel a good deal better. I wish so many times I could see you and Jim and hold you on my knee, one on each knee.

It is winter here and there are lots of sleighs and bells on the street. Hundreds of men are cutting ice on the Kennebec River, where your grandpa was a little boy and your great-grandpa, too.

We ride on the cars every day, and Thursday we must ride all night and all day too.

I liked your letter, though it was short, and I hope you can soon write more and tell me about everything you think of. Won't it be nice when we get back all of us to dear old Buck Shoals and the Mizes?

> With 2,500 kisses right here I must say good night to you and write to Jim. Kiss your dear Mamma for me and be her Man in Papa's place.

My sisters were attending boarding-school in Asheville, and so Buck Shoals was closed and we spent a few weeks with Mrs. Glaser at Mountain Cottage, where my mother received this letter, written at Bangor, Maine, on January 30:

> It is snowing great guns and has done so all night and all day. We are not sure that we shall get safely out of Maine without being snowed under, but the doughnuts and baked beans hold out first rate and so we do not worry.
>
> Everywhere the elderly lady who was a Nye or a Loring or a Teague [names connected with the family history] looms up on my port quarter wearing a Paisley shawl which smells of doughnuts and dried apples. She has little to say but generally looks at me fixedly from head to foot, estimating the probable cost of my English clothes and raising the question of whether they are all wool or not.
>
> I rather enjoy it when I'm not too weary. One of them was the wife of an undertaker. She was also a Teague. The two things together did not help her to win my heart. A nice old man of the Josh Whitcomb type drew me into conversation the other day. He knew Isaac Teague, he said, who was my granduncle. He thought a long time, trying to get hold of something pleasant to say about Isaac. Finally he hove a sigh and said:
>
> "Well he was—a schemah!" That's the best he could do for Isaac. Our houses are big and *very* good, nice and respectable, and they come to "larf." We like them very much, and I have to return again and again.

Hawley is improving. Somehow there's a terrible restlessness connected with this business which is almost impossible to manage. You want to eat or drink or smoke or do something all the time. I've analyzed it down to that, and that's what ails Hawley.

Your last letter touched me very much, for I hate to know that you have had to cry—and that I could not be there to get some of it in my neck. I'm glad that you are going home in a few weeks, for surely you will be glad, too, and the boys as well, to get out of the crowded and highly "sensitive" atmosphere of Mountain Cottage.

I'm *very* well, and if all our travel and hotels were no worse, we would be quite content. Thearle says, however, that we have no severe work this year, and I hope he has not lied, for I hate to see a man whose father was a Baptist preacher turn in and lie.

A letter to Cousin Clara gives more intimate observations of his running-mate:

We are having loads of success, both $$ and in applause. Smith is a plain unassuming man, and when he passes through the car, most of the watches stop. But he is not vain—that is, not too vain, and we get on real well. He is a little cranky about what he eats and is now eating Mellin's Food. I asked him if he intended to publish his portrait in the magazines as a Mellin's Food Child Wonder. He eats Mellin's Food for health and then eats everything else because he is hungry.

He was rather wakeful the first week out and used to calm himself by means of some Peoria rum which he carried with him. I called a physician, who advised me to take the rum away from him, which I done. It did not hurt me because I was perfectly well, but with his phyz-

zeak he ortn't to of hed it, and when he sent home for
some more I took charge of it for him until such time
as he should be nice and well again.

He is a real good man and talks constantly of his wife,
who does not appeal to me the least bit, being, as my
Uncle Hosea of Bangor would put it, as homely as hell
is wicked.

He was real homesick for a week and wanted me to
stroke his brow of nights. I stroked it with one of his
socks filled with bituminous coal and besought him to go
to sleep.

He has with him crocheted collar-box and cuff-box and
crocheted night slippers and pulse warmers made in
Peoria, Ill., and when he does go to sleep at last, possibly
with a homesick tear on his concave cheek, he looks like
one of the Ptolemys of Cairo, Illinois.

The clouds were beginning to close in, and though there
were glimpses of the sun to come, the fragment of Bill Nye's
life remaining was written in a minor key.

A month of the lecture grind sufficed to cause a relapse in
Nye's health, and he had to take a few days' rest. He tells
of it in a letter to Cousin Clara, written on February 26,
1894:

Your letter came at a very welcome juncture. Do you
know what a juncture is? I do not. Nyether do I care
a tinker's damb. Aunt Fanny is with me having fun.
The press cannot kill us off yet. Of course I had a little
mild congestion of the thinker a week ago but was on the
road again the following day, and now talk in a lucid way
off the stage. On the stage that is not necessary.

Aunt is enough to make a feller glad he was born. She

is one of the best and most indispensable women on the face of the earth. She is a *comrade!* That's what!

She is not solely an ornament to society, a tutor continually pointing out the "better way," a mentor with sweet words all the while and a bed slat up her sleeve for her husband, but *real* palpitating, humid about the eyes, and yet so genuine and so unselfish that a visit from her cuts our long journey in half, as Max says, and I enter on the last half with courage and delight, swearing a great big Etruscan oath, with plush frogs on it, that I will never, never speak a piece again after this trip.

For sixteen years I have been on exhibition to the stare of the manager and the public. I have done it for my family, and yet they have begged me not to do it. Bess writes me that she'd rather be poor, and I believe it. As those I have done it for beg me not to, I would be a fool to continue.

You say to Winifred that the more I hear people wrangling with a piano the more I *know* that I like to hear her play better than anybody else I have ever heard. She hits me in a place where nobody else ever did, and she seems to *sprinkle* the music in the air with those limber fingers of hers just as an angel might scatter holy water on a lot of thirsty, dusty souls. This is not flattery, for she would see through it if I dared any experiment of that kind. I wish that such a daughter might grow up in the Nye family, but I am afraid we will not grow a great musical genius at Buck Shoals.

April 20 found Nye at Buck Shoals. Four days later he wrote:

I closed a week ago, sending Smithy home via St. Louis.

Smith ate shrimp salad with his custard pie and did all sorts of Peoria things. When his wife joined him, he had been so boastful for two weeks that all looked forward to her arrival. I had seen her, however, and was prepared. She wears huge spectacles and short hair. Together they look as though they had walked out of an almanac, both being "befores," not "afters."

The History is going beautifully, and my *best* endorsement has come from the South, on account of my treatment of the war. Ain't I glad I had my way and insisted on the publication of that part without alteration?

I've also got my Author's Club autograph book ["Liber Scriptorum"]. It is large and beautifully done with 109 authors into it with pen and ink signatures to each article. (Price $100.) Thus we have put $15,000 into the building fund. Lippincotts have bound for me a volume *de luxe* of the History that is a corker. On the 19th I run up to Philadelphia to be the guest of the Art Club, and 1,000 invitations have been issued. It will be a proud moment. Then I run up to look over the N. Y. flats and have some repairs done and home to stay a long time. Aunt Fanny never looked so well. Mize is still patenting fresh additions to the English language, and Bess and Win are quite gay. They straw-ride and German and horseback-ride and are really seeing life.

In the late spring, misfortune struck nearer home. My mother was very ill. There were more nurses and doctors than I had seen before. For the first time in my recollection my father looked worried. The house was still and there was an air of impending tragedy.

One day Cousin Winifred Smith took Max and me for a long ride up Mills River. May-apple blossoms were in bloom, and we gathered a huge bunch of their white flowers and verdant leaves.   As we drove homeward, Cousin Win, in the most natural and sympathetic way, told us that she had hoped to have a very pleasant surprise for us, but that things had gone wrong.   We had a little brother, but he had not entered this world alive.   When we returned home, we were taken into the guest-room, where we saw the little fellow peacefully but forever asleep and there left as our silent tribute the armfuls of flowers we had gathered.   How near we had come to losing our mother we did not know, but my father makes it plain in his letters. My sisters were now at school in Washington, D. C., where Bessie received this troubled note:

> You don't know how much good your letter has done us both and especially poor mother.   And when you said you remembered her every two hours at night it made her cry, for it's in the long, long nights that she suffers, lying wakefully.   She is gaining, but no one can tell how she suffers with nervousness and sleeplessness.   No one can do much for that, but it is after all the worst agony one can go through.   She is brave and good—the same mother she has always been.
>
> Think what a little tragedy we have gone through since we saw you and Winnie!
>
> Do not work too hard and take good care of yourselves.
>
> I am afraid you could not read my last letter to you, it was so broken and disconnected.   I ought to write twenty more letters, but when I take up the pen I am paralyzed.
>
> Bye and bye I can be more calm, I hope.   Mamma is very grateful for the letters she gets and especially when you and Winnie write her.   Dr. Fletcher is a great comfort.

A little later in June he writes more cheerfully to "Cousin":

> After a few days Fanny's recovery has been perfectly marvelous. She sleeps pretty well and has a nurse that might have been sawed out by Mary E. Wilkins; angular, sweatless, and one upon whom you would naturally say that garters would have no effect; just the kind that should have screw hooks all along up her shins and spinal column, to hang raiment on—and yet she is a *real* good first class Bellevue nurse and is worth and owns $15,000 (born within 15 miles of this place) and a shrewd "*smaht*" woman.
>
> The boys are perfect little angels, though of course Heaven is so arranged that the angels have better facilities for being aired than North Carolina has.
>
> The old windmill and pump bring people from a long distance to see her *hyst*, and we are very proud of it. Your Aunt is a wonder, though I think there are some long sorry hours in the night when she claims to be asleep but when she is really wishing that little brown curly head was over there to cheer her up.
>
> When she can get out and ride we are going to have a six-seated carriage made to order with wide seats and a brake and room for things inside and under the seats. You may ride into it if you will come.
>
> Winifred is just fitting into her appointed place, and not a yap or yahoo echoes in the halls of Buck Shoals. I am general manager, Mize is Farm Superintendent, Winifred is General Smoother, Noiseless Overseer, and reader by special request. William [the butler was studying theology] represents the cause of the Redeemer, and

wears out my old pantsies. Write when you can, and you will notice an improvement in my work.

Bill Nye met and took a fancy to young John Fox, Jr., who, like Nye, was doing so much to acquaint the American public with the Southern highlanders. Fox wrote of Nye and a trip they made together:

Buncombe County is enriched by the kindly presence of Edgar Wilson Nye. He is not far from Vanderbilt—"Neighbor Vanderbilt," as Nye professionally calls him. The river sweeps below him in a semicircle, and breaking into shallows, makes Buck Shoals, the name of his "Shatto," as Nye styles his country place.

"They call shallows 'shoals' in this country," said the sage of Buncombe, "and the deer used to go to that point 'mossing'; so I took the name that was already there."

Several mountaineers passed us. They wore shapeless hats and carried old-fashioned squirrel rifles. Two or three long-eared deer-hounds and a coon dog followed them.

"I can't get very close to those fellows," said Nye. "I'm told they have some fun in them, but they shrink up when I come around."

"They are shy," said I, "until you get to know them: then they have a good deal of humor. It's rather rough usually, but it's keen and subtle sometimes in the women, who have more humor than the men."

We drew rein at Kersbrook, which is a little mountain cottage three thousand feet above the sea and just across the road from a singing trout stream.

Nye climbed from the buggy. "Well, I'm paid by that ride," he said, "if we don't catch any fish." But we did catch fish and aplenty.

We carried back that night a large appetite apiece, and we

obeyed with alacrity when we were called in to eat our trout
by a pretty mountain girl whose eyes danced like the brook's
water at the source, and whose cheeks had the rose flecks of its
trout; and then we sat out on the porch with two long pipes
and were happy.

Nye told bear stories to the pretty girl's little sister, and a
mountain boy came in and made an old banjo talk tunes several
hundred years old. After he was gone the girl sang a song
that Nye said he had not heard for many years. It made him
moody and taciturn, and he said nothing more until just as
we were going to bed, when I asked him if he would climb old
Craggy with me the next morning. He had lived many years,
he said, eight thousand feet above the sea. He had not gone
up there to look down. He was not in the habit of climbing
five thousand feet up anywhere just to look down, and he was
blamed if he was going to begin now.

The next family tragedy came in September with the
death of my mother's brother, Uncle Day K. Smith. My
father's ill health would ordinarily have kept him at home.
But Uncle Day was a beloved brother-in-law as well as a
brother Mason. And so to Kansas City went Nye to comfort and advise Aunt Margaret and our cousins.

A letter from Kansas City shows that symptoms of my
father's poor physical condition are multiplying:

> I'm going on to Chicago in a few days and thence
> North if I keep well. On arrival here I was taken with
> severe pains in the back, and analysis shows a serious
> condition of things. In fact it is important that I should
> be careful hereafter or I may get a chronic trouble set-
> tled upon me.

When my father could leave Chicago, my mother, Max,
and I went with him for a visit in Hudson as the guests of

the Humphreys. It was during this visit to the Northwest
that there happened a little adventure in politics which has
never ceased to tickle my Uncle Frank. He has told this
story better than any one else could:

The only time I ever heard Bill Nye make a political speech
there wasn't a line of politics in it, but it did the business. Joel
P. Heatwole was running for election in the Third district.
Governor Nelson had been billed to talk at a town in this
district, but at the last moment it was deemed advisable to
have him appear in Minneapolis, where the fight was getting
hot. The State committee picked me to fill the engagement,
and without knowing what I was getting into I prepared for
the trip.

My brother dropped into Minneapolis an hour or so before I
was ready to leave town. I hadn't seen him for about seven
years, and I compromised the demand for party loyalty and
brotherly devotion by inducing him to come along with me.
We had the train journey and the night to visit in, and looked
for no untoward circumstances to interrupt us.

We hadn't pulled into the depot yards of the town before
we saw trouble ahead. The magic name of the governor had
been a lodestone. Excursions from every part of the district
had been run into the town, and there, awaiting the chief executive, was a reception committee, prominent citizens in car-
riages, and a band. The reception committee was "put out,"
to say the least, and it did not attempt to conceal the fact.

"I'm ready to make quite a speech myself," I modestly said,
"and my brother Bill Nye is here, and when I get through,
maybe he will consent to say something." This didn't seem to
impress the chairman much.

"We have with us this evening Mr. Nye, of Minneapolis,"
said the chairman, "who has been sent by the State committee
to speak to us on the issues of the campaign, and we will listen
to him shortly. And there is also here," he added, as an ap-

parent afterthought, "Mr. Nye's brother—I believe he is called
Bill Nye—and he may add a few words."

I saw some of the people prick up their ears, as though the
name of Bill Nye was not entirely unknown to them. But at
this point Joel Heatwole took up the tale of woe, and his
remarks also were not calculated to greatly arouse the enthusiasm of the audience. He referred feelingly to the keen
disappointment which all felt over the failure of the governor
to appear, and painted Republican prospects in anything but
brilliant colors.

I was introduced, and we settled down to a quiet little evening of campaign talk. I guess I talked for an hour and a
quarter, and there were as many in the hall when I got through
as when I started.

And then Bill got up. I never knew him to be in better trim.
He didn't talk a word of politics, but he hadn't said a dozen
words before they were shouting; and when he had concluded
a fifteen-minute talk there were men actually rolling on the
floor.

We broke up amid a storm of demonstration, and Bill and I
escaped and went to the hotel for the long delayed visit. We
had hardly lighted our cigars when there was a rush in the
hall, the door burst open, and in bounded Joel Heatwole.

"Frank!" he cried, as he slapped me on the shoulder, "we'll
carry the county by five hundred."

We did carry the county by a good majority, and I think
Bill's speech did it.

The success of Frank and Edgar as a team suggested
joint lecturing possibilities. I have often regretted that
they never made a tour together, for Uncle Frank was successful as a serious lecturer in later years, and his style as
a speaker is such as to have been in excellent contrast to
that of his brother.

My father refers to the political incident in this letter to Bessie:

Will you excuse this small sheet of paper that was sent me by a gent who desired an autograph? I have mislaid his address and used his stamp, so he will have to write again.

I went over to Minneapolis last Tuesday, and Frank and I made two of the most beautiful speeches on Thursday ever heard in the State. He did the eloquent act, and I spoke a piece that was facetious in places.

Max and Jim have just gone to their studies with May Swanson, for they lost a day in Minneapolis. They have recovered from the feeling of depression they had when I refused to let them burn the R. R. bridge on Hallowe'en. They are real good boys now, and look fine.

Mollie is getting tired of my stories, but I tell her they go along pretty well with "Fresh Life" [the name of a composition for the piano which my mother played even more frequently than my father retold his stories].

Back at Buck Shoals, early in November he wrote my sister:

I want to send you some copies of my "pieces," the first that I have done in seven weeks and the only spare copies I have.

Mollie is getting breakfast, and so I know we will have something *re-al* good. I have had to jolt Mize up since I came home but he promises to do better.

He and Eller have adopted a 1⅛ year old boy and they are most tickled to death. Poor Max and Jim have broken noses but Nyether one nose it. They see that

the fickle Mize hardly notices them, but they are so innocent that they turn in and do everything for the little
chap and want to give him everything they've got 'cause
it pleases Mize.

Well, I 'spose you've heard the news—Election news,
I mean! Wasn't it beautiful? North Carolina was
utterly lost by the Democrats.

A bad man said that everything but Texas and H—l
had gone Republican, but since that Texas has knocked
out the Democrats, and we get Congress easy by 140 or
150 in the House.

After I made that speech in Minnesota I was telegraphed for and sought after by the Republicans on that
account, (and because I did not charge any admission).
Once St. Paul sent a special over to Hudson for me and
the engineer walked into Judge Humphrey's parlor for
me as I sat playing "Cinch" with Mrs. Humphrey.

On November 15, a letter to my sister Winifred:

It is almost dinner time now, and Gosh, how hungry
I am!

I am looking for the meal time most of the day.

Mollie makes a good cook, and I go out to the kitchen
and play I am a policeman. We have all the boiled eggs
and hash that we can eat. Also nice hot corn bread and
cream. Jim and Max have a scrap once in a long while,
but generally it does not last long and we let them settle
it themselves.

Every little while, Max and Jim write something with
their fore-fingers in the air and want to know what *that*
spells. One has to be pretty quick to do it. They can
read each other's aërial penmanship better than I can.
Jim occasionally varies these exercises by writing the

words on the top of my head and asking what *that* spells. I can read it better than when he crosses his t's and dots his i's by punching holes in the air.

You should steal in and see Max's *technique* on the piano. When he thinks that he is by himself, he just throws himself and seems to sit on a coiled spring. It reminds me of Winifred Mitchell playing something of Gre-e-eg's.

I'm going to write a History of England next year. The U. S. History passed its seventh edition some months ago.

A few days later, to the "girls":

By all means go and hear [Joseph] Jefferson. I have written a card which you may send in to him by an usher if you want to meet the dear old Dutchman. Do just as you like. I know you will be welcome. He likes nice girls.

We allow to start [for Washington] on the *3d. prox* or *ult* or whatever next month is. The Holiday U. S. History has 150 colored pictures. It's a P E A C H. . . .

Mollie sends love and is making mince pies (I can smell 'em). The boys have a pup. Its name is Hazel and I named it.

A letter written November 22, 1894, to his publisher is full of his plans for the "Comic History of England":

Dear Mr. Lippincott:

The school history of England is here and just the thing exactly. With that and the big history and Dickens, I can get along, I'm sure.

Regarding the time, I can hardly say, but I thought we would hardly care to turn this one loose before next

September or thereabouts, though of course I *could* do it earlier. I'd like to see the U. S. History have a chance this season by itself; still I do not know but the two would play into each other's hands. By the way, I got hold of a very nice notice of the U. S. History the other day from Manchester in which the author was described as "by far the most original American Humorist without doubt."

I think I can beat that book the next shot. I *know* I can beat that preface. I've got two or three chapters on England already that with a little editing will be O. K. George the Third, for instance . . . Darn him!

I feel just like it and will make it a *chief do over*, as the French say (if I have spelled it correctly).

I hope we will be fortunate in an artist, but I don't care a cuss what the critics say. All of them have unpublished MSS. in their old trunks, and they can't forgive anybody who gets out a book. Was there ever a critic who was not a stillborn author or dramatist with an old funky play or unborn book lying like a dead polecat in the attic of his abode?

On November 14, 1894, Nye writes in appreciation of several new books from Riley:

My Dear Jamsie:

You will be surprised and pained to know that I am home again, having *came* through Indianapolis without telegrafting you, but I tried from Chicago to your justly celebrated city to get off a message which read as follows:

Catalpa and I will pass through your place at 2:50 P.M. on Big 4 train.

16 pd.   WM. NYE.

BILL NYE'S SON, FRANK WILSON (JIM) NYE, ARRANGER OF THIS BOOK

But eyether the accursed operator could not be found or the Western Union Office was up town at the very few points where we stopped. Suffice to say that when I got to the beautiful Union Depot I still had the telegraft in my hand but yet looked out at window as who should say, "Mayhap the cuss will be down here missing trains today and I'll watch for him."

Your delightful books are here and not "an old favorite" amongst the lot. All are new and fresh as the dew. How dew you dew it? as a reporter once asked me regarding my works.

"Armazindy" is about the best of all from title *rôle* to tail piece—humorous or pathetic the author is equally at home (e.o.d. tf).

"Rabbit in the Crossties" to the magnificent Decoration Day Poem, all, all are strong and beautiful as human language and poor weak etymology, syntax and prosody can make them. Just as the carping and flatulent critic is about to say, "The air is getting a little heavy here. He is getting in too many dead children," here comes "Ringworm Frank," and ere we know it, with a pang, we butt our eager brows against the *envoy* and with a sigh look up at the old clock, which is crowding 4 A.M.

I shall let no lectures this winter, I wot, but like to carry around the applications and look at them "between the walnuts and the wine." You will be glad to know that I am extremely well and fat and that with a little damp weather my hair would sprout and thus ruin my business.

We had 25 bushels sweet potatoes this year and sold 1,200 cabbages. All the barn lofts and corn cribs are full, and so is the Georgia Sand Walloper, who did it under my direction. We had one 60 lb. watermelon and

oodlins of 30, 40 and 50 pounders. If you will come here
next summer, I'll have John Fox, Jr., the author of the
"Cumberland Vendetta," and we three can have a good
deal of moral fun. Just ice tea, Panatella Cigars, Star
Tobacco, sunshine, *Dolce Farina*, as they say in Italy, and
6 miles of river to spit in. Whassay, Wess?

Seriously I wish that you could and would try it, and
when you get weary of it there are trains that will take
you away. You can oversleep yourself—if you want to,
overeat yourself or over-spit yourself—all will be forgiven. I forgot to say your Dickens prose story is bully
and reads as if written on Gad's Hill, and I know for
I'm a student of Dickens for over 30 years. Goodbye,
my dear boy, with love to Doc. Hays and the friends.
Ever,

Yours,
BILL.

P. S. Tomorrow we kill a hog, and if you could be
here you might have his tail.

Nye did not want to go stale. Rural life at Buck Shoals
provided much good copy, but there was danger of monotony. Lecturing with its hardships provided change, stimulated new thoughts. There was to be no lecturing this
winter. My sisters were at school in Washington, and as
my father had always liked the capital and joyed to be
close to the fountainhead of government, we took up our
abode there in December. The fact was soon reflected in
my father's weekly letters.

Washington in many ways is the most delightful city
for residence in the Union, as everybody knows.

Still there is an air of intense anxiety here, a sort of
hurried glance over the shoulder, ever and anon, before

doing an important act, as if to discover what one's constituents will think of it. The only really happy man here is out of politics and without hope of an appropriation.

He that seeketh an appropriation during this session will have redness of eyes, ringing in the ears, palpitation of the heart, apprehension regarding the future, vertigo, and thoughts of self-destruction long before the money is brought to his boarding house in a neat package by a special messenger.

The vice president was speaking the other day to me on board the Asheville and Washington sleeper of the old-time political stump speaker, and among other things told of Dick Oglesby's methods of dealing with the currency question.

"Gentlemen," he said, "we now come to the currency question, of which the Democrats talk to you so much.

"Now, they ought not to do that. They don't understand and never did and never will understand the currency question. Why, gentlemen, the plain goddlemighty's truth about the currency question is that it's as much as the Republicans can do to understand it."

My father went to New York, writing:

I came on here to assist in a dinner to Conan Doyle and emitted a speech on that occasion, together with such rising young men as Depew, Noah Brooks, John Burroughs, and General Horace Porter.

Doyle is a big gent, of the Sam Jackman style, and talks like a basswood man with elmwood teeth. But he is a good feller.

I had John Burroughs on one side and Noah Brooks on the other, at the Doyle dinner, and made the first

speech after Doyle, with here and there slightly humorous remarks.

A letter to Uncle Mitchell, written Christmas day, gives
a good idea of how my father was enjoying his vacation
from the lecture platform:

1101 K Street,
The Strathmore Arms.

My Dear Alick:
    The box arrived yesterday, and everything hit the
bull's-eye of appreciation. I appropriated the umbrella
because I just exactly wanted it, although there was no
name on it.
    The boys got a "Safety" bicycle, and I need not say
that they are clinging to it with great difficulty but grimly
determined to ride it before 24 hours go by. They have
hardly slept for a week, worried for fear they had not
been good enough to secure it. They made a great effort
and really deserved it.
    This evening we are to have the five-cent Xmas tree
and lots of "spawt," I dare say. We have delightful
people here, thirty perhaps; among them Commander
Wilde of the navy. We are quite independent in the matter of sunny large rooms and a table to ourselves. There
is a fine smoking-room where we *all* go of evenings, play
cards, smoke pipes, tell stories and have *real* fun by the
bushel.
    We are renewing acquaintance with Vice President Ste-
venson and daughter, and last evening the U. S. Treas-
urer called, by Gosh! We have no idea of being lonesome
for a minute. I've had a box (complimentary) to the
shows: so far the Knickerbockers and De Wolfe Hopper.
All the good things seem to come here. Did I write you

about Dean H——? Guess I did. He and I have struck up a friendship and are *real chummy.*—Just fawncy.—He has given me a warm invitation to come and visit him at the Deanery.

It's only an hour from London and in the old historical neighborhood of Robin Hood, Dickens, and the rest. He was a friend of Dickens, Gladstone, Thackeray and Leech, the artist.

He wants me to go with him on a lecture tour to California, but I think one cannot be too careful about traveling with a stranger that way. Isn't that so?

Frances and I attended services at the Church of the Immaculate Collection this morning. It was superior to the service at Buck Shoals, and we enjoyed it in a pious way. A whole *passle* of boys did the singing and wore white wrappers. So much time was taken up with miscellaneous dialogue and specialties that the preacher only had fifteen minutes for preaching purposes, which suited me to a dot. The History is selling like hot cakes, and Brentano has sold out several times here.

We have scaled the Monument and are going to visit Mount Vernon. Have lunched with the Daughters of the Revolution, and I've been "interviewed" till my heart aches. Thearle wants me to promise him next season, but I haven't done so, though I yearn for the taels, francs, pounds, shillings and pence.

CHAPTER XXIII

SHIPWRECK, THE PATTERSON INCIDENT AND THE STAG PARTY: 1895

You may be sure that the winter in Washington was a big season for Max and me, despite the humiliation of attending the primary department of Mount Vernon Seminary for *young ladies*.

Our father devoted many afternoons and holidays to personally conducted tours of the capital city for our benefit. He had been living in the country for the better part of four years and, for a change, seemed to delight in the society of the other guests of the Stratford Arms. The theater, the shops, and the governmental activities also stimulated new interest. Most of the time he was gay and sparkling.

Late in January Nye sailed from New York for the Bahama Islands. The last few years of my father's life give the impression that destiny had marked him for a tragic end and was sniping at him from ambush with ammunition of various kinds. In February Fate's choice of weapons was shipwreck. I shall give first my father's account of the accident in his letter to my mother:

On Schooner *Good Will*.

We are rescued from the wreck of the steamer, and I can write a few lines to send by our Consul. I cannot tell you how glad I am to be alive, nor can I write the details of the wreck. I do not want any more experiences like it. We will get to Nassau, I hope, today, but cannot return before two weeks. Our ship struck yesterday

374

A. M. and in ten minutes my stateroom had filled breast high, for I was astern and she settled rapidly there. I got most everything but "Thelma" [the novel]. She went down. My telescope was filled with salt water and everything ruined.

We had great difficulty in getting off the ship by small boats. The first one was swamped, but women and all were gathered up by another boat, owned by native sponge gatherers, who afterward took the rest aboard this schooner. We were all day getting to Harbor Island, where we were made comfortable last night. Of course we are pretty well shaken up nervously, and I could not sleep—none of us could—for all night we were going over it again. There were two little babies and fifty-two passengers beside the crew. I dressed swiftly and was the first passenger on deck. For two hours the steamer was settling and likely to go to pieces, with not nearly enough small boats to hold us and no safety even for them to go ashore in the dark, over the immense reefs. But with daylight and the aid of the natives who had seen our rockets, we began to feel a little more chipper.

The night before I could not get to sleep at all till two o'clock, and to get sleepy I repeated the Lord's Prayer over 1,000 times, so, you see, when we struck I had that all attended to and could give my attention to other things.

Seriously, though, I never had a closer call, for if we had stopped on the first reef instead of going *over it* we would have gone down at once, as she would have broken in two. But our momentum carried us over it and up on the second reef. The water rushed in and put out the fires in the engines in eight minutes.

Bless de Lord it was no worse. I was so comfortable

to know that you and the children were safe on Terra Cotta instead of being with me, that I almost *enjoyed* myself. When I saw the little chaps (there were three boys like Max and Jim), all so good, and yet so likely to go down, I felt pretty well pleased to know that our little fellers were not along, nor you, Mollie.

The doctor prescribed grog in small quantities for every one when we got off the wreck safely, and I asked him if the grog made by old man Mumm would answer. He claimed that it would, and so, as the doctor himself ordered it, I just shut my eyes and swallowed it before I had time to taste the wretched stuff. Some of the passengers are still following up the treatment, and Father Lavelle was so much improved that he told me a little parable which I shall have to tell Mr. Smillie, Commander Wilde, Mr. Childs, Mr. Davis, and Major Hopkins [smoking-room companions at Washington]. I was going to tell Ford, but he is too young.

The papers of March 9 carried Nye's own detailed story of his voyage and the wreck. Those who read the account thoughtfully will see in its seriousness plain evidence of the severe nervous shock which he sought to hide:

I was somewhat late in securing my stateroom, so had to take one extremely aft. I was the last one to get quarters, and that is why they were so aft. No one was after than I.

When we retired on Sunday night, the sea was moderately calm, and no one was ill. All the mal de mer of the trip was forgotten as we went to bed knowing that we would land at our Bahama port in the afternoon of Monday.

I could not go to sleep readily. I read and smoked

and rolled about in my berth till 2 o'clock and then slept rather lightly. At 4:45 A. M. there was a scrape on the keel of the vessel like the low, hoarse growl of a bull-dog in the basement, and I awoke thinking I was at home and that a burglar below, in hunting for my cider barrel, had stepped on Towser.

A moment afterward a deeper growl from the keel and a jerk of the vessel showed that she had struck. I dressed hurriedly, but took time to put on an extra suit of flannels in case I should have to spend a few weeks on the ocean in an open boat. In a few minutes my stateroom had been flooded and a good suit of lecturing clothes had been placed on the bargain counter.

I started back once to get my hairbrush, but the water met me half way, and I returned to the upper deck. The weather was thick, and the rain came down in gusts, while all about us the noise of the surf breaking over the sharp reefs could be heard. The steamer settled rapidly and the captain ordered the lifeboats made ready.

The passengers were put into the boats, women and children first, and the most touching picture was that of the separation between wives and husbands and parents and children, for we could not be certain that the boats would safely hold every one. The first boat which tried to cross the reef was swamped at once, and women, children and crew thrown into the sea.

We had grown to know and to like each other in our four days' voyage, and to see those agonized faces turned toward us and the pale and horrified fathers and husbands on our deck forced to see their families go down within forty yards of us, or be torn to pieces by the serrated edge of the reefs, and their bodies given to the waiting sharks, that was the trying time with us.

Some people in such a calamity run around wildly looking for a toothbrush or an umbrella. Others try to get something to eat. Others think of their wives, but their natural instinct is to think of themselves. These passengers almost without exception behaved like born ladies and gentlemen.

To sit in a lifeboat that is tied up on the flank of a wrecked ship which may go down to the bottom at any moment and know that the chances are ten to one that your boat will not live five minutes when she is launched is not a pleasant method of passing the time.

I sat in one for half an hour by order of the officer, and then I got out and stood on the deck.

Finally a boat was sent out by Captain Hoyt, under First Officer Smith, in search of an opening in the reef, but after two hours' hard work it returned unsuccessful.

The steward made hot coffee and a fine hot steak for each of us, which we ate with our fingers, on deck, and in our life preservers.

With the approach of day, Mr. Van Winkle of Newark, N. J., from the bridge, saw with his glass a schooner of 62 tons (though I took her to be about 62½ tons) several miles away and tacking, it seemed, to get to us in answer to our gun rockets. For a while I feared that she might be one of the ships that pass in the night, and I said so to a deaf man with a tin ear, but he rebuked me for being gay in the presence of death. Now, will the reader please tell me what death has ever done for me that I should show him any attentions in the matter of etiquette?

Soon another sail hove in sight, and with the approach of daylight 30 or 40 craft, manned by blacks, mostly sponge fishers, appeared to the eastward. They managed, with their light boats and perfect knowledge of the shore, and their skill, to cross the reef, and before long the captain of the *Good Will*, the 62 ton schooner, had arranged with Captain Hoyt to take us and our ruined baggage to Harbor Island.

We were 30 miles off our course and should not have been there. A steamship is made to run on water, not on land. The moment you try to ride around over bare ground in a steamer you get yourself in trouble.

The following week's story continued Nye's account of his adventures in the Bahamas.

As these lines are being penned the good ship *Cienfuegos* is going to pieces on the rocks, and the mullet, the angel fish, the yellow-tailed snapper, the cowfish, the spikefish, the jewfish, the shark, the smelt, the mackerel, the skate, the flounder, and the eel are sailing up and down the gilded saloon and criticizing the architecture of the ship.

There is no cow on Harbor Island, and goat's milk has to suffice. We were taken by the rescuing schooner to Dunmore Town, a little hamlet on Harbor Island, and were met by all the inhabitants, who asked me to lecture.

Those who were capsized in crossing the reef were fitted out as well as possible with dry clothing and gladly took what came along. A prominent Philadelphian appeared in a sponge fisher's overalls, and a New York lady cheerfully rolled up the bottoms of a pair of flannel trousers and paced the deck with a glad smile.

The officers said we were the best behaved party they ever saw at a wreck. This is a high compliment considering that we had never attended anything of the kind before.

On Tuesday morning we went aboard the schooner and

started for Nassau, 52 miles distant, but the wind died
down about 10 o'clock, and we were becalmed. I told
Captain Sweeting repeatedly to luff, but he seemed to
think he knew his own business better than I did.

However, the *Santiago*, bound for New York, and a
sister ship of the *Cienfuegos*, hove in sight just off the
wreck and took us in tow, so that before sunset on Tuesday the Hog Island light, off Nassau, could be seen, and
the white breakers shooting up 30 or 40 feet into the air,
with a background of palms and the white walls of the
fort.

The people of Nassau are divided into two classes; *viz.*,
those who do absolutely nothing and those who solicit
pence.

The Bahamas soon began to bore Nye, according to indi-
cations in a third instalment of his log:

I might like to spend a honeymoon here or recover
from gout, but otherwise I would not hanker for this mad,
mad life, which consists mostly of walking from the hotel
down to the dock, where you spit thoughtfully into the
beautiful water and return to the hotel again. It is restful, but it does not improve one intellectually. If I had
a brand new bride and feared that some one more attractive than I—we will just suppose this for the sake of
argument—might win her from me, if I mingled too much
in Saratoga, I would bring her here, where I would have
no rival. I would keep the money and return tickets in
my own possession and threaten to leave her here if she
smiled on another.

But, thanks to the fatal gift of beauty, I do not have
to do that! My chief difficulty now consists in keeping

the moths from scorching their beautiful wings in the
bright glare of my massive smile.

There was no temptation for Nye to prolong his stay
in the Bahamas. The journey had had its share of thrills,
but the mountains of North Carolina began to call, and,
as quickly as expedient, the call was answered.

The welcome of the prodigal son was as nothing to that of
our "Tod" when he returned to Arden. He brought back
many interesting photographs and curios, including a linen
table-cloth, upon which those who had been wrecked with
him had recorded their autographs. These were duly trans-
lated into embroidery by the skilful needle of my mother.

A letter to Bessie in the early spring:

Well, I suppose you want to know about the trees!
They are putting out leaves at a great rate, and the boys
wanted to know how much I'd pay them per wheelbarry
load to put old leaves all around the new trees. I said 5
cents per load but little thought they would want to
carry (or tote rather) more than 10 loads, but now they
have shet Tom Mize off and propose to do it all themselves. They almost discharged Mize because the other
day he put a load around some rosebushes. Half the
time I have to put Mize and Pinner to the plow so Max
and Jim can have the two wheelbarrows. You ought to
see them play whist in the evening after a long hard day
hauling autumn leaves. They play together and kick
each other under the table and beat us most every night.
Mamma thinks they are horrible, for they make Martha
read to them after they are gone to bed. They claim
to be asleep first, long enough to allay apprehension,
and then the quickest one suddenly covers the other's

| head with the quilt and holds it there till he cries for
| fresh air. Mamma thinks such boys get shot most gen-
| erally, but they do not. In a year or two they will be-
| have as sweet as Johnnie Couch or Pinner.

The March, 1895, number of the "Ladies' Home Journal"
contained an illustrated page story of Buck Shoals and
"The Family of a Humorist." The story is full of Bokian
touches, and there are some inaccuracies. One of the illustrations is from a photograph of Bill Nye taken during
his last visit to London. It happened to show him about
to light a cigarette; certainly this would not come under
the head of a "Bokian touch." These details by way of
explaining a letter to Bessie which follows. But first let me
quote from the story:

Mrs. Nye received training on the piano, and has an excellent contralto voice. She sings at Calvary Church, near Buck
Shoals, and has been an Episcopalian always. She is essen-
tially a good housekeeper, a good wife and a good mother.
She is one of Mrs. Rorer's pupils, and, as her husband ex-
presses it, "likes to construct a new salad or experiment with
a new design in pie."

Mrs. Nye has always been a comrade, and the good fellowship and bonhomie existing between the husband and wife have
made him cautious about falling short from any cause in the
estimation of his wife. This good fellowship has made "Bill
Nye" also a poor clubman and man-about-town. As was said
by a member of the Lotos Club, and as Nye likes to repeat,
when urged to stay late he put on his overcoat and said good-
night. "You are the best fellers in the world, except my wife.
There is no one else I'd leave you for."

The poor of the mountains know Mrs. Nye far and wide, and
all have known well of her judicious benevolence. Food and
clothing go silently to the deserving poor, and Nye says when

he goes to bed at night he bids good-by to his clothes, fearing that he will see them next on a sad-eyed mountaineer.

There are four children, Bessie, aged sixteen; Winifred, fourteen, and Max and Jim, aged respectively eight and seven years. They have their father's eyes that seem to see a funny thing a long while before any one else can. And that they can run faster, walk further, catch more squirrels than any other boys of their age, tells the story of their strength and their preparation for the work of men.

The children are very fond of their father. They call him "Tod," and there is between him and them the most absolute confidence and companionship. This letter was written just recently from Jim to "Tod" out West on a lecturing tour.

"Dear Tod:
"Mize shot a squirrel; stuffed it and gave it to me, I send a kiss.
"Good-by.   "JIM NYE."

Winifred is the book-worm of the family. Bessie is very companionable to her mother, and has a positive talent for entertaining children, which she turns to account for the amusement of the boys, whose instruction is now carried on at home.

The house, according to Mr. Nye, is a sort of Colonial Queen Anne, "with a Watteau back." It is a handsome cottage of twenty rooms, finished in the oak, ash, chestnut, curly poplar and Georgia pine, which grows there; has open wood fires in every room, wide porches and all the luxuries and comfort of the American summer home. It is abundantly lighted with electricity, the power for which is furnished from an old mill further down the slope, upon which the farm rests. The grounds, too, have the electric arcs, and are lovelier than a dream when the sun goes down. Back of the house stands the carriage barn, frescoed with pigeons; and a pair of matched, black, carriage horses from Lexington, Kentucky, and two saddle horses, constitute the stud.

Within the house are the things well and affectionately known to readers of Bill Nye, among them the dog whose tail "wags in harmony with the dictates of his heart." Mr. Nye's writing is inspired by household occurrences, and the world laughs at the familiar happenings which wake sympathetic echoes in every heart.

And it may be added: "No one in the world has a more harmonious or congenial home circle, or one dominated by a woman more fitted to make a happy home than Mrs. Edgar Wilson Nye."

The next letter to Bessie gives the aftermath of the article:

I have just finished a couple of fine Jack o' lanterns for the boys, made of gourds with a hinged door at the back for the candle to go in. They are quite lum-tum. The roads are vile at present and jolt the daylights out of one with perfect ease. Between here and Asheville the roads are lined with cast-off daylights.

Max and Jim are riding their roller-skates on the porch while I write, and the roar mingles with that of Buck Shoals. By the way, our mail is mostly relative to that article in the Ladies' Home Journal. Begging letters and letters criticizing my cigarette come pouring in on every mail.

Frank and Storm are in good condition and when you come home in June—oh, how I wish it could be June *now* —we hope to be ready to give you a hearty welcome in our country home "lighted by electricity and surrounded by palms."

I haven't got so as to eat mince pie with impunity yet or even by itself.

We are happy and proud to know that you are both so industrious and altogether lovely. Nobody else has a

CALVARY EPISCOPAL CHURCH AT FLETCHER, N. C., WHERE NYE IS BURIED

MEMORIAL WINDOW TO NYE, ERECTED BY MRS. NYE SOON AFTER HIS DEATH

MEMORIAL, ERECTED IN CALVARY CHURCH YARD IN 1925

Standing from left to right, Frank Wilson Nye and his two children, Lorraine M. and Edgar Wilson, second; also Mrs. Eugene A. Pharr (Bessie Nye).

family quite like the one that Toddie is at the head of.
Tell me if you need more means and I will sell a turkey
and send you some.

In his press letter written a little later Nye again ac-
knowledges the publicity bestowed upon our family by the
editor of the "Home Journal":

A good friend wrote up our home here and spoke of us
so sweetly and of how generous we were with our wealth
that over 1,800 applications came in at once for help.
Everything was ordered, from my last season's dress suit
to $1,000 in cash. On top of this came the income tax.
One girl wrote that she needed $1,000 very much, but
feared that if I sent it to her through the mails some one
might discover it, and then her proud heart would break.
So I did not send it to her.
The description of our humble home and sweetness of
disposition was printed in the "Ladies' Home Journal,"
and I had never believed before that it had 750,000 circulation, but I now think that it is even more than that,
for I have two typewriters at work alone on the applications of bright young invalids who wish to take me to
Europe, meantime extending to me the hospitalities of
my equilibrium at the bank.
I am generous but I am intimately acquainted with the
lives and histories of a regiment of those who are deserving of assistance, and I do not have to get affidavits on
that point. If there should be a congestion of wealth
around the house sufficient to impede vegetation, after
these are attended to, I will then seek avenues elsewhere,
but those whose nearest and best friends will not buy them
an upright piano to cover their nakedness will not succeed much better with strangers.

My wife is really the more generous of the two and has
unlimited means. (This is done as a bit of pleasantry
and to open up a friendly correspondence between her
and the United States.)

For several seasons now Nye had been lecturing under
the Redpath Lyceum Bureau's management, but he still
wrote to Major Pond occasionally. On July 4 a letter to
the Major refers to the death of Burbank:

Poor old Burbank, I was about to say, but why should
I say that when he is taking a grand old rest after a
rather thorny trip? There never lived a more unselfish
gentleman than he. There are mighty few comrades that
can go through dark alleys and dangerous stage entrances
that are kept locked against the lecturer and only open
to the call of the felonious loafer who comes to shift your
scenery—only a few comrades, I say, who can go through
frosty towns and bitter weather cheerily, as he did—
noble old man! And there's no such test on earth to try
a feller's mettle, is there? I think it's a good idea to reform and abandon such a life before the hearse is actually
at the door waiting for one. I am cheerily preparing to
say farewell to these triumphal tours which wreck both
soul and body at so much a pair.

In a letter of April 24 to his Aunt Maria Field, my
father throws an interesting light upon his thoughts when
he writes:

I hardly think anybody up home realizes what a seri-
ous-minded funny man I have become the past year.
Manny things have combined to knock the trifling elements out of me, and I feel a good deal more in earnest

than ever before—not in a sentimental semi-annual way, but in a practical way that more befits a man approaching 45 years old.

I've been *almost* burned up, blowed up, shipwrecked, poisoned, shot and God knows what, but not quite. Always there has been an angel in ambush to prevent the full completion of what was apparently fatal.

These things have conspired, along with Fanny, to show me a hunk of horse sense concealed behind a tree and which I have socked into a vacancy which I found exactly fitted it. But enough.

Late in the spring I had a light case of diphtheria. Though uncomfortable for a while, I felt quite important, as in this case I had the distinction of being the only member of the family on the sick list. Also I had a trained nurse and much attention. It was many years later that I first read my father's sympathetic letters written during the quarantine.

Dearest Becky:

It is quite serious at best to have diphtheria in our home and patient old Jim off there in one corner of it. But it is not so gloomy as you might think, for we are all determined *not* to have it so. In the first place Jim is gay as a lark and could not gain faster. The nurse too is better than most physicians for diphtheria.

Jim works at arithmetic and has written out all the tables, eats like Johnnie Couch, and yesterday was singing like a bird. So you must not worry too much. We can correspond with him and "cut up" on the grass when nurse brings him to the window. He sends his love, and would divide his "goggle" with you if you would care for it. Yesterday he had a squab and ice cream. He looked at the squab, ate it, and the nurse said, "How did you like it."

"Oh, all right," say he, "but pwecious little of it."

I have been sent for by Mr. A. M. Palmer of New York and Paul M. Potter who dramatized "Trilby," to come this evening and meet Mr. Potter in Asheville, to arrange for writing with him a comedy for Mr. Palmer's theater to open in September. Isn't that gay? I hope "my life will be spared the remainder of my days" so that I can do the lots of work I have to do next season, and this summer.

Another letter written during my illness says:

Max and I have to play a good deal together and hunt azalias by the river's sedgy brim. We leave the brush full of interrogation points where he has shed them all along our trail. If he should remember all he finds out, of me, he will be one of the best informed men of the twentieth century.

The last two letters suggest what a good pal our "Tod" was to Max and me. His attitude was always fraternal rather than paternal. He seemed to have as much fun playing with us as we had cutting up with him. And there never was any sport better than that.

There was nothing patronizing about his contact with us. A child is quick to sense anything forced about a grown-up's attentions. We were just three care-free kids together. Tod made no secret of the fact that our society was as pleasant to him as that of our elders. The twinkle in those gay and kindly brown eyes put us and kept us at our ease. If family discipline needed enforcement it was our mother who made us toe the mark.

Tod loved to be a boy again by showing us how to make Jack-o'-lanterns, squirt-guns, and sourwood whistles. When he could spare the time he would take long walks or rides with us and delight us with his whimsicalities. We felt less constrained than when called upon to play with the child of a neighbor.

Once he invited us to take a journey to Spartanburg as his guest. Spartanburg, South Carolina, is several hours by rail from Fletcher station. We had never been far south of Buck Shoals and often asked questions about the country lying beyond that edge of the horizon. Spartanburg was a city of dark mystery to us. To our father it was just another dull little town. Railway travel was the last thing he yearned for. But he knew the trip would give us a major thrill. And so when he could get away he joined us in this exploration.

Nowadays a trip around the world would not begin to stimulate such delight as did this expedition. We caught an early train, spent an hour or so in the Mecca of our dreams, and returned the same evening. It was only a day's excursion, but what a day! How entertaining and mature we were made to feel! For one day we were men. To be sure, Tod bought us little railway lanterns filled with varicolored candies and everything else that a juvenile heart could covet. But the point was, he bought the same things for himself, and he seemed to enjoy them quite as much as we did. His letters show how it tickled him to be a youngster with his youngsters. This we felt, and it put the finishing touch of enjoyment upon our own good times.

His nearest approach to punishing us was on a certain memorable occasion. The family drove away to be gone all the afternoon. As soon as the carriage was well out of sight Max and I built a nice bonfire under the side porch. We did not burn the house down. We did not even scorch the paint. We realized our occupation was extra-hazardous, and, accordingly, we were extra cautious.

The fire was blazing merrily when, much to our surprise, the family, having changed their plans, returned and caught us red-, or, rather, black-handed. Very gravely, Tod approached us. "Boys," he said, "right after supper I want you to report to the library." It was then early afternoon, and hours must pass before our terrible suspense would be appeazed. By the gravity of his mien we knew that there was something unusual in store for us. Throughout the afternoon and at supper we sat thoughtfully with hanging heads, wondering what form of punishment would be ours. When at last we were called upon the carpet, we were invited to remove that part of our apparel which might tend to dim the recollection of what was about to be administered. This being done, we listened to one of the most exclusive and eloquent lectures our father ever delivered. At its conclusion we were told that we could bring our trousers back to normalcy without the actual administration of corporal punishment, as our preceptor felt that we had learned our lesson and would not build any more fires. We never did. Nor did we forget. Exactly the desired reaction was achieved, but it was done in good humor and with all kindliness. Had we not been so awed, I am sure we should have been highly amused at the no doubt humorous remarks included in the lecture.

A letter to Clara Mitchell:

I'm tickled to say that Jim has been out several days. He is the same old happy Jim, ever and anon killing a snake and bringing it in and laying it on my desk— always thinking more of my pleasure than of his own.

"Atty Nye" [my mother] had a sore throat yesterday. I pried it open and looked down it as far as etiquette would permit but could see no signs of anything serious, and so she and I took the fiery Kentucky saleratus blonde hoss Dandy and the yaller cart and went to Arden in order to be among people more. We were overtaken in our topless cart by a thundering mass of rain which saturated us generally, though I had an umbrella at which the elements seemed to smile in their sleeves—having them made large for that purpose. But the ducking cured the sore throat in 15 minutes. Today Fanny is plumb well and looks real sweet. A happy marriage has preserved her youth and buoyancy of spirits—like everything. Doubtless you know that I am in up to me eyebrows fooling with industry again—writing books, plays, lectures, magazine articles—farming, growing fruit, small grains, roots, fruits, nuts, berries and herbs in their season, yet phat, well, and moderately pious.

And to Uncle Mitchell, on May 23:

Yours of some days ago was gladly received. It found us absolutely well, and "he who hath his health hath four-fifths of all that God gives to man."

We go soon to Suffolk, Va., and several towns where I will assist at some college commencements. We will go first and get Becky and Winnie, thence ride down the coast by boat to Norfolk and be the guests of some nice folks, visit the Dismal Swamp, by boat and with high gum boots, and get home about the 9th of June. I hope that it will be smooth all the way. Max and Jim will take care of Buck Shoals, and Mrs. W., Jim's diphtheria nurse will take care of them. The boys would a damp site rather stay here than go most anywhere. Mize, the little tin Deity, will be near them, and they will help him with the craps.

Yesterday we got four and a half gallons of nice strawberries, and we've a nice new red cow, and with two redder cows to assist her, berries and cream for the young and growing as well as the aged and tottering will be the rule. I am now weighing almost 200 pounds, and on well-water and salt mackerel at that.

I've signed the contract with Palmer (for the play) and got a check from him to start with, so it looks like business, and if you want a leading part you must be ready by August 15th to attend rehearsals. Can I depend upon you?

A gossipy letter to my sister Winifred contained some good advice, characteristically worded. Nye lived before the "repression" of children was a live topic. But his method of getting results with his offspring was quite modern in that he did not indulge in scoldings, don'ts, and punishment. The friendly counsel to my sister Winifred was as close as he came to admonishment.

The Mize horse has a little coltie with a star in its forward. Mollie is looking tip top and has made herself a lot of new bonnets during the rainy days. They are quite swell and not large by any means. A jet button, with a hole in it for a hat pin to run through, makes a good bonnet for evening and keeps off the night air which is so injurious. We should always avoid the night air, I think, even if we have to hold our breath till breakfast time.

I didn't think I scolded you at all in Bessie's letter. Probably you are mistaken about that, but I don't want you to get as Max did so that he counted on his birthday dollar from me about a year ahead and had it laid out in advance, 'cause I might suddenly decide to give you a calendar or something useful, instead of a check. However, I think you must see by this time that whether you have much or little it can all evaporate for no especial good and for trifles, so that when one's laundry bill falls due there is no "shot in the locker" to meet it with. This is good advice and not scolding by any means, and I put it here so that there will be nothing of the kind to say when I see you. The money at present is of far less importance than the idea itself.

P. S.—In order that there should be no *hard feelings* in \$\$ matters I enclose a few dollars for you both. Advice is a good thing but I'd rather give most anything else to my dear delightful daughters.

At commencement time, my parents made the contemplated trip to Washington, Virginia, and the Dismal Swamp, bringing my sisters home for the summer. Thereafter Farmer Nye was soon immersed in hay-making, mostly from the front porch.

My new hay rake is three feet wider than my farm, and I had to get a right of way over an adjoining farm or have trouble.

Mine is a very slim farm, and the crops are similar in some respects. We have a new colt on the place, but he is not yet accustomed to his new legs. He can barely stand up when propped against the lunch counter of which his mother is the proprietor.

Of course I do not claim to make the farm pay. It is all I can do to make anybody pay, but the farm as a farm has never paid unless you estimate that the board of six people on the farm is worth \$7,200, and even then

we must take out of that $200 for taxes and insurance
and $9,000 for groceries and pop, of which we are pas-
sionately fond.

No; I did not take up farming as a means of livelihood,
and I can no longer conceal that fact from the public. I
took up farming in order to prove to my wife what a free
and independent life it is, with its golf, its tennis, its
pure air, rich cream and insolvency.

A letter to his mother of June 30 shows that despite
repeated red lanterns along the track, Nye had allowed himself to undertake responsibilities and a program of hard
work that would have been arduous for a man in the pink
of condition. Can it have been that he was blind to the
repeated warnings of the approaching breakdown? Such
undertakings were contrary to the earnest urging of my
mother. She at least knew that the family breadwinner
was taxing himself beyond his strength. And every member of the family but its head joined in the hope that he
would soon take things easier, no matter what readjustment
our standard of living might have to undergo as a result.

I am working very hard and do not try to keep up
any correspondence at all regularly as I have no one to
assist me. Am writing a play, getting two books ready
for the printer, writing a new lecture, a Sunday letter,
and running a farm, besides answering fifty letters a
week. This will pass for my busiest summer in forty-
five years.

I have agreed to go out twenty-two weeks with a cartoonist to assist me. I go on a guaranteed amount per
week with 33 1-3 per cent over a certain amount of receipts; that is the best arrangement I have ever made.

Max and Jim are tall and big for their ages and, on

the whole, very good boys. They have had a rather scattered education so far but are in fine health and can read and are crazy to learn. They are swift in mathematics and have just been in here to exhibit a little book of *poems* that they have issued with the aid of Martha (the colored maid, who writes and reads splendidly).

A letter to Cousin Clara in the early autumn:

I'm almost down with a sort of grippe or influenza which destroys 4 handkerchiefs and one large damask table-cloth per diem.

The play is going to be produced the latter part of October. I have the History of England two-thirds done. The publisher says it knocks the socks off the U. S.

In the dim distance I hope to combine on lecturing with my brother Frank, who has developed into a sweet-voiced orator of the Demosthenes variety. It may not be, but I am hoping for it one day.

I am a national director of the Lyceum League of America too, Coz, an organization for the benefit of the young citizen—for debate and study of political economy, local study of town, city and state politics. There is no hope for the old political bums, but the young man and woman (she's in it) may pull us out of our degraded position. There are just 500,000 members, and local Lyceums are asking by telegraph for charters. Me and Ed. Everett Hale is two of the directors, and Theodore Roosevelt was first President. Enough of Ego Nye, however.

A letter to Bessie after my sisters' return to school in the fall:

Mr. P. Potter took the completed "Stag Party" [the new play] in his little grip and started for New York. It will doubtless be November 15 before the play is produced in N. Y.

Meantime I've only two more weeks at home, and as the boys go to school or to lessons and only get back at 2 o'clock the *shatto* is like a deserted robin's nest of '85. But go way! How gay she looks in her *new paint*. It looks as big as the "Anthropological," as Mamma used to say, and very *ricochet*.

The boys and I were to go to the circus on Monday, but they ran away today to Geo. Lance's to play with Mr. Baker's little boy with whom they had a fight day-before-yesterday and yearned for yet another. So they will be excused from Buffalo Bill's show.

Cousin Winnie plays each evening, Mamma sheds tears and I smoke. I feel powerful good to get my Drammer done, but Gosh how lonesome hit is! We will surely be in Washington the 26th. We open the lecture season at Newport News the 23rd and are in New York and Philadelphia before the holidays.

I dread the first week very much indeed. Oh, *so* much.

A few days later another short note to "Fet":

I miss your merry laughter sadly, for as you say I have to laugh to myself at myself, and that is tedious as gosh. Hang it all, how few they is that really does know what is humorous! ·

I am leaving the "World," at an advance of 50 per cent on salary, by cracky, and going to the "Journal" (N. Y.), which has been bought by Mr. Hearst, my California friend, and will be run by Sam Chamberlain, my editor friend, and Charlie Palmer, my old business manager friend of the "Examiner," San Francisco. So times is not so scarce as what they was.

I'll enclose pass for you and Win and two more for the 26th, but am very nervous about the Show, of course. Do not be critical.

We all send our love. I am sorry Win has to wear glasses, but if they are becoming of course it will be all right. Girls could wear telescopes if they were becoming. But still we like 'em, I figgers. Don't we, Fet?

(Girls, I mean).

Bill Nye's last lecture, "For Laughing Purposes," was thus described by Mr. Thearle:

Mr. Nye has been for several seasons the best drawing card on the Lyceum platform; there seems to be no limit to his popularity, and his return dates are almost invariably to increased business. In selecting Mr. Bert Poole, cartoonist of the Boston "Herald," as Mr. Nye's companion entertainer, we have secured an artist who, in addition to his cleverness with pencil and crayon, is a humorist himself.

While Mr. Nye is taking the audience into his confidence and exploding many of the common beliefs and cherished romances of farm life and farming generally, Mr. Poole will be decidedly busy drawing brilliantly colored cartoons of the most ludicrous kind, aiding and emphasizing Mr. Nye's exposé.

But the new lecture experiment was ill starred from the first. The public's favorite, who had never failed to ring the bell in ten years of public appearance with Riley, Burbank, Smith, and others, who had tickled audiences in every important city in the country and hundreds of small towns, misfired completely in the fall of 1895. To his mother Nye wrote:

Your letter via Chicago came to day. I am home after a fine old fizzle out of a lecture trip. I never yet was quite so disgusted, or the people either.

I'm more calm now, but for a few days I was biling. We had a real nice rotten show, but the eggs were perfectly good. When I see you I will tell you about it. I was quite noticeably sober.

However—I hardly think that I shall resume the trip —surely not without another partner, though we had the best business booked that we have ever had. I am only sorry that we did not quit sooner.

The new play opens December 2. Of course I am very anxious about it, and should it succeed I'll have to go at another in January.

To go into a little more detail than my father does in this letter, the new lecture, opening at Newport News, traveled north. The new program was a radical departure from anything that Nye had tried before. Evidently it was an attempt to make his talk even more like his weekly letter by adding the humor of caricature and cartoon. But it failed to provide the relief from laughter that had rested the audiences and relieved Nye in the past, when his partners alternated with the humorist in taking charge of the program.

At Paterson, New Jersey, there was an unsympathetic audience. My father was ill, and everything went wrong. He faltered. His nerve, which had buoyed him up so long, could support him no longer. The audience showed its disapproval. And the next day one or two of the papers, which may have thought it good business to attack a man who was building circulation for rival journals, said some untrue and some unkind things.

When Riley heard of the trouble at Paterson he wrote in a private letter to a friend:

Our gentle friend Nye's real trouble was the result of his old spinal affliction. No one who knows the man-martyr and the hero he has ever been conjectured otherwise, no matter how the pitiless dispatches read. But he will be well again, thank heaven, and his true and faithful friends will be prouder of him than ever in all his victorious past, is my prophetic faith in my old comrade.

My father's manager, Mr. Pardee, made the following statement to the press:

"Mr. Nye is afflicted with failing eyesight," said he. "On the day and evening that he appeared in that place he was perfectly sober, and if he imbibed at all it was not noticeable. For two weeks Mr. Nye had been suffering from some ailment that affected his head and caused nervousness. In stepping on the platform he stumbled over some obstruction, owing to his near-sightedness, and this undoubtedly gave the audience the impression that the lecturer was intoxicated. His condition must have been indicative of drink, but his strange actions were due solely to the temporary nervousness.

"The auditors did not manifest disapproval, with the exception of a few tough characters who are constantly endeavoring to disturb meetings of any character. Nothing out of the ordinary occurred until we had boarded the train that was to carry us to our next stopping place, New York. Then a few members of the rowdy element of the town stepped upon the platforms and opened the doors at either end and commenced their onslaught, which was kept up until they were driven away."

Outwardly Bill Nye took the blow to his pride philosophically. But he never got over it. And when, on top of other misfortunes, his new play fell flat, it seemed to make him feel, for the first time in his life, that the battle was not worth the effort. A letter to Clara Mitchell:

You have doubtless heard of the celebrated Paterson Denooment—and Ovation.

Some of these was God's—but the alcoholic report I saw in one paper was a wicked and cruel lie—not that I have ever been confined entirely to branch water whilst lecturing—by no means—but in this case my conscience is absolutely clear. But a nimble prevarication is hard to overtake.

Suffice it that our show was decayed and pus-infisted from the start, and doomed to an early grave. I only regret that I gave it so much rope wherewith to execute itself.

I'm in fine health and actually glad, for the agony is over and I am again free from a most unhappy and ill-starred entanglement. Sorry about our method of eggsit but tickled to be free.

I am proud to tell you just between you and me that your greatly celebrated Uncle is just as good as ever if not better for this sorry jolt.

Frances is gay and debonair. She came to New York, and we shopped and went to the the-*a*-ter and snapped our fingers at fate and often referred to the dumb thing as a mere bagatelle, though nerry one of us knows what the likes o' that is.

Win and Auntie are decorating Calvary today for the lamb—Mary Lamb wedding. She will be placed on the altar tomorrow and become a Smith. I once went to see the Supreme Court in Washington, and the first case on the Calendar was the U. S. *vs.* Smith. Heartsick and hopeless over the unequal contest—and bidding good-by to the struggling Republic, I came away shedding a hot tear at every jump.

Two days later:

My dearest Fet:

We are all extremely well and the boys are just about starting off on horseback to their studies. Max has a sort of wine colored or maroon sweater and Jim a kind of tan color. Yesterday they dressed up to kill, for the Mary Lamb nuptials. Jim said, "I'm going to dwess after dinnah and I'll look like a Pwince." They are in "fwactions" now. I have given them a start at home. We all play baccarat evenings, and last evening both boys got too fresh and Max quit and Jim cried. He had lost heavily and got so that he demurred paying his debts and scorned to borrow. So we "hed" quite a circus.

"Tahntah" [Mrs. Nye] is real chipper and joyful, seems to be glad the old show burst with a loud newspaper report—as it were. By the way, you *must* get me the Post that you referred to. If you don't, you get no Xmas present, see? When a newspaper says I'm good, I want to subscribe.

There's nothing new in my line. I have told Thearle I'll not go out again on the road with anybody I know of, so I hope that settles it.

In his last letter to his mother, dated January 6, 1896, Nye refers to "The Stag Party":

I suppose I told you of the play? It is in the scrap pile after a very sad career of two weeks. However, we cannot always hit it. Some of the children of the brain are liable to be Gill Withams or Fred Swartouts.

"The Stag Party" was produced before the days of musical comedy and was called vaudeville in several acts. For Nye and Paul Potter it was a tragedy. My father liked the man who had dramatized "Trilby," but the two did not get on as collaborators. There were a good many Bill Nye lyrics in the piece, and some of them had merit, but evidently both authors were determined that this play should not suffer from the same complaint as "The Cadi," that is, too much Nye. I did not see the play, but I have read it, and most of the Nyesque touches seem to have been ironed out.

Eighteen ninety-five had been an eventful year in the Nye family, but few of the events had ended happily.

CHAPTER XXIV

THE SILENCE FALLS: 1896

LATE in January Edgar Nye wrote to his brother what seems to have been the last personal letter he penned:

My dear Frank:

Your letter was received some days ago, and I started to answer it on the 16th, but was interrupted and so did not resume it, for I can never begin where I left off in such a matter.

I see that you are making a record as an after-dinner speaker or *post prandial* orator, as I see it called in my paper. That is indeed a great gift, and I have no doubt that the descendants of Joe Choate and C. M. Depew will in future years point proudly each to his illustrious ancestor and say, "He was the Frank M. Nye of his time."

I would like real well to hear your melodious voice after a good square meal in Delmonico's big banquet hall with a lot of the alleged orators of New York and Washington sitting about smoking their *see-gars.*

With the dearth of good speakers now at large, I think that Minneapolis is peculiarly blest for a city of its size in having you all to herself. As an orator I am more on the Frank Crawford order, being more amusing than convincing, and in seeking to show how destructive Fire is, might refer to the destruction of the Tidd school-house or the holocaust which with tongue of flame licked up the line-fence between Fuller and Musser during the present century.

Did I write you that I am about to exchange the New York house for 3000 acres of timber and coal lands in West Virginia? At least I go next week to see the land. It is either a big thing or a very small affair. I shall take along a timber man in whom I have a good deal of confidence and go on his judgment very largely. It is in a coal belt where it crops out all along the creeks, and if the timber is as represented, there is no risk in buying, especially as the price is very low. Iron is also found there; salt and petroleum too are all about that region. I've had enough bad luck lately to make me hope that this is not all an empty vision.

But how many mirages we see before we actually lay our hands upon the real and true! How many times we clutch the empty air and groan through parched lips before we hear the tinkle of running streams and smell the dewy grass whence comes the chirp of the cricket and the song of the bobolinks.

Many a weary league of dust and alkali and burning plain must drink up our smarting tears before we may cool our beating pulses in the blessed shadows that hover about "a great rock in a weary land."

As we grow older and we stagger against selfishness a little oftener and a little harder all the time, the sun beats hotter and the miles seem longer It is then that we are tempted to get a little soured on humanity and to generally ferment, especially if we have the "Uncle Lyman" [acidity] as we call it here.

I wish we might see you in this country next summer. In some ways it would please and interest you, and the lazy, hazy atmosphere and the desire to postpone every thing until next week or next fall is extremely restful to the Yankee who has been on the jump for years and years.

We all send love to the family and to yourself. Tell me your plans and what is likely to happen in a political way. *Write* whenever you can and I will answer promptly.

Ever your Brother,

EDGAR.

My father's last stroke was a severe one, and there was no quick rally as there had been before. He became weaker and finally lapsed into unconsciousness. During the first part of his illness he used to send for Max and me, and he seemed to enjoy having us in the sickroom. But it was very depressing to us, for he did not seem like our old Tod at all. I think my mother feared the worst from the beginning, but the seriousness of his illness had been carefully hidden from us, and finally when my sisters returned from Washington and we all gathered at his bedside to bid him good-by our hearts were completely broken. Death had never been a reality to us before. I shall not wipe from my memory the agony of witnessing my father's last struggle against death. The only comfort was the knowledge that temporary victory for our Tod would probably mean paralysis.

And so on Washington's Birthday, 1896, my father died at Buck Shoals.

Only a few days before his death and after a night of care and anxiety for the nurse and doctor he jokingly said:

"Forgive me for not dying last night."

The last article he had written for the papers appeared on the day of his death and, by a strange coincidence, it contained this paragraph:

Sometimes it is perfectly tiresome waiting for a man to die so that you will feel safe in saying what you think of him, but if he happens to be a large, robust man, it certainly pays to do so.

The funeral took place on Tuesday, February 25, at Calvary Episcopal Church at Fletcher. The church was crowded with hundreds of his friends from near and far. The service was read by our rector, the Rev. H. H. Phelps, assisted by the Rev. Thomas C. Wetmore. The pallbearers were Dr. William D. Hilliard, E. P. McKissick, Major William E. Breese, Dr. George W. Fletcher, Oliver M. Rutledge, and Robert B. Blake.

Uncle Frank and his wife had arrived from Minneapolis a few hours after the death. This brother, who had been Edgar's closest chum for more than half his lifetime, gave a statement to the papers:

I am constrained to offer to the public a few words of simple tribute to the life and character of Edgar Wilson Nye, a brother as dear to me as life itself. We were nearly of an age and up to the spring of 1876 were scarcely separated for a single month at any one time.

He was a child of the sunlight. His life was a lesson of good will toward men—a constant song of kindly mirth—underneath it, the broad philosophy of universal brotherhood. No one was beneath him. The humblest child of poverty and distress found comfort in his welcome smile and stingless jest. He loved his fellow-men and bade them be of good cheer. His very presence was a rebuke to all despondency. He could not live in an atmosphere of gloom—he rose above it and took others with him. He did more than make the world laugh. His mission was beyond the momentary amusement of mankind. Those who knew him best felt, beneath the ripples of resistless fun, the ocean currents of his great good nature, his generous heart, his loving soul.

By a manner and style of exaggerated expression, indefinable, but natural and seemingly careless, he drew a striking picture of the ludicrous side of men, of times and of customs. He caricatured the follies and the weaknesses of men. This he did in a general, and never in a personal way. There was no element of bitterness in his nature. He cherished no enmities. He had no time to hate. His nature and his disposition were as sweet as the breath of a summer morning.

He was youthful always, a boy in spirit and disposition to the last. He never changed from childhood, except to grow. He spoke and wrote and conversed after he became known to the public the same as he always had. Time only developed— it did not change him. His characteristics were as marked and pronounced in childhood as they were in manhood. His droll expressions, his apt stories and his unexpected jokes were the surprising but ever welcome guests of our little country home and neighborhood. Whether at the unpretentious party, the spelling school, the lyceum, or in the threshing crew, he was the central figure. He drew to him the old and the young. There was beauty in his homeliness, gentility in his awkwardness, philosophy in his jests, good nature in his anger, buoyancy and good cheer in his adversity, wisdom in his youth and youthfulness in his age. In all his life he was genuine, sincere and true.

He had no idle dreams of great personal achievements. He had little, if any, conceit as to his own abilities to reform mankind or make them better. He did not seek to measure his own influence upon mankind in what he did or said or wrote. His life was a simple message of good cheer. He knew this message could do no harm—he hoped and believed it would do at least some good.

We measure men's influence and comprehend their work better after they have gone from us, and the world will better understand him now. He brought the smile, he dispelled the frown. He who does this should find a niche in the temple of enduring fame. The fragrance of the flower lingers after its welcome blush and bloom have departed.

My brother, to your dear memory I bring this tender garland. It is all my breaking heart can give.

My father's last public appearance had been at the opera-house in Asheville in an entertainment given for the Episcopal Church.

Dr. Hilliard, the family physician, said later that my father had been under his care for three years and that he had been anticipating the end for some time. He further stated that great injustice had been done Nye while on his last lecturing trip, his nervous system being then in such condition as to render him incapable of undergoing so severe a strain.

When Bill Nye's death became known the press blossomed with tributes of verse and prose. Riley immediately issued a short statement to the press:

Especially favored, as for years I have been, with close personal acquaintance and association with Mr. Nye, his going fills me with a selfishness of grief that finds a mute rebuke in my every memory of him. He was unselfish wholly; and I am heartened, recalling the always patient strength and gentleness of this true man—the unfailing hope and cheer and faith of his child heart—his noble and heroic life and pure devotion to home—its sanctity of love—mother, brothers, wife, children, friends—his deep affections, constant dreams, plans and realizations—all in happiest action and development. So I cannot doubt but that—somehow, somewhere—he continues cheerily on in the unbroken exercise of these same capacities—as marked an endowment of his spirit nature as was his peculiar gift of genius intellectual.

And this was soon followed by the beautiful sonnet:

BRONZE TABLET ON BILL NYE MEMORIAL

BOULDER AT NYE'S GRAVE. PLACED THERE BY THE AMERICAN SUNSHINE SOCIETY

The saddest silence falls when Laughter lays
    Finger on lip, and falteringly breaks
    The glad voice into dying minor shakes
And quavers, lorn as airs the wind-harp plays
At wane of drearest winter's bleakest days.
    A troubled hush, in which all hope forsakes
    Us, and the yearning upstrained vision aches
With tears that drown ev'n heaven from our gaze.
Such silence—after such glad merriment!
    O prince of halest humor, wit and cheer!
    Could you speak yet again, I doubt not we
Should catch your voice, still blithely eloquent
    Above all murmurings of sorrow here,
    Calling your love back to us laughingly.

I shall quote from only one more encomium. Of the scores of tributes that my mother collected after my father's death, this one stands out for its sincere and discerning appreciation. Unfortunately the writing is not signed, or if it was the name was lost. I should like to know who had so true an estimate of Bill Nye and with it the gift of language to record. The tribute is long, and I give only part:

A great American citizen is dead; a man who held no civic honor and wore no badge of official distinction, and yet who held a great place in the love of his countrymen, has been touched by the silence of death, and a nation mourns the loss. He was a common American citizen without rank or title, and yet for his death the world is inestimably poorer, even as for his life it was vastly better.

I never knew Mr. Nye personally, and yet as I think of him while I write, it seems to me that he had been my dear personal friend for many years. I cannot remember when I first began to read his sketches, but for several years I think I never missed anything he wrote. When I first learned of his death I was

reading his last article, which I believe was written but a short
time before his death. But a few short weeks ago I had the
pleasure of hearing his old friend, William Hawley Smith, talk
lovingly and admiringly of Mr. Nye, and his words inspired in
me an even greater admiration for the dead humorist.

I believe that it can be said with absolute fairness that he
made more people laugh than any man who has written in the
English language since Artemus Ward; and to those who followed his work closely there came positive evidence of the real
sublimity of his life. Under the lightest sentence that he ever
wrote there lay concealed some deep and significant truth.

There are many who will insist that he was not a literary
artist, and who will deny to him an abiding-place among the
master-builders of modern American literature. Nevertheless,
I am willing to believe that his work will prove to be more than
a transitory performance, and that in years to come his achievements will be accounted an authentic contribution to the lasting literature of the Republic. He himself, I am well aware,
had little if any idea that his work was of a permanent character, and yet surely in his lifetime he must have known that
he had secured a wonderful hold upon the hearts of men. Quite
possibly literary critics may reject his work, but that is at best
a matter of small moment. It cannot be believed that the American people will soon forget him or his work; and Mr. Howells
spoke wisely and well when he said that a people's love is a
much safer place for any writer's reputation than is a critic's
admiration. Much that Mr. Nye wrote will be forgotten, but
when all is sifted much will remain that cannot wholly pass
away. What he wrought, so seeming careless of any future
fame, will, yea, has already, bound him inseparably to the heart
of American literature, as his kindly nature has won for him
the love and admiration of the world.

He made men laugh, and that means that his heart was
beautiful and his life lovely. It means that all the time he loved
his fellow-man and believed that life was good. It means that,

above all else, he managed ever, amid all changing conditions, to keep on good terms with himself, and surely that is an heroic thing. He made men laugh because he himself knew how to laugh, and very few men know how to do that. Many people believe that humor is shallow and betokens lack of solidity, but they err. Laughter and tears lie very close together, and that man who laughs well is easiest moved to tears. And the tears that mingle with the laughter of the heart make the rainbows of human life. No true humorist is ever shallow. Nay, rather it will be found that under the rippling surface lie the calm waters of true wisdom and philosophy; the peaceful depths of true beauty and true joy. I believe that there was much more to Mr. Nye than ever was apparent in any of his work, even the most serious. But he filled a divine mission in the world, for he carried sunshine with him and scattered it everywhere carelessly, extravagantly and unconsciously, as naturally as the rose scatters its perfumes everywhere. That is the secret of human influence—the secret of the star's glory —of the sunset's splendor.

Sleep on, O gentle humorist, crowned thus with the dignity of death; sweet death, that unto such a soul as thine could be but a warm, warm coverlet of love. Sleep on, thus wrapped about with the beauty of Mother Nature, who all thy lifetime had thee in her gentle keeping. Sleep on, thus crowned with the applause of men, and lovingly homed in the great warm heart of humanity—wreathed with the benediction of the common day.

Amid the rush and hurry of these headstrong days death becomes a mere matter-of-fact event, and to the great world there comes but little thought of change or difference when such life has ceased among us. Happily, however, there still remains a gentle few of kindred heart and sympathy with whom memory shall abide of such a life as this. To those who have loved this kindly man until they seemed to know him as a friend, he remains forever a memory wholly lovable and immortal.

The death of such a man cannot cause the pain that so often accompanies the visitation of the Great Master of Silence; for all his life he was telling mankind by the serenity and beauty of his living that for so true and simple a life tears were not the fitting crown and benediction.   While the bereavement is great, it leaves not with us any sense of utter loneliness and loss, but rather a feeling of unutterable joy and thankfulness for the blessing of such a career.

No—he is not dead.   Such souls no more die than does the sunshine when the eventide comes.   Certainly he belongs to that "choir invisible of those immortal dead who live again in minds made better by their presence," and "whose music is the gladness of the world."   He is not dead—

> "He has but taken his lamp and gone to bed,
> We stay a little longer, as one stays
> To cover up the embers that still burn."